On Computing

On Computing

The Fourth Great Scientific Domain

Paul S. Rosenbloom

The MIT Press
Cambridge, Massachusetts
London, England

MIT Press books may be purchased at special quantity discounts for business or sales promotional use. For information, please email special_sales@mitpress.mit.edu or write to Special Sales Department, The MIT Press, 55 Hayward Street, Cambridge, MA 02142.

This book was set in Stone Sans and Stone Serif by Toppan Best-set Premedia Limited. Printed and bound in the United States of America.

Library of Congress Cataloging-in-Publication Data

Rosenbloom, Paul S.
On computing : the fourth great scientific domain / Paul S. Rosenbloom.
    p.   cm.
Includes bibliographical references and index.
ISBN 978-0-262-01832-6 (hardcover : alk. paper)
1. Computer science. 2. Computer science—Research. 3. Computer science—Philosophy. I. Title.
QA76.R657   2013
004—dc23
2012013852

10 9 8 7 6 5 4 3 2 1

For Elaine, Florence, and Michael

Contents

Preface

Computing isn't simply about computers (hardware) or programming (software). Nor is it merely about the act of determining the results of numerical expressions (calculation) or the development of tools (applications) for use by others. It is an exciting and diverse, yet remarkably coherent, scientific enterprise that is highly multidisciplinary while maintaining a unique core of its own. It has a future that promises to be as rich and momentous as its revolutionary past has already been.

This book is about the *computing sciences*, a broad take on computing that can be thought of for now as in analogy to the physical sciences, the life sciences, and the social sciences, although the argument will ultimately be made that this is much more than just an analogy, with computing deserving to be recognized as the equal of these three existing, great scientific domains—and thus the *fourth great scientific domain*. In eschewing the common phrase *computer science* and using instead a relatively unfamiliar phrase,[1] the goal is to transcend the normal boundaries and modes of thinking about both computing and its study, capturing each in its broadest sense. This then becomes the basis for a new perspective on computing that is open and expansive yet fundamentally coherent and that has major implications for how computing is viewed both in and of itself and in the larger context of the global scientific enterprise.

At one level down, a multiplicity of interrelated purposes have shaped this work, making for a potentially complex narrative and the likelihood that some readers will resonate with only particular segments of the overall story. Yet the story remains most compelling when told all of a piece, so that is how the reader will find it here. To help tame the complexity, five primary purposes have been articulated and associated with classes of readers for whom the purposes may be of most interest. This then yields a map of the overall structure and content of the story while also guiding those with more focused interests toward what is likely to be of most relevance to them.

The five primary purposes are as follows:

1. Introducing the *relational approach*—comprising a *relational architecture* and the accompanying *metascience expression (ME) language*—for structuring and characterizing the computing sciences, yielding a novel way of looking at them and how they relate to the other sciences.
2. Conveying the excitement of the present for the computing sciences and the revolutionary potential they continue to possess for the future.
3. Providing a broad multidisciplinary perspective on the computing sciences as a counter to the narrow and frequently self-limiting views of computing that are too often encountered.
4. Exploring three forms of *macrostructure* afforded by the relational approach for structuring and understanding complex multidisciplinary topics and organizations within computing.
5. Defining a dynamic, inclusive notion of a great scientific domain and arguing for the computing sciences providing the fourth such domain.

As listed, the first of these primary purposes is to introduce a new approach to understanding computing in terms of how it relates to both itself and the rest of science; in particular, the physical, life, and social sciences. The architecture and language derived from this approach form the core technical contribution of this book. The term *architecture* is most familiar colloquially in the world of buildings, where it refers to their design or structure. Within computing, the term is most familiar in the context of computer architecture, where it denotes the design and structure of hardware that computes. However, it also plays a role in software engineering—in the form of software architecture—and in cognitive science, where cognitive architectures model the fixed structure underlying intelligent behavior. As used here, the focus is on structure rather than design and on the structure of the field of computing rather than on the structure of computers.

The relational architecture provides an organization over the field of computing in terms of two relationships—*interaction* and *implementation*—that reveal hidden structures and connections among its diverse disciplines. It also exposes the domain's natural role in the larger world of science and engineering while highlighting an inherent symmetry between what are traditionally viewed as central versus peripheral—or core versus multidisciplinary—aspects of computing. The unidisciplinary[2] aspects of computing end up accounting for only a rather limited subspace of its overall coverage.

Architectures within computing typically induce useful languages. A computer architecture, for example, induces a machine language that enables programming of the computers based on the architecture. Likewise, software architectures may support architecture description languages, and cognitive architectures may yield languages for building intelligent systems. The relational architecture does not induce an executable language in which programs can be run, but it does yield a language—the ME language—that supports the analysis and description of computing disciplines and organizations in terms of the domains they comprise and the relationships that are implicated among these domains.[3]

The primary audience for such an architecture and language is likely to be both computing professionals—whether in industry or academia—and students who are interested in a new perspective on the domain of computing, its component parts, and how all of it can be seen to fit together into a coherent whole with a well-defined place in the overall scheme of the sciences. Although not written explicitly to be easily accessible to a broader audience, this perspective may also be of interest to people outside the field who seek a new way of understanding computing and as well to anyone interested in the structure of science as a whole. The architecture has predominantly been developed and explored in the context of computing, but it reflects a symmetry across the sciences that suggests the possibility of broader applicability and utility.

The relational approach arose from a computer (and cognitive) scientist's reflections on computing. Although it is natural and appropriate for an expert in a field to reflect on his or her field in such a manner and to want to share the results of such reflections with the broader community should they appear useful, my reflections by necessity led me deeper and deeper into philosophy of science in order to consider such topics as what science itself is and what makes a great scientific domain. I am an amateur in philosophy, so there is an inherent risk of philosophical naïveté in such an endeavor, yet such excursions became necessary to fill in the whole story. These latter topics are at the core of the fifth purpose, but they also impact aspects of this first one. For example, the idea of symmetrically relating computing to the physical, life, and social sciences assumes that there is at least some form of equivalence among them, while the appropriateness of the term *metascience* for the accompanying language depends on taking a broad view of science.

Earlier drafts of this book placed this philosophical material before the architecture to set the stage for its introduction. However, this led to two problems. First, the strong early dose of philosophy proved to be a deterrent for many people within computing—the primary audience for this book—making it difficult for them to get on to the more accessible and relevant material to come. Second, this ordering may have been construed to imply that the utility of the architecture depended on the validity of these excursions into more controversial aspects of philosophy of science. If either the notion of a great scientific domain or the proposal that computing is the fourth such domain ultimately fails to pan out, some of the sense of fundamental rightness about the architecture may go away, but its usefulness as a tool for understanding computing may remain. Similarly, if the attempt to broaden the standard notion of science should prove unworkable, the ME language could still be a useful tool even if the term *metascience* in its name becomes inappropriate. In consequence, the architecture is now presented up front, in chapter 2, with most of the more philosophical material delayed until chapter 6. Only as much of the philosophy as is necessary to understand the architectural material is included early on, such as the discussion of the nature and scope of science, which can be found as part of the introduction to the computing sciences in chapter 1.

The second listed purpose—of conveying the excitement and potential of computing—has a situational aspect. Computing has been in the doldrums in many ways since the dot-com bust. In combination with this bust, a focus on the mundane in computing—what can be considered the *trees* of its currently successful computing products and applications rather than the *forest* of its full scope and potential—has led to a growing concern that the excitement is gone from the field, or at least that the world perceives this to be so. In academia, this has been manifested most dramatically in a drop in undergraduate enrollment, but it also is evident in everyday interactions with people from both within and without the field. In response, various individuals and groups have attempted to reconceptualize and rearticulate the nature of computing, along with why it remains a vital and exciting intellectual endeavor with broad societal implications. One prime example is an effort to identify the *great principles of computing* as a vehicle for refocusing the field on its fundamental scientific principles.[4] Another is the explication of *computational thinking* and its pervasive impact on the world at large.[5]

Part of the motivation for the second purpose is to contribute to this ongoing discussion about the nature and vitality of computing by surveying, in chapters 3 and 4, much of what is exciting in the present and future of computing. But the survey isn't solely a response to the doldrums within computing, which as of mid-2011 we are already beginning to see turn around, at least with respect to undergraduate enrollment and high-flying valuations for computing companies. To illustrate the application of the relational architecture, help better understand the field of computing, and infuse additional novelty and interest into the survey, it is structured according to the relationships used within the architecture, with chapter 3 covering implementation and chapter 4 covering interaction.

The survey concentrates on what can be called *dyadic computing*, the combination of computing with one other domain; as is seen for example in computing's combination with the physical sciences in computer hardware and with the social sciences in human computer interaction.[6] Much of what is most familiar in computing over the past few decades fits into dyadic computing, but there is also a range of newer and less familiar topics that show up here, such as brain–computer interfaces and the use of DNA for biocomputing. Beyond dyadic computing is *polyadic computing*, which includes the full breadth and richness of computing that arises from its combination with an arbitrary number of other domains. Examples here include intelligent robots and cyborgs and worlds that tightly intermingle the real and the computational/virtual. Much of the current leading edge in computing, and even more of its future, falls within the scope of polyadic computing. Aspects of polyadic computing are included in the survey when there is a single dominant relationship by which we can classify the area at the top level. Other pieces are included in chapters 5 and 6 in support of later purposes.

Because so much of the future of computing seems to lie in multidisciplinary areas, and because such topics are too often given short shrift within the field, the survey concentrates more on such aspects of computing than on traditional core topics. Within this overall focus, my own background in artificial intelligence (AI) may have led to AI and robotics being somewhat overrepresented in both examples and descriptions—as my home base at the University of Southern California may have led to examples from there also being overrepresented—but the explicit goal has been to be universal and inclusive. Whether biased or not, the survey's broad multidisciplinary focus implies that it also contributes directly to the third purpose. ME expressions are assigned to the individual topics to make explicit the diversity of domains—and the relationships among them—involved in each topic, while also helping to identify where the topics fit within computing, and science, as a whole. Readers uncomfortable with formal or semiformal languages or who simply do not want to try to puzzle out what particular expressions are intended to denote are more than welcome to skip over them during the survey.

The survey is potentially relevant to anyone concerned with the first, second, or third listed purposes, including professionals working within the field, students just learning about or considering entering the field, and people outside of the field who have an interest in it. However, the level of detail provided on the topics surveyed and the amount of background assumed in their presentation can have a major impact on the survey's accessibility for each potential audience. It seems likely that both the level of detail desired and the amount of background that can be assumed will decrease as we proceed across these three potential audiences. The survey provided in chapters 3 and 4 mostly assumes a level of understanding corresponding to the first audience while leaving open the possibility that sufficiently motivated or guided members of the other two will still find it useful. In contrast, a very detailed survey is beyond what is necessary to support any of the three listed purposes, so the survey proceeds at a relatively high level.

We have already seen how the survey contributes to one aspect of fulfilling the third purpose, but more broadly the third purpose is concerned with countering a too common tendency to construe computing in an overly narrow fashion, potentially limiting its overall scope, significance, and future. It is not surprising that many people tend to view computing through the lens of what they see on a regular basis. Thus, to much of industry and the general population, computing becomes about the hardware and software they use. For academic computer scientists, it becomes what is covered by the traditional disciplinary structure. For scientists outside of computing, it becomes the tools from computational science and informatics that they use in pursuing their own research. These individual views all derive from what should be a positive—the pervasive utility of computing in helping people accomplish their personal and professional goals—but even in combination these topics fall short of its full richness and of what makes computing an exciting and crucially important scientific enterprise. A true understanding of computing should enable the nature and potential of the field to be explained properly, both to the general public and to our colleagues, students, and selves.

Much of the argument here derives from definitions that will be provided in chapter 1 plus the relational architecture in chapter 2 and the dyadic survey in chapters 3 and 4. Together these foster a view of computing that is broad, frequently multidisciplinary, and symmetric in how it relates to the other sciences. So, for example, although the provision by computing of tools for the other sciences fits naturally within the architecture, this topic is far from all there is to the architecture (or the survey). Some of computing's relationships have nothing to do with providing tools, and the symmetry of those that do implies that the other scientific domains may stand just as much in the role of providing tools for computing as the other way around. In addition to the relevant material in chapters 2–4, aspects of this argument will also be covered in chapter 5 (section 5.2), as part of a broader discussion of the use of computing in science. The intended audience for this discussion is anyone who wants to expand their view of what computing is, subject to the same accessibility qualifications that were mentioned previously.

The fourth listed purpose seeks to leverage the relational approach in exploring forms of higher order coherence, or macrostructures, over complex computing topics and organizations. Three such forms of relational macrostructure are examined in chapter 5: (1) two-dimensional tabular, (2) complex expression synthesis and decomposition, and (3) layered hierarchical. Topics that will be analyzed include mixtures of real and virtual worlds, methods for the pursuit of science, computing research institutes, and academic computing. The intent is to leverage these four analyses to provide new insights into the topics analyzed while simultaneously exploring and illustrating the utility of these macrostructure forms and providing further feedback on the applicability and utility of the relational approach for understanding complex aspects of computing. This is of potential interest to anyone concerned with understanding complex scientific areas and organizations in general, understanding any of these four specific topics in particular, or simply understanding computing as a whole better.

The fifth listed purpose focuses in chapter 6 on the development of the notion of a great scientific domain, plus the argument that computing forms the fourth such domain.[7] This particular notion of a great scientific domain is a new one, but it is intended as an elaboration and refinement of the long-familiar division of the sciences into broad domains that study the physical, living, and social worlds. These three existing great scientific domains are the crown jewels of human intellectual achievement. Each covers a broad swath of the understanding of our world and ourselves while simultaneously enabling the development of technologies that ever increasingly alter the world and us. Although computing has undoubtedly spurred massive technological developments, it is most often viewed as a form of engineering rather than as a part of science that is on a par with standard disciplines such as physics, chemistry, biology, or psychology, not to mention any question of parity with an entire domain such as the physical, life, or social sciences. So it is a rather large leap to propose that computing forms the fourth such domain. But, if it is true, it provides an even stronger argument than the survey for the importance and future of computing.

A key part of this is by necessity a discussion of what science is. There are many extant definitions of science, covering a range of senses from "a particular branch of knowledge"[8] at the broad, permissive end of the spectrum to "a system of acquiring knowledge based on scientific method, and to the organized body of knowledge gained through such research"[9] at the narrow, restrictive end. Yet, none quite matched the way I as a practicing scientist think about science. Continued pursuance of the reflections on computing that originally produced the relational architecture have led to a very broad and rather nonstandard answer to the question, one that incorporates both *understanding* (as is the focus in most traditional science) and *shaping* (as is the focus in engineering and other professions) and includes essentially anything that increases our understanding over time.

Both this discussion and the definition of a great scientific domain may be controversial. They are due to a philosophical amateur who may be both ignorant and naïve in key ways; they bulldoze through many of the traditional ideas and arguments about science; and they embody a form of circularity in which reflections on computing lead to notions of science and great scientific domains that are then used to make claims about computing. But the intent here is more to initiate a conversation on these topics than to provide final answers. Backing down from raising controversial claims because not all of the *t*'s can yet be crossed nor all of the *i*'s dotted would not do this, nor would waiting until the evidence is so solid that the claims will be accepted with little dispute. My concern in including this material is therefore not so much with ultimately being proved right about these claims but with providing food for thought in service of accelerating the field's progress toward compelling answers.

There is a need and a role for professional scientists to consider and speculate about the natures of their domains and not just leave it to philosophers. My hope is that computer scientists, and possibly other scientists and members of the general population, will find this discussion thought provoking, even if not authoritative from a philosophical perspective. Getting something out of this material will however require a willingness to deal with its philosophical nature.

The overall structure of this book follows from its purposes. Chapter 1 defines and scopes computing and the computing sciences, including a necessary prefatory discussion about the nature of science; chapter 2 introduces the relational approach, as composed of the relational architecture and the ME language; chapters 3 and 4 discuss and survey the implementation and interaction relations; chapter 5 focuses on macrostructures and analyses; chapter 6 covers the more controversial topics, including a second pass on the nature of science, the definition of a great scientific domain, and the claim that computing is the fourth such domain; and chapter 7 concludes. Yet before we get started on this material, this preface wraps up with a note on writing style, a section on the history and background behind this book, and acknowledgments of those to whom I am most indebted for help with it.

This book contains a wide diversity of material that varies in its nature, the style in which it is written, my level of expertise concerning it, and the types of citations included for it. The background and acknowledgments sections are, for example, personal, and therefore are written in such a style. But I have also felt free elsewhere to resort to personal anecdotes when they seemed apropos to the point being made. In contrast, the relational architecture and ME language are technical in nature and are presented in a more professional style. The survey is more of a mixed bag. The presentation style here is a mixture of description and gee whiz, with a dash of technical, as befits the material and the purposes for its presentation. I have expertise in some of the areas covered in this book and a working familiarity with others but have had to learn about some of the topics from scratch in service of fleshing out the respective sections. The citations here reflect this, sometimes being appropriately scholarly but at other times citing more general sources, such as Wikipedia. Although thus not always authoritative, the survey still hopefully fulfills its intended purposes. The philosophical material is written in a more polemical style, opinionated and undoubtedly controversial. It captures a working scientist's, rather than a professional philosopher's, views on the material, with the citations limited to the relevant sources consulted during these reflections. I have also felt free to resort to a combination of personal and polemical styles for a few non-philosophical topics—such as the discussion of academic computing—where personal experience has led to a particularly strong opinion.

Background

If I were to go back to the late 1990s and try to predict what the future would bring for me professionally, it would have been quite unlikely to include this book. At the time, I was a confirmed AI researcher with a long-term commitment to understanding the architecture of cognition; that is, the fixed structure underlying thought in both natural (e.g., people) and artificial (e.g., computer) systems. I was just coming off a successful multiyear project funded by the Defense Advanced Research Projects Agency (DARPA)—which is probably best known for having given the Internet its start—to use such an architecture in building simulated pilots and commanders for large-scale virtual military exercises.[10] What occurred then, however, was a classic case study in *desires and diversions*, as outlined in Allen Newell's last public lecture of that name.[11]

In his talk, Newell—one of the four founders of AI—reflected on styles of research careers, with a particular focus on his own style, the all-encompassing desire to answer a single ultimate scientific question; in his case, understanding the nature of the human mind. Such a question can inspire a life-long scientific career, obscuring from view—or at least from serious consideration and investigation—all other topics. Yet, diversions do inevitably occur, generally for social reasons, and may last for years. For Newell, these diversions included foundational work on computer architecture, speech understanding, the psychology of human–computer interaction, and hypertext systems. To him, the important point was ultimately to make such diversions count, not only by significant contributions to the subject matter of the diversion but also by salvaging something for the central question. Given that this book is about all of computing, with a strong focus on multidisciplinarity, it is notable that the ACM/AAAI Allen Newell Award was created after his death to honor career contributions that have breadth within computer science, or that bridge computer science and other disciplines.

Until 1998, I followed a research path that was closely tied to Newell's, working closely with him from the time I entered the graduate program in computer science at Carnegie Mellon University in 1976 until his death in 1992, and continuing to work on what had become a large-scale joint research project until 1998. He was initially my PhD advisor but later a friend, mentor, and collaborator. One of the reasons we had such a successful working relationship over so many years was that I was driven by a scientific question that was closely related to his and on which he had done much of the seminal work. In my case, it was the understanding of cognitive architecture. I was particularly interested in seeking a uniform architecture that could yield the full richness of intelligent thought and behavior from the interactions among a small set of very general mechanisms—essentially what could be considered cognitive Newton's laws. The uniform approach to cognitive architecture was not, and still is not, the dominant paradigm, but to me it had an irresistible appeal both scientifically and aesthetically.

In the early 1980s, John Laird, Allen Newell, and I instituted the *Soar* project to develop, understand, and apply a new cognitive architecture—eponymously called Soar—that would capture our best joint understanding of the mechanisms necessary for producing intelligent behavior.[12] Laird was a fellow graduate student and Newell advisee whose PhD thesis developed the problem-solving model at the heart of Soar, and my thesis focused on a model of human practice that would become Soar's main learning mechanism over most of its history.[13] Soar continues to be developed and applied to this day under Laird's leadership at the University of Michigan, roughly thirty years after the first version was built. But my own active participation ended in 1998, after spending much of the 1990s working on the DARPA project mentioned above, and then spending a sabbatical year exploring, largely unsuccessfully, the role of emotions in Soar.

I left the project because I had hit a wall; a metaphoric wall to be sure, but it still brought progress on my central research desire to a halt. I no longer felt that I was making a significant difference on what I had hoped and expected to be a career-defining question and had little enthusiasm left for the chase. After painful and extended soul searching, I concluded that a major change was necessary, but whether it was simply to be a diversion—of whatever length—from which I would ultimately return or a permanent shift was unclear at the time.

When Herb Schorr, executive director of the Information Sciences Institute (ISI)—a large research institute in Marina del Rey that is part of the Viterbi School of Engineering at the University of Southern California (USC) and where I had pursued much of my own research during the prior decade—offered me a chance to play a leadership role in ISI's New Directions activities, I jumped at the opportunity it afforded for refreshing my understanding of the broader world of computing and for working all around its cutting edge. At that time, ISI engaged in research and development across much of computing, spanning computer science (software), computer engineering (hardware), information science (information), and information technology (applications). It had been quite successful since its inception in 1972, with notable contributions in networking—such as the development of the Domain Name System (DNS), which associates hierarchical names with resources on the Internet, and the attendant creation of the initial top-level Internet domains, such as .com and .edu—AI, grid computing, software engineering, computer architecture, and high-performance computing. But, as a soft-money research institute that was totally dependent on external contracts and grants, ISI could only remain large and successful by continually striking out into new areas of value.

My role during what ended up as a decade (1998–2007) of leading New Directions was to help understand where computing was heading and where ISI should be going, as well as to lead, instigate, and facilitate new efforts in these directions. This meant working across a broad range of computing disciplines, both within ISI's existing areas of expertise and in new areas of potential interest. It also meant working extensively at the interfaces between these areas of computing and an even wider diversity of critical topics and problems outside of computing. At various times this included interactions with the Getty Center about technology and the arts; Paramount Digital Entertainment and the U.S. Department of Defense (DoD) about combining computing and entertainment for military training, culminating in the creation of the U.S. Army–funded USC Institute for Creative Technologies (ICT); the Southern California Earthquake Center (SCEC) about the development of a community earthquake modeling environment; USC's Keck School of Medicine about biomedical computing; the National Science Foundation (NSF) and others about responding to unexpected events, both natural and human engendered; and a panoply of academic disciplines and industrial sectors about automated building construction. (ISI has continued down this path in more recent years as well, with for example the creation of a quantum computing center, in conjunction with Lockheed Martin and D-Wave, to house a 128-qubit quantum computer.)

As I reflected on the breadth of topics and interactions with which I was involved, I began searching for any form of commonality, coherence, or structure that might be lurking behind what initially appeared to be nothing more than a hodgepodge begotten from a liaison between need and opportunity. Just as with the earlier work on cognitive architecture, I was inexorably driven to investigate whether this diversity of topics was merely the complex surface manifestation of an underlying coherent whole—what I eventually began to think of as an architecture for the domain of computing—that might itself be explained uniformly in terms of interactions among a small set of general principles. The relational approach ultimately emerged from these reflections.

The first exercise in disseminating the results of these reflections was a short article published in *IEEE Computer* in which a precursor of the relational architecture—referred to as a framework at that point—was proposed as a basis for the rational reconstruction of the sibling disciplines of computer science and engineering.[14] The positive responses to this article helped encourage me to continue, but other responses pointed out the potential for controversy in such an endeavor. More will be said about this latter bit in chapter 5 (section 5.4).

A desire to introduce this overall perspective to students who were in the process of developing their own views on the field led to a subsequent graduate seminar in which the framework was further developed and used as a vehicle for introducing to them many of the new and exciting developments in the field.[15] This in turn, along with further external encouragement and the opportunity of an upcoming sabbatical, led to the idea of a book that would make the ideas available more broadly. Originally, this was conceived of as following the structure of the course and for an intended audience of everyone from the technically interested layperson to professionals in the field, but with a particular focus on students considering a career in computing. Reality, however, in the form of feedback from publishers and from family and friends who had tried their best to make it through early drafts of the introductory chapters, forced a change: It was made clear that I needed to retarget, and reduce, the intended audience along the lines mentioned in the previous section.

While writing this book, I realized that the relational architecture implicitly assumed a symmetry between computing and the physical, life, and social sciences. The process of understanding and justifying this symmetry led to the notion of a great scientific domain and the idea that computing was the fourth such domain, although it took the enthusiasm of Peter Denning—a former president of the Association for Computing Machinery (ACM) who has been leading the push to identify the great principles in computing—to make me realize that this latter idea was not just a supporting point in the development of the architecture but a critically important point in its own right. This led to a joint column on this topic in *Communications of the ACM*.[16]

Formulation of the notion of a great scientific domain and the need to establish whether or not computing was one also led me to think more about what computing is in the abstract; that is, what distinguishes the subject matter studied by the computing sciences from that studied in the physical, life, and social sciences. Although the resulting definition of computing as *information transformation* is neither terribly novel nor controversial in its own right, its combination with the notion of computing as a great scientific domain has led to the controversial proposal that mathematics should properly be viewed as part of the computing sciences. These thoughts yielded a recent contribution to an ACM *Ubiquity* online symposium "What Is Computation?"[17] The definition of computing is discussed further in chapter 1, but the controversial nature of the proposal concerning mathematics, and the fact that the rest of the book does not depend on this proposal, have led to deferring its discussion until chapter 6.

I have also been tempted by several opportunities to apply the relational approach further and further beyond my core expertise in computing. In one case, this led to an article analyzing the relationship between science and society[18] and in another case to a discussion of the digital humanities.[19] The latter article includes a potentially controversial claim that is analogous to the one about mathematics, but here proposing that the humanities should properly be viewed as part of the social sciences. As with the proposal concerning mathematics, this one is discussed further in chapter 6.

This brings us back up to the present and the culmination of this more than decade-long diversion into new directions in computing and the nature of the computing sciences. One of my personal hopes in writing this book is that it will help make this diversion count by challenging readers to rethink their own assumptions about computing and assisting them in attaining a better understanding of it, its nature and structure, its role in the larger world, and its potential for the future. When I teach or mentor students, what I value most is the opportunity to expose them to new ways of thinking. New facts are essential for progress, but if they just fit into existing, well-trodden paths, they too often miss their latent ability to transform. The current contribution may be short on new facts, but the hope is that it will provide a fresh perspective on those already known while helping to illuminate a path toward the future.

From a more local and personal perspective, this diversion has already counted through the new directions that we were able to initiate at ISI. But I am also in the process of seeing what I can salvage from it for my own ultimate scientific question. Writing this book has made me realize how absolutely central the metaphor of Newton's laws—of finding a small core of essential regularity across diverse phenomena and integrating this core uniformly into a coherent whole—is to my whole intellectual life. Without such a focus, I struggle to make progress and too often feel like I am not making the kind of difference that I most value. In summer 2008, I returned to my core desire of understanding cognitive architecture, but with a new inspiration for how to create architectures capable of producing the broad diversity of intelligent behaviors from a small set of principles. In a second bit of salvage from my decade of new directions, this new research is being pursued at USC's ICT, an institute I helped to create in the late 1990s. The results from this new effort are promising,[20,21] and I am excited about its future.

Acknowledgments

I would first like to thank Allen Newell, who taught me to be a scientist, inspired my approach to science, guided my early career, and who has always stood as an icon of the true scientist to which I could only aspire to approximate in my own career. I frequently play a video of his "Desires and Diversions" talk to groups of students, both in classes I teach and in more informal settings, to help get them started on thinking about their own research styles and future scientific careers. It inspires me to reflect anew on my own career each time I see it.

These re-perusals also keep reminding me that in the talk, he warned against attempting multidisciplinary science without being a professional in all of the fields involved. I kept this advice in the back of my mind as a warning as I pursued forays into philosophy and areas of polyadic computing in which I have little to no real expertise, but I have not been able to resist including such material here. Only time will tell whether I am right in doing so or whether this is another case where I would have been better off following his advice.

The meat for the initial reflections in this book came out of my decade of involvement in New Directions activities at ISI. Herb Schorr offered me the opportunity to lead these activities at a time when I needed a major change from my existing research path. He further provided critical inspiration, support, mentoring, and encouragement over the years of my involvement. I am also, however, indebted to researchers from across ISI and other organizations with whom I was able to work on these new directions and from whom I learned a lot about many aspects of computing and its interactions with other domains.

Peter Denning has provided a range of helpful interactions about this book's topic and material, encouraged the overall enterprise, forced me to rethink and revise a number of aspects, suggested the name of the relational architecture, and provided the insight that the identification of computing as the fourth great scientific domain was a major point in its own right rather than merely being a supporting point in the development of the relational architecture. He has also repeatedly cautioned me about the more controversial aspects of the book, such as the proposed subsumption of mathematics within computing. This has helped me decide how such material should be presented, but otherwise I'm afraid I have treated it like Newell's advice on multidisciplinary work, keeping it in the back of my mind while still pushing forward with what seemed right to me. Here, too, only time will tell who was right.

A range of family and friends made dogged attempts to read early drafts of the introductory chapters and to provide useful feedback as I unsuccessfully struggled early on to write a book that would be accessible and of interest to a general audience. This included Pam Fenton, Sharon Elaine Lee, David Nagy, Anne Rosenbloom, Florence Rosenbloom, Kate Rosenbloom, and Michael Rosenbloom. Several anonymous reviewers for MIT Press also went through a similar exercise, either with just the initial chapters or a full early draft. I want to thank them all for their efforts and apologize for their difficulties. They did provide an invaluable service in helping me get this book on the right track.

I would also like to thank the students in the class I taught at USC on this subject, who helped debug some of the ideas and deepen some of the insights; my colleagues at ICT who have helped further broaden my understanding of the computing sciences; Julia Kim of ICT, in particular, for reading through a full draft of this book and, among other useful pieces of feedback, suggesting the shift of the more philosophical material to near the end; and my colleagues in USC's Computer Science Department who listened to my early ideas on this topic and lived through a multiyear experiment in restructuring the department along lines suggested by it (more about which can be found in chapter 5, section 5.4).

Neither this book nor the new research project on cognitive architecture could have been begun without the sabbatical support provided by USC's Viterbi School of Engineering during the 2008–2009 academic year. That year gave me the time to concentrate on these two new challenging efforts and really helped get both off to flying starts. Likewise, this book could not have been completed without the ability to write it as part of my normal faculty responsibilities or the opportunity of a second sabbatical unusually soon after the previous one. USC's Dean of Engineering, Yannis Yortsos, also provided helpful last-minute pointers to several newly published, yet highly relevant, books.

The Web in general, and Wikipedia[22] in particular, have been invaluable resources in writing this book, providing background and pointers on topics I needed to know about but with which I previously had little experience, along with specific facts, quotes, and figures that have been incorporated directly into the text as appropriate. Dictionary.com[23] also proved invaluable in clarifying concepts and providing alternative ways of expressing them, and Engadget[24] and Slashdot[25] helped keep me abreast of some of the latest discoveries and inventions. The diffuse impact of these various sources is acknowledgeable though not citable. Specific reuse is cited where appropriate.

1 The Computing Sciences

Anyone conversant with science is likely to be acquainted with the physical, life, and social sciences (figure 1.1). Each is a significant domain of intellectual endeavor that seeks to understand a broad but distinctive swath of reality. The physical sciences study physical, nonliving systems, from the smallest subatomic particles to the immensity of the universe—or multiverse, if our universe turns out to be just one among many. Disciplines within the physical sciences include physics, chemistry, astronomy, and geology. The life sciences study living organisms, which may be unicellular (e.g., bacteria), multicellular (e.g., plants and animals), or noncellular (e.g., viruses, which exist on the margin between living and nonliving). Disciplines within the life sciences include biology and ecology. The social sciences study human behavior in individuals and groups, both past and present, and both organized and not so organized. Disciplines within the social sciences include anthropology, economics, history, political science, psychology, and sociology. Together, these three scientific domains cover much of reality.

The content of each of these domains comprises a distinct combination of *structures* and *processes*. Structures are the *things of interest* in a scientific domain. In the physical sciences, a partial list includes particles and energy (physics), atoms and molecules (chemistry), stars and planets (astronomy), and rocks and rivers (geology). In the life sciences, we see everything from organic molecules to cells, organs, organisms, and social groups (for nonhuman organisms). In the social sciences, the structural focus is on people, their minds, and the artifacts that they produce and use.

Processes actively alter structures over time. In the physical sciences, we see elementary forces and their consequences (physics), chemical reactions (chemistry), the birth and evolution of the cosmos and its major components (astronomy), and the creation and evolution/erosion of land masses and bodies of water (geology). In the life sciences, we see the creation,

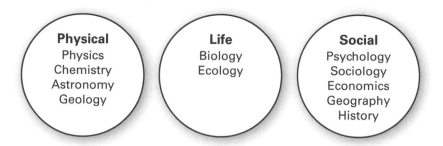

Figure 1.1
The three traditional great scientific domains.

evolution, and maintenance and death of organisms and their components (biology). We also see the interaction of life forms with their environments (ecology). In the social sciences, we see varying genres of cognition and behavior, such as individual and group cognition (psychology), past behavior (history), monetary behavior (economics), group behavior (sociology), and group behavior in a physical context (geography).

The distinctions among these domains are of course not without problems. For example, the question of what is life, and thus what fundamentally separates the life sciences from the physical sciences, is a difficult one. It will likely just get more difficult as humans increasingly tinker with creating life, or at least its near facsimile. The discipline of artificial life is focused on just such an enterprise, whether in organic/biological or inorganic/robotic hardware technologies or merely in software.[1] In the reverse direction, there are also emerging fields, such as DNA nanotechnology, in which core biological molecules are being used as the basis for extraordinarily tiny machines.[2] Such machines are made of the essential stuff of life but would generally not be considered alive. This kind of work may ultimately force us to rethink the boundary between these two great domains.

This is not the only such problem of course. As one further example, consider the dividing line between the life sciences and social sciences. This division reifies a form of the mind–body distinction, with the body and brain within the domain of the life sciences and the mind situated within the social sciences. The disciplines of cognitive neuroscience[3] and cognitive neuropsychology[4] are concerned with bridging this divide from its two sides by investigating how cognition arises from the workings of the brain. But they currently represent only the tip of the iceberg, as more and more of human behavior becomes firmly grounded in the workings of the body.

To some extent, such boundaries are thus social constructions,[5] although distinguishing among the domains is still useful to the extent that they differ strongly in both their core subject matter and how this material is studied and as long as we do not let such distinctions cause us to lose sight of the underlying unity of all of nature and thus of the unity we also ultimately should demand from science (what has been termed *consilience*[6]). A bigger problem from our perspective is that none of these domains covers the study of computing. Matter, energy, and force can be used to implement computing, just as they implement life, but neither computing nor life is best studied as a purely physical phenomenon. They each introduce new kinds of phenomena that enable, and in fact demand, new approaches to their study. The basic phenomena of computing are also not directly identifiable with biological organisms and the processes that support their lives or with people and the social processes that make them human. As with the physical domain, there are interesting overlaps between these domains and computing, which we will spend considerable time mapping out later in this book, but these multidisciplinary connections should not blind us to the core fact that the basic phenomena of computing are neither biological nor social.

So if computing is not part of the three traditional domains of science, what is it? One possibility is that it simply isn't a science. Some would argue that it is properly part of engineering rather than science, with more of a concern about building things than understanding them. Computer science did after all grow out of electrical engineering at a number of universities. According to this view, some science may go on in service of computing, but such *engineering science* is a subsidiary activity that does not rise to the level of a true science. A second possibility is that computing is part of mathematics—the original home for computer science at many universities where it did not come out of electrical engineering. But then mathematics has its own issues concerning whether or not it is science. A third possibility is that computing forms an additional scientific domain in its own right. This book explores this third way, hypothesizing that computing is not only a science, and the basis for a scientific domain that is distinct from the traditional three, but that it also forms the basis for what can be called a *great scientific domain*—the *computing sciences*—that is the equal of the physical, life, and social sciences.

Computing isn't simply about computers (i.e., *hardware*) nor is it just about programming (i.e., *software*) or formal principles (i.e., *theory*). Although all three of these topics are important—hardware provides the physical devices that enable computing to occur, software enables the specification of what should be computed, and theory answers questions about what is computable and how efficiently answers can be computed—the computing sciences comprise much more than just these bare essentials. Computer science, one of the traditional disciplines within the computing sciences, also includes for example such topics as artificial intelligence (AI), with its goal of developing computational systems capable of human levels of intelligent behavior; human–computer interaction, with its focus on facilitating human use of computers; networking, with its emphasis on communication among computers; and graphics, where researchers investigate visual rendering of both real and imagined scenes. But this list still just barely begins to scratch the surface of conventional topics within computing, particularly when we look beyond the discipline of computer science to other computing disciplines, such as computer engineering, information science, informatics, and computational science.

Such a list fails even more miserably when it comes to the rich space of more exotic multidisciplinary topics currently being explored in computing and related fields, such as monkeys controlling robotic arms by pure thought (figure 1.2)[7]; quantum computers of heretofore inconceivable power[8]; technology-enabled superhuman intelligence (what is now consid-

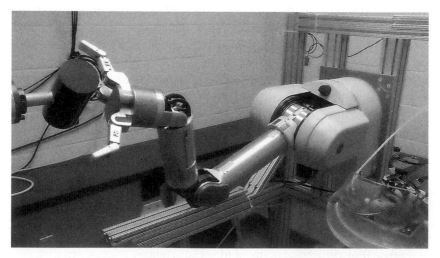

Figure 1.2
Monkey reaches to grasp doorknob-like object via thought control of a robot arm (University of Pittsburgh).
Image courtesy of UPMC.

Figure 1.3
Simulated humans combining virtual bodies, minds, emotions, and language for virtual reality training of soldiers in cross-cultural interaction and negotiation (University of Southern California).
Image courtesy of Arno Hartholt, USC Institute for Creative Technologies.

ered as part of the *singularity*)[9]; the deep intermingling of the real and virtual worlds, as people start to interact with each other and with virtual people in computationally created environments (figure 1.3)[10]; robots capable of constructing houses automatically from blueprints and raw materials (figure 1.4)[11]; and the possibility that the entire universe is itself simply a massive computer.[12] Such notions may read like science fiction, but they are all under active investigation.

Yet, neither does computing merely consist of an ad hoc catalog of topics relating to computers, although it is possible to come away with such an impression when reading such lists or even when examining the online self-descriptions of many of our best computer science departments. Computing forms the basis for a diverse but fundamentally coherent scientific domain. It is a domain that has already made substantial contributions, both intellectual and societal; that has gone through some recent doldrums due to the burst of the dot-com bubble; but that is as exciting

Figure 1.4
Robotic gantry capable of rapid, automated extrusion of concrete walls (University of Southern California).

as ever in terms of the work that is going on and its revolutionary potential for the future.

This book comprises an extended attempt to articulate the nature, structure, current excitement, and future potential of the computing sciences, culminating with an evaluation of the hypothesis that computing is the fourth great scientific domain. The approach will be unconventional. There is a minimal introduction to how computing works, and not much at all on its history. For those who want a better introduction to its basic principles, St. Amant's *Computing for Ordinary Mortals*,[13] Hillis's *The Pattern on the Stone*,[14] and Biermann's *Great Ideas in Computer Science*[15] take complementary approaches. Denning's work "The Great Principles of Computing" is also relevant.[16] A range of books on the history of computing can be found simply by searching online via Google or at an online bookstore such as Amazon.com. Beyond these gaps, there will also be no serious attempt to justify computing's status as a science via arguments about the depth or fundamental nature of its discoveries. I am content to leave that to Peter Denning and others.[17] Nor will we focus to a great extent on the traditional disciplinary structure within computing, except as necessary to relate it to the organizational concepts to be introduced here. What we will do is first discuss the nature of computing and the scope of the computing sciences in the remainder of this chapter before moving on to an inherently multidisciplinary, *relational approach* to understanding the domain of computing as a great scientific domain.

Understanding the nature of computing in terms of a succinct definition is essential for scoping both the field in general and this book in particular. Without such, we cannot know what to include in the computing sciences or how to argue for their amounting to a great scientific domain. We cannot even adequately explain to our scientific colleagues in other fields, to our students, or to the public at large what it is we do. The definition of computing we will settle on is conventional and mostly uncontroversial. The approach to scoping the computing sciences, in contrast, begins with a largely conventional—although still possibly controversial—proposal, and then proceeds from there through a succession of less conventional and likely more controversial alternatives.

The relational approach to understanding computing is novel in both its structure and implications. It suggests a strong parallel between what is generally viewed as core versus multidisciplinary research. It assumes and exploits a symmetry between computing and the other three great scientific domains. And, most critically, it provides a distinctly different way of understanding the individual topics within computing, how they relate to each other, and how computing as a whole relates to the other domains. These differences are leveraged to provide a new kind of multidisciplinary overview of the domain of computing, with a strong focus on what is most exciting for the present and future. They also provide insight into several forms of macrostructure that can be defined over the domain. The ultimate result is a surprisingly diverse yet coherent perspective on the domain of computing that can be leveraged, along with an excursion into philosophy of science, to evaluate the hypothesis that computing comprises the fourth great scientific domain.

1.1 What Is Computing?

Existing definitions of computing tend to focus on particular disciplines within the overall domain, such as computer science or information technology, rather than on the domain as a whole. However, there is a core motif woven through most such definitions that can be distilled out as the essence of computing as a subject for study. Let's start with definitions of computer science, which has a long and often distinguished tradition of attempts to define it[18] dating back to at least the late 1960s.[19] Informally, computer science studies computing and information, both in the abstract and in real implemented systems. It focuses on theory (the mathematical and logical foundations of computing), algorithms (sequences of instructions to be followed to perform tasks), and all kinds of software systems and issues. It may also include work on computer hardware as well. Typical efforts to define it include "the study of (the phenomena surrounding) computers,"[20] "the study of algorithms,"[21] "the field of computer hardware and software,"[22] and "the study of the theoretical foundations of information and computation, and of practical techniques for their implementation and application in computer systems."[23] There are not as many attempts at defining the other disciplines within the computing sciences, but typical ones consider computer engineering to be "the science and technology of design, construction, implementation, and maintenance of software and hardware components of modern computing systems and computer-controlled equipment,"[24] information science to be "the scientific study of the gathering, manipulation, classification, storage, and retrieval of recorded knowledge,"[25] and information technology to be "the development, implementation, and maintenance of computer hardware and software systems to organize and communicate information electronically."[26]

Perhaps most directly on point has been a recent symposium in the Association for Computing Machinery (ACM) online publication *Ubiquity*, which attempted to answer the question, *What is computation?* One contribution defined it as process,[27] another as symbol manipulation,[28] a third as the transformation of representations,[29] and several—including my own—focused on information transformation.[30,31] The common motif running through most of these and the earlier definitions, either implicitly or explicitly, is that computing involves the *transformation of information*. This can be expressed alternatively as *information processing* or simply referred to as *information and computation*, where computation is understood to be the process of transforming information. The particular focus in any individual definition may be on the fact that transformation is occurring, or on the abstract specification of transformations (i.e., algorithms) or on the concrete hardware and software that enable the transformations to occur in the physical world, or on the maintenance of information, or on its denotational aspects. But, no matter how this motif is modulated, it sits at the core of all of computing and thus should serve us well as a definition of the subject matter of computing.

The technical definition of information itself derives from information theory, where it is structure—patterns of binary choices—that resolves uncertainty. A single such choice amounts to one *bit* that is capable of being either 0 or 1. One bit is sufficient to resolve whether an unbiased coin comes up heads or tails. More bits can resolve larger sources of uncertainty, such as distinguishing this book's name out of the set of all possible strings of English words. But information need not be literally expressed in bits. More broadly, it can be thought of as any content expressed in some medium—whether electrical signals in wires, magnetic domains on disks, or marks on paper—that resolves uncertainty. This can consist of bits. But it can also consist of numeric values and measurements, such as the balance in a checkbook, GPS coordinates, or seismic data from an earthquake. It can consist of strings of characters—fragments of text— covering everything from short nonsense strings, such as *ax5q*, to web pages, to the contents of this entire book. It can consist of online audio and/or video files encoded in some format, such as MP3 for audio files. It can consist of knowledge about the world, such as the generalization that *all men are mortal* or the mostly true statement that *books are found in libraries or bookstores*. It can consist of models of how things work, such as a computer-aided design model of an airplane or car, or a model of circulation within the earth's atmosphere. Or it can consist of programs; that is, content that specifies sequences of operations to be performed by computers. Content can be about our world—and be more or less accurate in the process—about imaginary or virtual worlds, or about no world at all.

In some of the definitions listed earlier, the terms *symbol* or *representation* were used instead of *information*. Both of the former terms focus on the relationship between two structures, where the first denotes the second— such as when the phrase *this book* represents, or acts as a symbol for, the book you are currently reading—rather than on structures that determine choices. Yet information is usually composed of symbols and thus represents, whereas representations generally comprise information. For our purposes here, we will not worry about subtle differences among these terms, simply going with *information* as our choice; but for those interested in this topic, a more thorough treatment of the distinction between information and representation in the context of defining computing can be found in my *Ubiquity* article.[32] For those wanting a broad overview of the topic of information—including its history, theory, technology, and impact—James Gleick's 2011 book *The Information* is a good source.[33]

Transformation then is the process of executing computational operations that alter such information. Such operations could increase a checking account balance by crediting a deposit, predict the climate later in this century, convert an audio file on an iPod into signals capable of driving speakers, or conclude by reasoning from the general rule concerning mortality and the fact that I am a man that I am mortal. The concept of transformation is general enough to subsume all of the other activities one normally thinks of as being associated with information, such as acquisition, storage, transmission, analysis, understanding, presentation, and application. Software and hardware concern the specification and execution of information transformations.

1.2 The Scope of the Computing Sciences

Given a definition of computing as the transformation of information, what then is comprised by the computing sciences? We will explore this question in two directions. First, we will look at the domain of computing in isolation, as a pure or unidisciplinary domain, and ask what is properly part of its scope. This discussion will by necessity delve partway into the question of what science is, and isn't, starting with a mildly controversial baseline and then proceeding to two proposals for moving beyond this baseline that, although they have come to be second nature to me, are likely to raise quite a few more eyebrows. We will then examine the status of multidisciplinary work that involves computing, asking to what extent such work should also be considered as part of the computing sciences.

1.2.1 Pure Computing

At a minimum, the computing sciences should include anything that applies the traditional analytical or experimental methods of science to understanding aspects of computing. Analyzing the complexity of algorithms provides a prototypical example of such an activity, but it is far from the only one. Much more pervasive is the use of experiments in understanding essentially all aspects of computing and all varieties of computing systems. However, even the classification of these kinds of activities as science is sometimes denied because of the largely non-natural, man-made origin of what is studied. Herbert Simon—another of the four founders of AI (along with Allen Newell, who was mentioned in the preface) and the sole computer scientist to have won a Nobel prize, albeit in economics—attempted to cope with this by referring to computer science as a *science of the artificial*, being the study of man-made artifacts.[34] Peter Denning has argued more recently that the modifier *artificial* is unnecessary and that computer science is simply a science like any other, given that we have recently come to realize that computing does show up in the natural world, including in a number of ways within our own bodies.[35]

I believe that we should go even further to accept that the distinction between natural and artificial is increasingly untenable and that it is past time it were dropped as a central distinction in science. The distinction seems to originate in a tradition that God created both nature and people, but with people occupying a special position outside of, and in a dominating position over, nature. Within this tradition, everything God created is natural, along with anything else engendered by processes in nature, whereas anything created by humans is somehow outside of nature and thus artificial. A beehive when created by bees is thus considered natural, whereas a similar structure created by people would be considered artificial. If, however, as evolution implies, people are merely one more fragment of nature, then their products are as natural as anything else.

Furthermore, although it has generally been easy historically to distinguish human products from natural products, this has become—and will likely continue to become—more and more problematic as our understanding of nature continues to improve and we are increasingly able to alter it at its most fundamental levels. Consider food flavorings. Both natural and artificial flavors may consist of identical molecules, with only the sources from which their atoms are derived differing. Similarly, plants first evolved without human intervention, and then under general pressure from human selection, and now via pointed genetic modifications. Are these plants really becoming more artificial? They are still made out of the same chemical and biological ingredients as the original "natural" plants. When doctors influence stem cells to become organ cells, are the new cells natural or artificial? The body cannot tell the difference. And nanotechnology now gives us the ability to alter both the living and physical worlds at the molecular level. The future seems likely to look more and more like this, where we will need to understand a world in which human and nonhuman effects are increasingly difficult to distinguish. Thus, even in these traditional domains, the distinction between natural and artificial appears to be heading toward the intellectual scrap heap.

Whether you accept computing as a natural science, or only as a science of the artificial, or you deny the relevance of the distinction, hopefully you will accept the baseline notion that the traditional kinds of scientific activities discussed so far fit appropriately within computing as a science and thus within the computing sciences. The next two proposals are likely to be more jarring but hopefully will make as much sense.

The first proposal takes off from a notion I have come to accept as a practicing scientist that science should include all activities that *tend to increase our understanding over time*. The standard analytical and experimental methods within science are geared toward generating conclusions that are valid to a high degree of certainty. Such levels of certainty can be critical when results are to be applied in real-world situations, but the process of understanding can be more gradual in general, with progress possible by a variety of methods that vary dramatically in the certainty they provide and the kinds of understanding they yield.

When I read a scientific article, what I care about is learning something new and important that I can be convinced is true. I am agnostic, at least in principle, concerning what methods were used to invent or discover the new thing or what methods were used to convince me of their reality, as long as they achieve the desired ends. Great science requires all three of these attributes: novelty, importance, and veracity. Good science makes some compromises. To many researchers, all that is important for good science is veracity, and work may be publishable with miniscule quantities of the other two attributes as long as there is sufficient evidence of—or methodology for establishing—truth. In contrast, I often learn more from sufficiently novel and important conjectures—even before there is a great deal of evidence or methodology in their favor—leaving me more comfortable in labeling such papers as good science than in applying such a label to traditional small-but-validated results. I do not learn of necessary truth from such articles, but they may still revolutionize my way of thinking about the topic, opening up new possibilities and plausibilities never previously considered.

This distinction is surprisingly reminiscent—at least to a devotee of English literature such as me—of an interchange in Jane Austen's *Persuasion*[36] between Anne Elliot and Mr. Elliot concerning the nature of good company. The former says that she prefers "the company of clever, well-informed people, who have a great deal of conversation," to which the latter replies "Good company requires only birth, education, and manners, and with regard to education is not very nice." Mr. Elliot then goes on to state with respect to Anne's notion that "that is not good company; that is the best." What is "best" in both company and science is substance that inspires and yields new insights irrespective of either the form in which it is clothed or whether it is based on novel facts or new ways of thinking.

The broader notion of science as understanding includes not only the kinds of explorations and conjectures discussed earlier, which identify new scientific possibilities, but also replacement of complex theories with simpler ones, even when this does not increase their ability to predict observable phenomena (a form of progress that has recently been central to my own research); and weak analytical and experimental methods that increase the likelihood of one theory over another even if the difference is not statistically significant. All of these can tend to increase our understanding over time and thus are fully part of science under this extended notion.

On the flip side, it is important that a scientific enterprise also not tend to increase our misunderstanding over time. Fortune telling, astrology, and religious prophecy can lead to correct predictions, particularly when ambiguity is combined with generous post hoc interpretations and rationalizations, but none of these ultimately has demonstrated any ability to predict better than random guessing. On the whole, they contribute much more to misunderstanding than to understanding despite occasional hits. Such activities are thus clearly not scientific, even in the presence of occasional legal rulings to the contrary.[37] Still, although the difference is clear here, there can be gray areas where it is difficult to determine whether some activity tends to increase our understanding and should therefore be considered within the scope of science. Work on a normative scientific method attempts to deal with this by prevalidating the approach taken to understanding. As long as the scientific method is used, what comes out of it will be science. The problem, of course, is that much of actual science does not proceed by such a method, and it would be greatly impoverished if it were forced to do so. Not to mention that much trivial science follows the method to the letter.

One key research-style dichotomy I have noticed among scientists of my acquaintance is whether they are more focused on *similarities* or *differences*. The former care most for identifying what is common across a range of diverse phenomena, whereas the latter are most deeply concerned with what distinguishes the phenomena. Science as a whole cannot proceed without both kinds of activities, but individual scientists often seem to fall into one camp or the other. The recognition of this distinction among research styles goes back to at least the mid-nineteenth century in biology, where it is known as *lumpers* versus *splitters*.[38]

Both this book and my earlier research on cognitive architecture identify me as a fully committed member of the lumper camp, focused on similarity and commonality. I cannot help seeing similarities as more important than differences, getting the most satisfaction out of uncovering hidden commonalities and looking to the benefits of integration over those of differentiation. This strategy is clearly a factor in the move to identify science with the full breadth of progressive understanding activities. The commonality among such activities and how they all contribute to our knowledge of the world becomes their predominant trait, with the differences among them, although still important, becoming a subsidiary concern.

The second proposal goes even further in this lumping process, proposing that great scientific domains should really be thought of as comprising a combination of understanding plus a general constructive activity that we will refer to as *shaping*. The task of shaping the world is generally considered the realm of engineering, whether the activity involves creating something new—such as a new computer, bridge, appliance, or chemical compound—or altering some aspect of the world that already exists; for example, by upgrading a computer or retrofitting a bridge. Traditional engineering disciplines focus on shaping the physical aspects of the world, with emphases such as civil, mechanical, chemical, electrical, nuclear, environmental, aerospace, and computer engineering. However, it would be wrong to conclude from this that shaping only occurs within the physical sciences. Shaping also occurs in the life and social sciences, just under different names, such as medicine and education. The use of the term *engineering* is conventionally limited to quantitative, mathematical approaches to shaping. As aspects of shaping diverge from this, there is more resistance to calling them engineering, but all progress in shaping is of consequence—not just the aspects traditionally labeled engineering—just as all aspects of understanding are of consequence.

The proposal here starts with this broadening from the traditional notion of engineering to the full scope of shaping, but then also includes shaping as a full, closely intertwined partner with understanding in the composition of great scientific domains.[39] Science and engineering, when considered together, are two closely interlinked faces of the same activity—somewhat like the Roman god Janus (figure 1.5)—both of which deeply embrace understanding *and* shaping. Science is most particularly about understanding the world, but it is also an inherently creative activity that shapes how we think and perceive the world through the development of new concepts and theories. It also physically shapes the world in creating the experimental equipment needed to investigate the world,[40] such as the massive Large Hadron Collider (figure 1.6).

Allen Newell used to talk about how the Computer Science Department at Carnegie Mellon University evaluated faculty for promotion based not so much on their publication record but on the extent to which they *pushed around the field*; that is, on how their work shaped the future of computer science as a discipline. This could involve discoveries that alter

Figure 1.5
The two-faced Roman god Janus.

how people think and what problems they work on, but it can also involve the creation of tools—whether conceptual, theoretical, computational, or physical—that enable new directions to be pursued, new discoveries to be made, and new tools to be built. It is the tools that make science cumulative, enabling later scientists to *stand on the shoulders* of their predecessors.[41] He even stated that all that really mattered in science was the tools. If other scientists could not, or need not, make use of your contributions in pursuing their own work, it was as if your contributions never existed, much like trees falling in the forest in the absence of witnesses. According to such a view, there can be no productivity in science without shaping of the domain.

Engineering takes the dual perspective from science, being most particularly about shaping the world but also inherently concerned with understanding what is being created and the principles underlying these creative acts and their outputs. There is a constant reciprocation between science and engineering, where they perpetually challenge and stimulate each other. Science provides theories and data upon which engineering can be based. Engineering in turn poses questions for science to answer while simultaneously evaluating the validity of scientific hypotheses by assessing whether technologies based on them succeed in the manner predicted.

Figure 1.6
The Large Hadron Collider, a 17-mile-circumference particle accelerator at the European Organization for Nuclear Research (CERN) near Geneva.
Image courtesy of CERN.

Within computing, it can be extraordinarily difficult to distinguish between understanding and shaping. One might think a priori that it would map onto the difference between computer science and engineering, but it mostly does not. Despite use of the word *science* in its name, computer science is frequently considered to be an engineering discipline in addition to or instead of a scientific discipline. My own computer science department is situated within a school of engineering—the USC Viterbi School of Engineering—as are computer science departments at many other universities. The development of algorithms and software systems, along with programming in general, are clearly engineering activities; yet, computer science is also inherently about understanding computation. As a computer scientist, I have always felt ambivalent about whether to consider myself a scientist or an engineer. I create new things—concepts, theories, and systems—and sit within a school of engineering, but my drive has always been to get to the bottom of things, to understand the *how* and the *why*.

Computer engineering focuses on computer systems, primarily hardware and aspects of systems software—software that is *close to* or integrated with the hardware. It overlaps extensively with both electrical engineering—the study of the flow of electricity, including through the kinds of semiconductor materials used in computers—and computer science. Computer engineering is in some sense more engineering-like than computer science because it is closer to the physical domain and thus also more amenable to formalization via traditional mathematics, but in the same sense it is more science-like as well. The distinction between the two disciplines is thus really more between a focus on software in computer science and hardware in computer engineering. Both include substantial aspects of understanding *and* shaping.

But the problem goes beyond merely confusion in labeling to permeate much of the field. Because computing largely understands what it creates, it is difficult in general to tell when shaping leaves off and understanding begins. This is often viewed as an embarrassment, contributing to the notion that computing is not science. To articulate more clearly the breadth and depth of computing's science base, academics continue to work hard at separating out understanding from shaping. But what if the more fundamental problem instead turned out to be that we have been looking at this issue backward all of this time? In other words, what if the inherent intertwining of understanding and shaping within computing were actually a strength rather than a weakness? Furthermore, what if this meant that computing is not a problem child within the sciences but a model for the future of the other sciences in terms of the centrality of such intertwining within great scientific domains?

In computing, this intertwining of understanding and shaping has actually been one of its greatest strengths rather than a weakness for which we should feel apologetic. It is a key factor in computing's astonishingly rapid development. Think for example of Xerox PARC in its heyday, when a ferment of exploration, experimentation, and creation combined to revolutionize the dominant paradigm of computing. Although not referring to computing, Richard Feynman—a Nobel laureate physicist—captured the overall notion well in a statement on his blackboard at his death in 1988: "What I cannot create, I do not understand."[42] The life and social sciences in particular have long suffered from their limited ability to shape their domains in conjunction with their understanding of them. As our ability to create and manipulate living and thinking systems continues to improve, the life and social sciences will have an increasing opportunity, and in fact an imperative, to embrace the intertwining of understanding and shaping that has so long been a major factor in computing. Although people have long shaped the physical domain, even there our ability to manipulate it at its most fundamental levels is taking a giant leap with the advent of nanotechnology.

We may have to wait until scientists from the other scientific domains fully appreciate both the inevitability and the power of intertwining understanding and shaping in their own work and domains before we can hope to see a broader acceptance of what computing has been both confronting and leveraging since its inception. But this may not be too far in the future, as intertwining increasingly becomes the norm across the sciences, just as it has been in computing since the beginning.

In the meantime, I have increasingly bonded to the notion that at the top level, the distinction should be between content domains—physical, life, social, and computing—rather than science versus engineering, with each such domain then being a blend of understanding and shaping. Science and engineering, as traditionally construed, are central to understanding and shaping, respectively, but are inherently more limited in presupposing particular domains of interest and methods for exploring these domains while disregarding most understanding or shaping activities that fall outside of the boundaries defined by these domains and methods. The traditional methods focus on experiments whose parameters can be controlled by the investigator, theories expressed in the language of mathematics, and more recently simulations implemented on computers. The domains of science and engineering tend to be limited to those that can be investigated via these methods. Deriving the meaning and significance of the works of Jane Austen is, for example, clearly an activity of understanding, but it is part of the humanities that is not generally considered part of science. Similarly, medicine and education shape our bodies and minds but are not traditionally part of engineering.

The notion of a great scientific domain, as it will be more fully developed later, assumes the intertwining of understanding and shaping. Defining a great scientific domain in this way is far from standard, but the centrality of this combination emerged directly out of my experience as a computer scientist. I have come to consider the computing sciences as comprising *the understanding and shaping of the transformation of information*. This subsumes the science and engineering of computing; basic and applied work with computers (including scientific computing and the many informatics disciplines); the academic disciplines of computer science and engineering; information science and technology; and the divide between academic and industrial computing. Understanding is more central in those segments of the domain characterized by such terms as *science*, *basic*, and *academic*, whereas shaping takes the lead in those segments better characterized as *engineering*, *applied*, and *industrial*. However, it is all computing science. I occasionally find myself debating with computer science colleagues whether work on the more applied side can form the basis for good academic computing research. In my view, it clearly can, as long as it yields something sufficiently novel and important concerning computing.

In the remainder of this book, we will assume that the computing sciences span the full breadth of both understanding and shaping and argue further (in chapter 6) that they amount to a great scientific domain. If your preference is still to keep science separate from engineering or to keep each defined more narrowly than what is implied by understanding and shaping, you can mostly substitute *science* for *understanding* and *engineering* for *shaping* in what is to come and also substitute *science and engineering domains* for *great scientific domains*. The fit will not be perfect, particularly when we slip outside of the traditional boundaries of science and engineering, but many of the concepts and messages will still apply.

1.2.2 Multidisciplinary Computing

To what extent does multidisciplinary work that involves some aspect of computing belong within the computing sciences? Multidisciplinary work in general often holds a tenuous position within academic departments, sometimes accepted, sometimes accepted only grudgingly as peripherally within the discipline, and sometimes considered outside of the scope of the discipline. I still vividly recall my experience in the 1980s as a young assistant professor at Stanford University, where I had a joint appointment in computer science and psychology working on cognitive architectures via a combination of psychologically motivated AI and computational modeling of human cognition. This had been my dream job, but the reality was that I was all too often viewed by psychologists as a computer scientist because I did not do experiments nor was I concerned primarily with the accuracy of fits to human data, and computer scientists too often viewed me as a psychologist because I explored psychologically inspired mechanisms rather than more formal methods (such as logic) and was not primarily concerned with core computational issues such as optimality. My concern instead was how to develop a single integrated model/theory/system with maximal breadth of coverage across the basic phenomena of intelligence. But, in the process I had managed to situate myself outside of the predominant paradigm boundaries in both of my home departments.

When it comes to great scientific domains, similar issues arise. Should work that spans two domains be considered as fully within both domains, as only within one domain—based on criteria such as which domain most benefits from the combination—or considered to be outside of both domains? Hopefully, most people will agree that the last alternative is self-defeating, particularly as more and more of the most exciting work within computing and the other sciences becomes multidisciplinary. If the boundaries drawn around domains and the organizations that investigate them are too narrow, multidisciplinary research falls between the cracks, a result that is dysfunctional both for scientific progress in general and for the individuals involved in particular. Similar risks also result when departments, disciplines, and domains become too focused on the benefits to themselves as a criterion for whether multidisciplinary work is within their scope. The relational approach, and in fact much of the rest of this book, can be viewed as an argument for the naturalness and importance of including within the computing sciences any work that involves significant understanding or shaping of computing, whether multidisciplinary or not; and we will proceed under this assumption as we make our way through the remainder of it.

1.3 Summary

If you accept the arguments in this chapter, we have a notion of computing as the transformation of information and of the computing sciences as a multidisciplinary activity that involves the understanding and shaping of computing. This yields a broad view of computing that spans what traditionally is partitioned across science and engineering, basic and applied, computer science and engineering, information science and technology, and academic and industrial computing. It also subsumes the distinction between pure and multidisciplinary computing—and core versus peripheral computing—bringing computational science and the plethora of informatics disciplines fully into the fold. Last, but not least, it sets us up for a discussion of the importance and vitality of the science of computing. Computing is not merely the handmaiden of the other sciences, nor is it just a pragmatic art or a form of engineering; it is a great scientific domain in its own right.

2 The Relational Approach

The relational approach to understanding computing derives from a simple core idea of examining the ways in which computing relates to itself and to the other three great scientific domains. It originally grew out of a desire to determine if there was some form of coherence lurking behind the wide array of multidisciplinary topics I was working on as director of New Directions at the University of Southern California's Information Sciences Institute (ISI), ranging from automated construction to technology and the arts, biomedical informatics, simulation-based training, and responding to unexpected events. Over time, this led to the development of the relational architecture and the accompanying metascience expression (ME) language, which together provide an inherently multidisciplinary perspective on computing.

Architecture is an integrative concept. Simply put, an architecture describes how a set of parts combine to produce a functional whole. It provides structure and coherence, enabling the resulting assemblage to yield more than just the sum of its parts. In the everyday world, its most common usage is in the design and construction of buildings. Within computing, architecture is central to the design and construction of hardware. It both characterizes the hardware to be constructed and specifies the instruction set in which the hardware is to be programmed. Within cognitive science—a multidisciplinary area that combines "Artificial Intelligence, Linguistics, Anthropology, Psychology, Neuroscience, Philosophy, and Education"[1]—architecture is applied to key aspects of integrated models of cognition. In analogy to computer architecture, a cognitive architecture specifies the fixed structure underlying cognition while also specifying a language that can be used to encode knowledge—the variable part of cognition—within the system.

Architecture becomes a core tool in science by supporting the processes of understanding and shaping. In the preface to the fourth edition of their classic text on computer architecture, Hennessy and Patterson state that their "goal has been to describe the basic principles underlying what will be tomorrow's technological developments," that their "primary objective in writing our first book was to change the way people learn and think," and that they "have strived to produce a new edition that will continue to be as relevant for professional engineers and architects as it is for those involved in advanced computer architecture and design courses."[2] The earlier classic text in computer architecture, originally by Bell and Newell, also had similar goals of providing a better understanding of the range of existing computers plus tools to assist in designing new ones.[3]

The discipline of cognitive architecture is less coherent, with the primary home for the understanding of (natural) cognition being within cognitive psychology and that for the shaping of (artificial) cognition being within artificial intelligence; although in artificial intelligence, the term *cognitive architecture* is often replaced by another term, such as *intelligent agent architecture* or *artificial general intelligence*, to avoid the *natural* connotations many place on the use of the term *cognition*. At one point, there was hope that cognitive science would be the home for work such as this that spans both natural and artificial cognition. However, its focus has narrowed to an emphasis on natural cognition, although insights are still welcome from artificial cognition as long as they bear on natural cognition.

In my earlier collaborations with John Laird and Allen Newell on the Soar cognitive architecture, we explicitly held the dual goals of understanding intelligence—whether natural or artificial—and shaping (artificial) intelligence. Our approach was based on a belief that these goals were best pursued in tandem, where they could cross-inform each other: Understanding human thought (the best working example we have of intelligence) can help guide decisions in developing artificially intelligent systems, and computationally implemented architectures can serve as key elements of unified theories of cognition[4] (integrated models of thought that combine both architectures and knowledge) to support experimentation and analysis and feed back into our understanding of the human mind. We were clearly outliers in taking such an approach but found it to yield a fertile ground within which to work.[5]

The rationale for the development of the relational architecture was to understand computing better, but the architecture itself is symmetric across domains and thus is potentially applicable in understanding any topics within science. On occasion in the forthcoming discussion, the concern will be with science in general, but mostly it will be with the architecture's application to computing. Science as a whole actually does already have a well-accepted architecture of a sort, based on its decomposition in terms of differing goals, methods, and subjects. Understanding and shaping, for example, can be viewed as alternative scientific goals that distinguish, respectively, the traditional scientific disciplines such as physics, chemistry, and biology from engineering and the other professions. Similarly, choice of methods—whether hypothesis testing, controlled experimentation, mathematical and computational modeling, statistical and computational data analysis, or other approaches—is sometimes used either to differentiate science from other intellectual disciplines or to distinguish among the sciences.

The boundaries engendered by distinctions among goals and methods tend to be fairly coarse, whereas differences in subject matter can occur at arbitrary levels of granularity. When fully elaborated, subject matter distinctions yield a traditional disciplinary hierarchy (figure 2.1). At the top of the hierarchy is the root node representing all of science. The four great scientific domains may then appear just below or there could be intervening layers; for example, first splitting out the natural sciences—the physical and life sciences—from the social and computing sciences. Below the level of great domains lies what generally becomes the departmental structure in universities, with such subjects as physics, chemistry, biology, ecology, psychology, anthropology, and computer science. Beneath this departmental level can be further subdisciplinary hierarchies, possibly going all of the way down to the narrowest of subspecialties.

Such a hierarchy provides a taxonomy, or ontology, over the sciences. It is a form of architecture that enables pigeon-holing of scientists and their work. The definition of computing provided in chapter 1 focused on

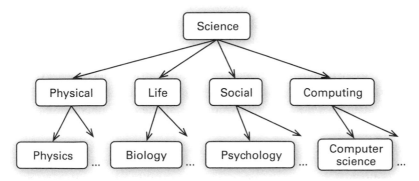

Figure 2.1
Top part of a disciplinary hierarchy for the sciences.

characterizing its content as a scientific domain, thus fitting neatly within this traditional ontological methodology, distinguishing what computing is from what it is not. When combined with the notion that computing is a great scientific domain, it also enables us to determine where computing fits in the hierarchy of sciences, as a distinct node within the first tier just below the root node. We can then further populate the hierarchy under this node with conventional disciplines and subdisciplines within computing, providing one form of organization over the domain.

Such an ontology thus tells us something about the *subclass* relationships among domains and disciplines, providing a structuring over computing and a place for it within the hierarchy of science. The relational architecture takes a different tack. Rather than being based on a static relationship—subclass—among subjects, it leverages a pair of active relationships between domains: *interaction* and *implementation*. Together, interaction and implementation provide insight into how scientific domains work with each other and how individual disciplines, subdisciplines, and research topics—essentially any node in the ontology—become defined by such relationships. A new organization for a domain such as computing then results from this, based on commonalities and differences among the domains and relationships implicated across this space.

In more detail, the first step is to analyze individual disciplines, subdisciplines, and research topics in terms of the great scientific domains out of which they are composed plus the relationships implicated among these domains. For example, human–computer interaction involves the computing and social domains in an interaction relationship. Artificial intelligence involves these same two domains, but here the computing domain implements the social domain; well, actually computing typically simulates rather than fully implements the social domain, but this is a subtle distinction we will return to later. To consider one more example, in weather forecasting, computing implements—actually, again, simulates—the physical domain. Such analyses can be performed for all of the classes in the hierarchy to yield dynamic models of scientific disciplines at all levels of granularity. The analyses reveal the essential multidisciplinarity of the topics studied plus how the subject matter of the component disciplines work together across disciplinary boundaries to yield the content of the class of interest.

The second step in the overall analysis is to compare the results from these individual analyses, looking for commonalities and patterns across topics. From just the three simple examples mentioned, we see that computing plays a central role in all three, but that each also includes one other domain plus a single relationship between computing and the second domain. All three are thus instances of what will be called *dyadic computing*, at the simpler end of the space of multidisciplinary forms of computing. Further comparison reveals that one pair of topics, human–computer interaction and artificial intelligence, involves the same two domains, just with different relationships, whereas a second pair, artificial intelligence and weather forecasting, shares the same relationship, differing only in which other domain is related to computing. These analyses thus reveal nonhierarchical similarities across the classes in the standard ontology.

The third step leverages these similarities to develop a new form of organization over science that is inherently multidisciplinary and nonhierarchical. When we are talking about dyadic computing, involving only one domain beyond computing and one relationship, it is possible to lay out the architecture as a two-dimensional table. Such a table will be provided later, in chapter 5, once all of the necessary groundwork for it has been presented. But understanding and presenting the full architecture requires the combinatoric flexibility of a language. Just as Bell and Newell, in writing their text, were impelled to create a new language—actually two new languages, Instruction Set Processor (ISP) and Processor Memory Switch (PMS)—in service of understanding and shaping computer architecture, a new language ultimately becomes necessary here as well. The ME language is a first stab at just such a tool.

Metascience can be thought of as *science about science*. The name of the language thus embodies the intent that it will assist in understanding and shaping the scientific enterprise. The focus here is on its use in understanding and shaping computing science, but as with the relational architecture from which it derives, the language is symmetric in how it handles the four great scientific domains. At bottom, the ME language is domain independent. Yet, because most of the experience with it to date has been in the context of computing, how useful it will prove outside of this domain—as well as whether it will require extensions adequately to model the full range of topics outside of computing—remains to be seen. Within computing, the ME language has so far proved adequate for all of the explorations in this book, although occasional discussions will come up about ways that it may at some point be worthwhile to extend it.

With the relational architecture and the ME language in hand, we can go beyond simply taxonomizing science to a deeper form of understanding and shaping of it. This can be by providing insights into the nature of individual disciplines, revealing hidden commonality across disciplines,

altering how we think more generally about disciplines and their relationships, or even influencing the creation of new disciplines.

The first possibility, of understanding individual disciplines better,
depends only on the initial step in the relational analysis—decomposing
individual disciplines into their component domains and relationships—
but the others all depend critically on the ability to make comparisons
across disciplines and ultimately to assemble all of the disciplines into a
coherent and understandable whole. In the remainder of this chapter, we
first look in more detail at what is involved in decomposing disciplines
into their constituent domains, along with how the implementation
and interaction relationships can recombine these components into
meaningful disciplinary representations. As it proves useful, we will move
back and forth in the process between a concern with science as a whole
and computing as a special case of particular interest. As domains and
relationships are discussed, bits of the ME language will be introduced as
they are needed. In the final section, the portions of the ME language
already introduced will be reviewed and the remainder of the language
presented.

2.1   Domains

In this section, the focus is on how disciplines are composed of combinations of domains. We will keep the concept of relationships among
domains simple for now, limiting it to a generic notion of *overlap*, in order
to focus on the domain combinations themselves. Let's start with one of
the simple examples from the introduction, the discipline of human–
computer interaction, which concerns the understanding and shaping of
the interactions between people and computers. Based on its name and
definition, it is obvious that this discipline involves at least an overlap
between the social and computing domains. But can, and should, we say
anything more about its composition in terms of domains? Without more
on relationships, there are still at least two ways that this decomposition
could be further elaborated.

The first possibility leverages the ontology of scientific disciplines to
narrow these domain descriptions down to those segments of the overall
domains that are relevant. Starting with the social domain, we could
narrow it down to psychology and perhaps from there down to cognitive
psychology, with its focus on human thought processes. Likewise, we
might narrow computing down to computer science and from there down
to graphics. In both cases, however, we would clearly be omitting parts of

the domains that are relevant, at least to some degree; for example, psychophysics—the study of human perception—in the social domain and the development of computer displays in the domain of computing. We could explicitly add such missing areas back in, so that we are considering a set of disciplines within each domain, or we could choose to move back up the hierarchy to nodes that are more inclusive. These are kinds of decisions that can arise any time one is modeling complex phenomena. What matters most? How much detail should be sacrificed for simplicity and clarity versus being included for completeness and accuracy? In exploring the relational architecture to date, the domain granularity considered has been restricted to just the top two levels of the ontology: the generic root node representing all of science and the four great scientific domains just below it. This has proved adequate for the work so far, while avoiding the complexity of constantly choosing ontological levels. However, it is a choice that could be revisited in the future should it prove necessary.

The second possibility is to include additional great domains in the decomposition when they play some role. Human–computer interaction is primarily about humans and computers, but their interactions are also mediated through both physical and living components. The computer side of the interaction involves physical input and output devices, such as mice and screens, whereas the human side requires biological perceptual and motor mechanisms, such as eyes, ears, and hands. A full characterization of the discipline would thus involve overlaps among all four great domains. However, it once again becomes a modeling decision as to whether or not to include such second-order domains and their associated relationships. The choice of which domains to include is at present left up to the modeler. In a specific situation, different people may make different choices, and the same person may choose differently at different times depending on the context and the intended use of the model.

One of the basic assumptions behind the relational architecture is that every node in the hierarchy of sciences can be analyzed in terms of the domains involved in it, just as was done here for human–computer interaction. We should therefore be able to proceed through the hierarchy node by node, focusing particularly on the subhierarchy for computing, and perform such analyses. In addition to this analytical approach, there is also a contrasting generative approach. Here, we start with the individual domains, then combine them in all possible pairwise manners, and then generate all possible combinations of three of them, and finally bring all four together. For each such domain combination, we can determine which topics in the hierarchy it covers and thus generate a systematic

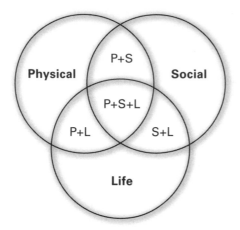

Figure 2.2
The overlaps among the traditional great scientific domains yield new disciplines at the forefront of today's research enterprise.

structure over all of science or just over all of computing if we limit ourselves to domain combinations in which it plays a role. Such a perspective provides an abstraction over the full relational architecture, missing as it does the differentiation among interdomain relationships, but like the full relational architecture it is intrinsically multidisciplinary and quite different in form from the standard ontology of scientific disciplines.

Figure 2.2 shows the space thus defined by the three traditional domains. Each domain is represented as a circle, with overlaps denoting generic relationships among domains. The figure introduces some notational conventions that we will build on as we move toward the full ME language. Domains are represented by capitalized initials: P(hysical), L(ife), S(ocial), and eventually C(omputing). The existence of a generic relationship between domains is denoted by the plus (+) symbol. As with the traditional addition symbol, this relationship symbol is commutative, so P+L and L+P represent the same overlap between the physical and life sciences. With just the traditional domains, the universe of science consists of three *monadic* regions (P, S, and L), three *dyadic* regions (P+S, P+L, and S+L), and one *triadic* region (P+S+L). The monadic regions are home to the core subject matter that makes each domain unique—concerned with physical, living, or social phenomena. However, much of today's most interesting work arises from the overlaps among these domains.

At the intersection of the physical and life sciences (P+L) lies one of today's most significant science and engineering revolutions: understanding and manipulating biology at the molecular level. Different flavors are studied under distinct subdisciplines—such as molecular biology, genetics (genomics, proteomics, etc.), and biochemistry—but they all have this overlap in common and are jointly contributing to our understanding of, and ability to shape, biological systems at the molecular level. Also within this same intersection are disciplines such as biomechanics, which seeks to understand aspects of living organisms as mechanical systems; mechanical prostheses, which attempt to repair or augment a living organism through physical means (such as the robotic arm controlled by the monkey in figure 1.2); and ecology, at least when the physical aspects of the environment are fully considered.

At the intersection of the social and life sciences (S+L) sit cognitive neuroscience and cognitive neuropsychology, the scientific counterparts of the long-standing philosophical dispute over the relationship between mind and body; that is, whether the mind is physical and coextensive with the body (physicalism) or is a distinct nonmaterial entity that can exist independently of the body (dualism). By sensing the activity of the brain at different spatiotemporal scales—individual neurons, groups of neurons, or whole brain regions—and relating the resulting measurements to human behavior, these disciplines are laying the scientific groundwork for physicalism.

In this book, we will distinguish between the mind and the brain, with the mind considered to be part of the social domain (S) and the brain as a component of the human body to be considered part of the domain of life (L). This is not intended as an endorsement of dualism as a scientific concept, rather only as an acknowledgment that the domains of study are traditionally distinguished in this fashion. As the understanding of the relationship between the mind and the brain continues to improve, a shift in the boundaries of the great domains may ultimately result. As useful, we will either focus on the dominant domain (S or L) in any particular situation or explicitly include both (S and L).

The overlap between the physical (P) and social (S) domains is more of an oddity. Unless one believes in direct spiritual connections between the mind and the world or in psychic phenomena such as mental teleportation, most relationships between the physical and social domains must involve the body, and thus the domain of life. However, if the involvement of the body is truly subsidiary to the roles of the mind and the physical world, such a relationship may be abstracted to a dyadic one between S and P, much as we abstracted away the involvement of P and L in human–computer interaction. One example of this might be global warming, which can be considered at the top level as a relationship between S and P, although L would also certainly play a significant role in a more detailed analysis. A second way in which we can end up with a dyadic relation between S and P occurs when the mind embodies a representation, model, or simulation of the physical world. We will consider such a relationship to comprise an approximate form of implementation and allow it to sit here.

In addition to pairwise relations across domains, it is also possible to consider such relations within individual domains; for example, physical chemistry concerns the application of physics (P) to the understanding of chemical (P) phenomena. It thus can be denoted as P+P. We will focus much less on within-domain relationships than on across-domain relationships in this book, but we will not completely ignore these relationships in computing, as they define crucial aspects of its complete architecture.

Going beyond pairwise overlaps among domains, the full understanding of a number of critical topics lies at the intersection of all three of the traditional domains (P+L+S). As mentioned earlier, global warming primarily studies the impact of human activity (S) on climate (P), but the interactions with plants, animals, and human bodies (L) are also critical for a complete understanding of climate change and to assess its potential for shaping the future of life. Geography, in its full sense, would also fit in this category.

To add computing to the picture, we need to increase the dimensionality of figure 2.2—from two-dimensional to three-dimensional—so as to enable moving from a triangular arrangement of circles to a tetrahedral arrangement of spheres (figure 2.3). Such a figure is difficult to present and annotate on a two-dimensional page, and the intricacies of the internal overlaps among the spheres are not easily discernible, but the intent should be clear. Fortunately, our particular focus on computing will let us bypass large regions of this space, narrowing our view to the portion circumscribed by the computing sphere and allowing the use of a simpler two-dimensional diagram of just those regions of science that overlap with computing (figure 2.4). Here, a computing circle engulfs the triangle of domain circles from figure 2.2. This is not intended to indicate that the rest of science is a part of computing, instead merely to provide a convenient two-dimensional representation of computing and its interactions with the other three domains. The outer region of the circle covers monadic computing, with the segments that denoted monadic domains in figure 2.2 now representing the pairwise combination of those domains with computing. Similarly, regions that previously denoted dyadic combinations are

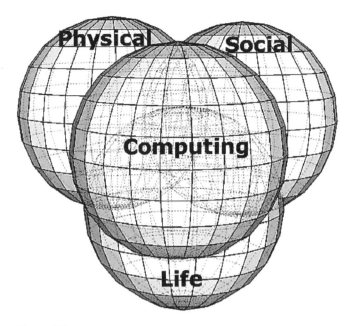

Figure 2.3
Three-dimensional tetrahedral representation of the four great scientific domains and their overlaps.

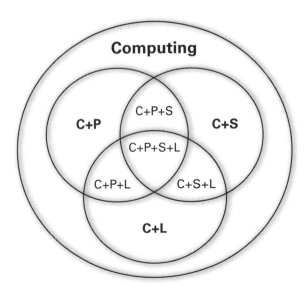

Figure 2.4
Two-dimensional representation of computing and its overlaps with the other three great scientific domains.

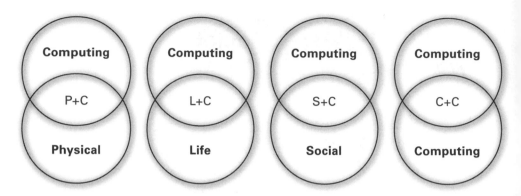

Figure 2.5
The four flavors of dyadic computing (C+Δ), where computing (C) overlaps with exactly one other domain (P, L, S, or C).

now triadic, and the unique triadic region becomes tetradic. This type of figure cannot naturally represent within-domain dyadic relationships, but for those dyadic combinations that involve computing, we can shift to a more piecemeal alternative representation that does include them, as in figure 2.5.

As with the other three great scientific domains, computing in isolation—what can be called *monadic computing*—is unique and interesting in its own right. It indeed constituted much of the field's focus during the early years and includes the study of algorithms and theoretical computer science plus aspects of computer architecture, databases, and programming languages. Algorithms are simply sequences of instructions to be followed in performing a task. They may guide the behavior of a computer, or a person, or any other type of entity that can follow instructions. In computing, algorithms provide the abstract plans that guide the development of programs; however, they are not the programs themselves.

Theoretical computer science studies the mathematical and logical foundations of computing. One of theory's central classes of questions concerns the *complexity* of algorithms; that is, how much time and space (memory) will be required to solve specific problems via particular algorithms. For example, given an unordered list of numbers of length n—such as the length-five sequence <5, 20, 1, 4, 3>—whether it will take time that is logarithmic [$\log(n)$], linear (n), quadratic (n^2), or exponential (2^n) in the length of the sequence (i.e., in n) to sort them from smallest to largest: <1, 3, 4, 5, 20>. For this relatively simple to define task of sorting, a surprisingly broad range of qualitatively different algorithms has been developed.

The most obvious algorithms require quadratic time (n^2) to sort a list, whereas optimal algorithms run in time that is proportional to $n \cdot \log(n)$. For our five-element list, this is $5^2 = 25$ versus $5 \cdot \log(5) \approx 11.6$ (using 2 as the base of the logarithm).

Theorists organize algorithms into complexity classes, such as **P** for algorithms that are solvable in time that is polynomial in the size of the algorithm's input; that is, in time that is proportional to n^k, for an input of size n and some constant exponent k. Computer scientists generally consider polynomial-time problems to be *tractable*. Even if it can take a long time to solve such problems, solution time grows slowly enough with problem size that if small problems are solvable, then larger ones should be as well. Problems that require exponential time—proportional to 2^n— grow so fast that even when small problems are easy, increasing the size just a bit can make them infeasible. For example, 2^{10} is only about a thousand—1024 to be precise—so an input of length ten isn't too bad for an exponential algorithm, but for each additional ten inputs the running time increases by a factor of a thousand. So an input of length twenty implies a million, thirty a billion, forty a trillion, and so on. In contrast, for a quadratic algorithm with an input of length forty, we only get forty squared, or less than two thousand.

Theorists use the class **NP** for problems whose answers—once they are found—can be verified in polynomial time, but which may require exponential time to find, and use **co-NP** for problems whose non-answers can be verified as not being answers in polynomial time. **NP-Complete** is the class reserved for the hardest problems in **NP**. If an efficient algorithm can be found for any problem in **NP-Complete**, then efficient solutions must exist for all problems in **NP**. The problem of whether **P=NP** (i.e., whether problems that can be verified in polynomial time can also be solved in polynomial time) is the most critical open problem in computer science theory.[6] The Clay Mathematics Institute has established a $1 million prize for whoever proves whether or not **P=NP**.

One prerequisite for performing a complexity analysis is that the problem be *computable* in the first place. There are precisely definable questions that cannot be answered even in principle; that is, functions that are uncomputable, such as whether an arbitrary program will ever halt on particular input data—what is known as the *halting problem*. No algorithm can solve the halting problem for all programs. Theoretical computer science studies computability as well as complexity. It also studies the relative computational power of different abstract models of computing. The Church–Turing thesis,[7] for example, claims that there is an abstract class of machines—*Turing machines*[8]—capable of computing any computable function. Going even further, within the overall class of Turing machines there are specific instances known as *universal Turing machines* that can emulate (i.e., imitate or *act as if*) they were any other Turing machine. This unlimited ability of a single device to emulate arbitrary Turing machines—and thus to compute any computable function—is the basis for modern stored-program computers.[9] Computers read programs stored in memory—while also reading and writing data in other portions of their memory—to *act as if* they are those programs.

Turing machines are abstract in the sense that they are conceptualizations used in understanding computation rather than physical machines used in performing computation; the definition of a Turing machine requires, for example, the existence of a tape that is infinite in length. But there are also other computational models that are equivalent to Turing machines, in the sense of being able to compute the same set of functions; for example, typical programming languages are Turing equivalent.

Computer architecture, databases, and programming languages are the means by which abstract concepts such as Turing machines are made real and become able to perform useful work. Computer architecture provides the blueprints for computers. It defines the basic instruction sets that are to be implemented by the hardware, along with the organization and connectivity among the computer's functional components (processors, memories, etc.). In the small it is a monadic discipline because instruction sets for novel computers can be designed and analyzed—at least with respect to some key questions—in the absence of any reference to the physical implementation. But in the large, computer architecture requires understanding circuits and other aspects of computer hardware (P).

Databases provide the ability to store, organize, and access large bodies of information. As with computer architecture, core aspects of database technology can be studied independently of any other domain, but when either their hardware support or their information content become a factor—or when databases are to be distributed across multiple computers—multiple domain instances are implicated.

Programming languages are the means by which algorithms are encoded to control the computations performed by real computers, providing the ability to define arbitrary transformations over information. In their full depth, programming languages cannot be investigated without understanding the nature of the computers on which the programs are to run (P), the capabilities and limitations of the people who will write the programs and interact with them (S), and whatever domains contain the content of the program. Still, there are core issues in programming languages—such as the specification of what a program means (i.e., its semantics)—that can be independent of extra-computing domains.

Although monadic computing remains of critical importance, and there are significant open problems in each of its various subdisciplines, much of what has been most intriguing in computing over the past few decades has involved *across-domain interaction*, and such across-domain interactions are where much of the exciting future of computing also appears to lie. For this reason, and because monadic computing is already well covered by standard texts, it is not our focus here. We will instead start with *dyadic computing*, where computing interacts with one other domain (which may also be computing).

Dyadic computing is denoted in general as C+Δ, where Δ can be thought of as representing the top node in the scientific hierarchy (i.e., all of science) enabling a simple expression to span the overlap of computing with all of the other domains (including itself). From a slightly different perspective, Δ can be thought of instead as a *wildcard* symbol that is replaceable by any of the particular domain symbols—P, L, S, or C—to yield a specific form of dyadic computing,[10] such as C+P for the overlap between the physical and computing domains that underlies computer hardware.[11] Figure 2.5 showed the four varieties of pairwise relationships that can occur between computing and one other domain (P, S, L, or C). As we progress through the remainder of this book, we will look at these overlaps in much greater detail, but a few quick examples are helpful in passing.

Quantum computing[12] investigates the implementation of computing via physical devices (C+P) that maintain quantum mechanical properties such as *superposition* and *entanglement*. Superposition, for example, enables parts of the world to be simultaneously in multiple incompatible states—Schrödinger's cat is famously and paradoxically both alive and dead at the same moment. Quantum computers based on superposition can solve some problems with time complexity that are unapproachable by normal computers. Consider the task of factoring an integer such as 12. Integer factorization involves determining a set of smaller integers that are not further factorable—such as 2, 2, and 3 in this case—which, when multiplied together, yield the original integer. The current best algorithms for integer factorization on conventional computers are exponential in the size of the integer; that is, time grows roughly according to the expression 2^n, where n is the length of the integer in digits (or bits). For quantum computers, Shor's algorithm can solve this same problem in polynomial time, where calculation time grows according to n^3.[13] Because n^3 grows much more slowly than does 2^n as n increases, it may be possible to use quantum computing to crack the cryptographic codes built on integer factorization that protect much of our critical data. Quantum computing is discussed further in chapter 3.

Artificial intelligence (AI), according to the Association for the Advancement of Artificial Intelligence, is "The scientific understanding of the mechanisms underlying thought and intelligent behavior and their embodiment in machines."[14] It is a classical combination of the computing and social domains (C+S), as well as of science and engineering. As with quantum computing, we will have more to say about AI in chapter 3, but for now it can be exemplified by two of its most publicized achievements in recent years, both due to IBM: Deep Blue beating a human world chess champion (figure 2.6)[15] and Watson beating a pair of human Jeopardy champions.[16] In 1957, Herb Simon predicted such a victory would occur in chess within ten years. He was right about the inevitability of such a

Figure 2.6
Gary Kasparov losing a six-game chess match to IBM's Deep Blue chess computer in 1997.
From http://commons.wikimedia.org/wiki/File:Deep_blue_chess.png. Creative Commons Attribution-Share Alike 3.0 Unported license.

victory, given the steady progress in both AI and hardware, but he was overly optimistic—a typical failing in new fields, where initial excitement and progress can mislead researchers about the difficulty of the full problem—as it actually took four times longer than he predicted. During the intervening years, some critics erroneously used this delay as evidence that it could not in principle be achieved.

A brain–computer interface, as underlies the behavior in figure 1.2, directly connects a brain to a computer (C+L), bypassing the body's normal sensory (eyes, ears, nose, skin, etc.) and motor (hand, arms, feet, etc.) systems. Figure 2.7 provides a schematic for how this works in one experimental setup with monkeys.[17] A surgically implanted brain–computer interface captures signals from the monkey's brain as the monkey moves a joystick in controlling activity on a computer screen. The monkey's neural signals are simultaneously transmitted in real time to a computer to control the movements of a remote robot arm. Figure 2.8 shows a

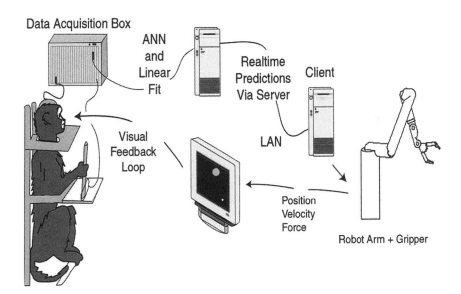

Figure 2.7
Architecture of monkey brain–computer interface for direct brain control of a remote robot arm (Duke University).
From figure 1A in Jose M. Carmena, Mikhail A. Lebedev, Roy E. Crist, Joseph E. O'Doherty, David M. Santucci, Dragan F. Dimitrov, Parag G. Patil, Craig S. Henriquez, and Miguel A. L. Nicolelis, "Learning to control a brain-machine interface for reaching and grasping by primates," *PLoS Biology* 1, no. 2 (2003): 193–208. Creative Commons Attribution License.

Figure 2.8
Noninvasive human brain–computer interface (NeuroSky).
Image courtesy of NeuroSky.

noninvasive brain-computer interface being explored for human use. This wearable device senses coarser neural signals through the skin and skull, enabling the computer to respond at some level to the human's brain activity. More on brain–computer interfaces can be found in chapter 4.

When computing overlaps with itself—C+C—there must be a relationship between two different components of computing. This could involve, for example, two computers communicating over a network or one software system that is executing on top of another one. These overlaps of computing with itself will be refereed to as *pure dyadic computing*—or *pure polyadic computing* more generally when there are two or more instances of computing involved—and overlaps with other domains will be termed *mixed dyadic (polyadic) computing*. As with monadic computing, much of pure dyadic computing has been around for some time and is generally well covered by existing texts. So, we will not focus on it a great deal here, either, beyond trying to understand how its subdisciplines fit within the relational architecture of computing.

The boundary between monadic computing and more complex forms of computing is actually rather fuzzy. We have, for example, included aspects of computer programming as part of monadic computing. But when the relevant physical (hardware), social (programmers and users), and content (knowledge and data) issues are taken into consideration, it can become mixed dyadic or polyadic. Likewise, although a program can be considered as a single fragment of computing at one level, at the next level of analysis down it can be viewed as the interactions among many smaller fragments of computing, whether procedures or individual lines of code. We will see the benefits of thinking about many topics within computing in terms of pure dyadic or polyadic computing in the next section, when we look at relationships in detail, but it is important to at least understand that at a high enough level of abstraction, they also can be thought of as monadic computing.

Beyond dyadic computing, we can talk about triadic and tetradic computing, but it will be simpler in general to just refer to everything beyond pairwise relationships as *polyadic computing*. If we want, for example, to represent the full richness of brain–computer interfaces, we need to look at overlaps among all four domains (P+S+L+C). These interfaces not only involve the brain (L) and computers (C), but also the physical devices (P) that mediate between the brain and the computer, plus the thought (S) that is reflected in the measured brain activity and that is ultimately to be reflected in appropriate control of the computer or whatever other devices are attached to it (such as the robot arms in figures 1.2 and 2.7). All four domains are also required for a full representation of human–computer interaction, as well as for the kind of virtual world shown in figure 1.3, where a computer (C) simulates a physical world (P) that contains intelligent virtual humans with both bodies and minds (L and S).

One of the hot topics recently has been the convergence of biotechnology, information technology, and nanotechnology, in what is succinctly referred to as bio-info-nano (although you can also find it listed as nano-bio-info and nano-info-bio). Bio-info-nano is a prime exemplar of triadic computing (L+C+P), in which the focus is on how the life, physical, and computing domains come together in the world of the very small. Sometimes you will even find it described as nano-bio-info-cogno, bringing in cognitive science—and thus the social domain—as well, yielding tetradic computing (P+L+C+S). Claims have been made that this is not just another form of interdisciplinary science, but rather a major phase change in science and technology.[18]

The definition of computing in chapter 1 identified it as the transformation of information. Monadic computing focuses quite precisely on this. However, any topic within computing that includes in its decomposition any domain other than computing (i.e., all forms of mixed dyadic computing, such as AI and human–computer interaction, plus mixed polyadic computing) must have a focus that extends beyond just information transformation. In keeping with the discussion of multidisciplinary computing later in chapter 1 and the further discussion to come in chapter 5 (section 5.4), we will consider any topic that includes computing as a significant constituent domain to be part of the computing sciences. That sounds almost tautological, as it should, but many people fail to recognize interdisciplinary topics as being within the scope of the disciplines out of which the computing domain is composed. Thus, a topic like human–computer interaction will be considered as part of both the computing and social domains, rather than being relegated to a state of limbo between the two. Or, in other words, computing spans the entire sphere that is so labeled in figure 2.3 and the entire circle that is so labeled in figure 2.4. Regions are not removed from this sphere or circle just because other domains also overlap with computing in them.

Although some may find it counterintuitive, we will also consider applications of computing to other domains to be forms of mixed dyadic or polyadic computing and thus as forms of multidisciplinary computing. A computer application in banking, for example, involves both the computational (C) and social (S) domains and thus would be denoted as C+S and considered as a form of multidisciplinary computing. The roles played by the individual domains determine the nature of the relationship between the domains, as we will see in more detail in the next section, but this basic notion of participation in a multidisciplinary activity is independent of role.

2.2   Relationships

Relationships describe how the domains out of which a discipline is composed are combined to yield a unitary body of content. While discussing domain combinations in the previous section, we made do with a relatively abstract, generic notion of overlap among domains. Identifying such overlaps helps to understand the inherently multidisciplinary nature of much of science, but it is essentially just another static relationship that, in and of itself, is not much more useful than the traditional subclass relationship. What is required to go beyond this is something like the architecture's pair of active relationships.

Consider quantum computing, for example, where the physical domain (P) overlaps with computing (C). Can anything more be said about the actual nature of this overlap? The overlap is clearly active, in that quantum properties are producing computation. More particularly, however, the physical domain is *implementing* the computational domain. Generically, to implement is to *put into effect*. Electronic circuits implement computing by providing a physical device—a computer—capable of computation. Likewise, quantum computing involves the provision of a physical device capable of computation, but based on quantum rather than electronic principles and components. A computer can in fact be implemented by any combination of structures and processes that interact to yield a device capable of information transformation. And, more broadly, one domain can be said to implement any other domain if structures and processes from the first domain interact to produce the elementary structures and processes that define a device or system in the other domain. The first domain puts into effect the second domain.

In AI, the computational domain (C) implements—or simulates, depending on your point of view—all or part of a mind (S); that is, computational structures and processes interact to produce a device that thinks, or appears to think. It can be quite tricky in general to discriminate between whether something is actually implemented (i.e., exists in reality) or is just simulated (i.e., is imitated or copied in some manner but is still lacking in some essential attribute or attributes). Within AI, it determines whether you are talking about *strong AI* or *weak AI*.[19] Strong AI maintains that a computer can actually be intelligent; that is, it *brings into effect* intelligence. Weak AI maintains that a computer may be able to *act as if* it were intelligent, using the flexible mimicry that derives from universal Turing machines, but cannot actually be intelligent.

This same distinction can arise in other contexts as well. In artificial life (alife), biological processes (L) are re-created computationally (C) to yield hard or soft alife, depending on whether it is based on hardware or software, or biochemically (L, P) to yield wet alife.[20] Is the result actually life or merely a simulation of it? The *strong alife* position claims that the result may be life, whereas the *weak alife* position denies this possibility, at least for dry (i.e., computational) alife.

Computational physics is full of simulations (C) of the physical world (P), but digital physics goes beyond this to ask whether the universe as a whole (P) is itself just an information process; that is, just a computer (C).[21] In *Wizard of Oz* experiments, a human pretends he or she is a computer, usually when a requisite computer is not readily available or when the available computers cannot be readily programmed for the task at hand. I recall Don Norman, a cognitive psychologist who was at the University of California, San Diego, at the time, telling a story in the late 1970s about a trip he had earlier taken to the Soviet Union, where on a tour he was proudly shown their computer simulator. Because the facility could not acquire a real computer, they had a human in a back room simulating the activities of a computer. But is the human merely simulating a computer or actually implementing one?

Although it is possible to argue endlessly about such questions, the answer must fundamentally come down to a combination of definition and science. How does one define intelligence, life, the universe, computation, and so forth, and is it possible to establish that a constructed entity meets the definition? It is too early for a definitive answer to many of these questions, but we can answer with respect to computing. If a computer is defined as something that processes information, then the human in a Wizard of Oz experiment is implementing rather than just simulating a computer, although he or she may at the same time be simulating a particular electronic computer. The term *computer* was, after all, first applied to people who calculated long before electronic computers were conceived. With such a generic definition of a computer, it is conceivable that they can be implemented via technology from any of the four great scientific domains. The field is most conversant with physical implementations of computers, but there are also approaches being actively investigated that are based on the life and social domains.

Computing can also implement itself. Compilers implement one language in another. Computer simulators and emulators implement computers that simulate the behavior of other computers. An emulation provides a real computer, it just isn't the real computer being emulated, and thus is a simulation of that other computer. For example, one may build in software an emulator of an old-fashioned Digital Equipment Corporation (DEC) PDP-10 computer that runs any software written for a PDP-10 just as would the original computer. Yet it still would not be a PDP-10, a physical device manufactured by DEC and on which I cut my computational teeth during graduate school in the 1970s.

Personally, I would be very surprised if either strong AI or strong alife turn out to be fundamentally wrong. The approaches currently being taken in AI and alife may or may not ultimately prove to be on the right track, but I see no fundamental barriers and would be astonished if any were now to emerge. I am less convinced by digital physics, given both the state of the field and my own understanding of it, but if I had to lay a bet it would be on the side of the universe ultimately being computational; that is, for what could be called *strong artificial physics*, in analogy with strong AI and strong alife.

An important qualification glossed over in this discussion is that it can be difficult to give precise definitions to concepts such as intelligence and life, and thus it can be difficult to assess whether an entity meets such a definition. We can try to define a concept: (1) *extensionally*, as a list of everything that is an instance of it; (2) *intensionally*, where the set of all such instances is characterized abstractly in terms of necessary and sufficient properties (yielding open-ended but still hard-and-fast category boundaries); or (3) *prototypically*, where neither an explicit list nor necessary-and-sufficient properties are provided, but there is an exemplar of the concept plus a similarity metric for determining how close other entities are to the exemplar (yielding a degree of membership in a class rather than a hard-and-fast answer). We could, for example, try to define a bird extensionally by explicitly listing every individual bird; intensionally as any entity that has wings, feathers, and flies (or that has a particular combination of genes); or prototypically by pointing to a particular robin and defining a similarity metric with respect to it.

An extensional definition implies that no newly constructed entity can be an instance of the concept and is thus uninteresting in distinguishing implementation from simulation. An intensional definition provides clear criteria, they just might be wrong; as is the case for, at least, the first intensional definition of birds given earlier. A prototypical definition leads to discussions about which attributes are (more) critical, and what is the nature of the similarity metric. We will focus here on a hybrid between intensional and prototype definitions, extending the intensional use of necessary-and-sufficient conditions with the notion of typical traits from prototypes, and view a simulation as an entity that captures some but not all of the necessary and sufficient conditions, plus any number of typical traits. A simulation may thus be a useful imitation, but it falls short of reality in some essential way(s).

A simulation is still an implementation of something, just not necessarily of a real thing in the intended domain. A virtual chair, in which a virtual human in a virtual environment might sit, is a real computational object (C). It also may possess many of the attributes of a real chair; however, we might hesitate in saying that it is a real chair (P) because it is impossible for a real person to sit in it. Thus, we could talk about a virtual chair either as involving the computational implementation of an aspect of computing or as the computational simulation of an aspect of the physical world. The former viewpoint has some utility, particularly if you are the developer of virtual environments, but the latter is more often what we care about. Rather than thinking of simulation as a new relationship between domains, we can consider it to be an approximate form of implementation, as long as we keep in mind that not all virtual entities need be approximations (and thus simulations); for example, a piece of art in a virtual world may be a real piece of art in and of itself rather than a simulation of a real-world piece of art—artists are now in fact selling virtual art for real money.[22]

It will also prove useful to consider *representations* and *models* as alternative forms of approximate implementations. A representation, as mentioned in chapter 1, is a structure that denotes some other structure. In the modeling and simulation community, a model is a representation of an object or process, and a simulation is what happens when the model is run to produce behavior. A model in this sense is a static structure, much like a representation, that is brought to life by simulation. In the rest of this book, we will use the term *simulation* as the generic term for an approximate implementation to emphasize how such approximations are in general active rather than static, but with models and representations explicitly considered as static subclasses of simulations. Many uses of the term *simulation* also connote that the model underlying the simulation represents something else. Although our simulations may have this property, it isn't a prerequisite here. All that is minimally necessary is that the simulation be an approximate implementation.

In contrast to quantum computing and AI, brain–computer interfaces are not based on an implementation relationship. The brain is not implementing computing in this case, nor is computing implementing the brain. Instead, there is an *interaction* relationship between the two domains. Interaction involves "reciprocal action, effect or influence."[23] When a rock (P) hits a person (L), the physical and life domains are interacting. When a person (S) gives a command to a pet (L), the social and life domains are interacting (if we think of the command as coming from the mind of the person rather than from his or her body). In human–computer interaction, people (S) use their normal sensory and motor systems (eyes, hands, etc.) in conjunction with computer input and output devices (keyboards, screens, etc.) to interact with computers (C). Brain–computer interfaces are much like human–computer interaction in purpose—enabling people to interact with computers—albeit rather more novel and exotic in bypassing the normal human sensory and motor systems and instead attempting to interact directly with the brain (L). In general, we can think of interaction between two domains as involving communication, or any other form of direct influence, between elements of the two domains.

As was done with domains, we will want to represent implementation and interaction symbolically. To do this, we will use an in-line division symbol (/) for implementation and an arrow (→, ←, or ↔) for interaction. So, for example, quantum computing becomes C/P, and AI becomes S/C. Likewise, human–computer interaction becomes S↔C, and brain–computer interfaces become L↔C. As implicitly marked by the symbols, implementation is inherently asymmetric, whereas interaction may be symmetric or asymmetric (i.e., directional). A non-touchscreen computer monitor, providing the ability for a computer to influence a human but not for the human to influence the computer, would for example be represented as C→S.

As mentioned earlier, the generic relationship symbol is the plus sign (+). It signals the existence of some relationship between a pair of domains but distinguishes neither its nature nor direction. As was earlier true with domains, it is possible to consider an ontology of relationships, with overlap (+) as the root and implementation and interaction just below it. The subclass relationship could also be a node at this level, and distinctions among directions of interaction would then exist at the third level (figure 2.9). There also could be additional relationships that expand the hierarchy in depth, based on finer and finer distinctions, or in breadth. We could, for example, consider simulation as a subrelationship under implementation. However, for simulation (as well as for modeling and representation),

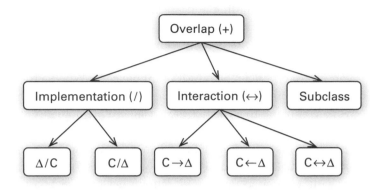

Figure 2.9
Top part of an ontology of across-domain relationships.

we will shortly introduce a different manner of distinguishing it notationally from implementation, for use when it is important to designate that something actually is a simulation. With this special case handled, we will be able to make do with just implementation and interaction in this book, in conjunction with the choice between symmetric and asymmetric—including the two distinct directions—for interaction. Whether these two relationships will ultimately be adequate to cover all of computing—and beyond that, all of science—remains to be seen, but when used singly for dyadic computing, and in combination for polyadic computing, they have proved sufficient for the areas examined to date.

A third relationship—*embedding*—was until recently also thought to be necessary,[24] in addition to implementation and interaction, but it was ultimately deemed to be superfluous given these other two and their combinations. Embedding focused on the encapsulation of one domain within another. A neural prosthetic, for example, is a computer chip (C) that is to be embedded in the brain (L) to replace lost or damaged functionality (although neural prosthetics could conceivably also be used to augment brain function). Figure 2.10 illustrates one specific variant, where a biomimetic computer chip (i.e., a chip that implements/simulates some aspect of biology) is developed to replicate the functionality of a portion of the hippocampus (part of the forebrain thought to play a major role in short-term memory and spatial navigation).[25] This chip is then ultimately to be embedded in the brain and connected to the neurons around it, as a surrogate for functionality that was lost when the hippocampus was damaged. Although the core focus in neural prostheses is on the relationship between the brain (L) and computation (C), it can also be considered to involve the

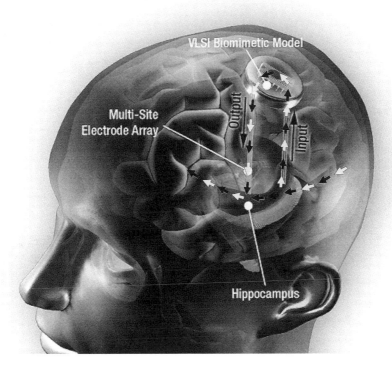

Figure 2.10
Concept for a hippocampal neural prosthetic; that is, a computer chip that simulates a fragment of brain function that is embedded into the brain to replace damaged functionality (University of Southern California).
Image courtesy of Theodore W. Berger, Center for Neural Engineering, University of Southern California.

physical domain (P), given the physical nature of the chip and its connections to the brain, and the social domain (S) if we grant the basic premise of physicalism.

Embedding does tell a neat story for neural prostheses, and it is also useful in talking about other forms of encapsulation, such as when a human (S) is embedded in a computational environment (C). The Amazon Mechanical Turk[26] is a good example here. The original Mechanical Turk—it was actually just called *The Turk*—was a chess-playing automaton developed by Wolfgang von Kempelen in the eighteenth century (figure 2.11).[27] It beat human players for decades until it was exposed as a hoax in the middle of the nineteenth century. The secret of course was a human (S)

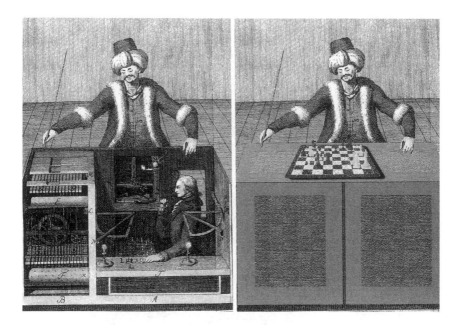

Figure 2.11
The Turk, an eighteenth-century chess "automaton" with a compartment for embedding a person.
From Joseph F. Racknitz, *Ueber den Schachspieler des herrn von Kempelen und dessen Nachbildung* (Leipzig and Dresden: J. G. I. Breitkopf, 1789).

wedged inside of the mechanical computing device (C) who performed the essential calculations for it. The Amazon Mechanical Turk is a web service—"a software system designed to support interoperable machine-to-machine interaction over a network"[28]—but which uses a technique called *crowdsourcing* to outsource to people the tasks that the computers cannot currently perform, effectively embedding people in the web services.

Despite the conceptual utility of embedding, I was never completely comfortable with it as an independent relationship type. Every attempt to explain what it was ended up spending too much time clarifying how it was not quite implementation or interaction. Embedding clearly has properties in common with both—for example, an embedded neural prosthetic (re)implements/simulates part of the brain while interacting with the regions of the brain immediately surrounding it—yet it is clearly not just one or the other. After exploring several alternative ways of thinking about embedding, I concluded that it would be best considered as a *compound relationship* that is built out of a combination of the two basic ones. So, a neural prosthesis should be thought of as a combination of a biomimetic implementation relationship, where computation (re)implements part of the brain (L/C) plus an interaction relationship where computation interacts via a brain–computer interface with neighboring brain regions (L↔C) to yield L/(L↔C). Likewise, in both variants of Mechanical Turks, the embedded human can be viewed as implementing/simulating computing while simultaneously interacting with the other bits of computational technology around them, C/(C↔S), whether it be the mechanical contraption in the original Turk or computers for the Amazon Mechanical Turk.

Every implementation in fact implicitly involves interactions among the elements in the lower domain. When the interacting elements are all from the same domain, we have a choice of thinking of this as a simple case of implementation or as a compound relationship involving implementation and interaction. This choice is analogous to the one discussed earlier between whether specialties such as computer programming should be considered as monadic or pure dyadic/polyadic computing. As was the case there, it is a modeling choice as to how much detail would be useful. A purchaser of a chair may, for example, only care about its being made out of wood, P/L, whereas an artisan might care about the details of how the chair is constructed out of interacting pieces of wood, P/(L↔L).

Given that implementations do involve interactions, it may make sense at some point to extract out the interaction component from implementation to yield a more orthogonal pair of relationships. Instead of implementation, the second relationship would then be something like *abstraction* or *aggregation*, which reconceptualizes a set of entities as some new kind of entity. Implementation would then be a compound relationship, much like embedding, comprising a combination of interaction, to yield a set of entities, and this new relationship to turn this set into a new kind of entity. This book does not take this approach, but it is worth considering for the future.

As with relationships across domains, within-domain relationships can be based either on implementation or interaction. For example, within the physical domain we can talk about how physics implements chemistry (P/P) because the particles and forces studied by physicists combine to define the atoms, molecules, and reactions studied by chemists. Similarly, two kinds of atoms or molecules may interact chemically (P↔P) such as when a sodium ion (Na^+) reacts with a chlorine ion (Cl^-) to create a salt molecule (NaCl).

These same forms of interplay among multiple elements of a single domain can also occur within pure dyadic computing. Two computers may communicate (i.e., interact) via a network (C↔C). Likewise, an interpreter is a program written in one computer language that deciphers and executes instructions written in a second, different language: C/C. An interpreter for the programming language *Lisp* written in the programming language C effectively implements a new computing system that processes Lisp instructions on top of an existing computing system that understands C.

A number of the subdisciplines of computing fall within pure dyadic/ polyadic computing, such as interpreters,[29] compilers (which convert programs in one language into programs in another language, while not necessarily executing either program),[30] operating systems (such as MacOS, Windows, Linux, Android, and iOS, which manage a computer's resources and services by providing the ability to run programs, store and retrieve files on disks, print files, interact with users, etc.),[31] networks (which provide intercomputer communication),[32] and distributed computing (which provides intercomputer coordination).[33] Given that, as with monadic computing, most such topics are standard in computer science education, we will not focus on them much more here except for including them in the overall architecture of computing.

One straightforward way to visualize the two basic relationships is via a spatial metaphor, in accompaniment with a pair of prepositional phrases, as in figure 2.12.[34] Implementation builds one domain *on top of* another, where combinations of structures and processes in the lower domain define the basic elements and processes in the upper domain. For example, the molecules and reactions studied by chemists (P) combine to yield the cellular components and processes studied by biologists (L). From chemistry to biology, this relationship is studied across such subdisciplines as organic chemistry, biochemistry, molecular biology, and cellular biology.

Beyond the implementation of individual objects, we can also talk about a whole domain or discipline implementing another domain or discipline. Consider the relationship between physics and chemistry.

Implementation   **Interaction**
"on top of"   *"next to"*

Figure 2.12
Spatial metaphor for the two basic domain relationships.

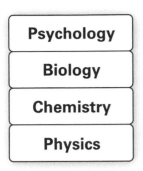

Figure 2.13
An implementation hierarchy among select sciences.

Chemistry studies atoms, molecules, and such like, plus the processes—chemical reactions—that interact with them. Physics provides the elementary structures and forces that define chemistry's structures and implement its processes. This is a pure dyadic physical relationship (P/P). But if we now look up from chemistry to see the implementation of biology (L), we find an across-domain dyadic relationship (L/P). By continuing upward from biology to its implementation of psychology (S), we start to descry a rich, multilayered implementation hierarchy across the physical, life, and social sciences (figure 2.13). This yields an alternative kind of hierarchy over the sciences from that in figure 2.1, based on implementation rather than decomposition. It also reveals how implementation relates to the traditional notion of reductionism in science.[35]

This hierarchy could easily be enriched with additional disciplines; for example, neuroscience (L) naturally slots in between biology and psychology, and cognitive neuroscience (S/L)—which explicitly studies the implementation relationship between neuroscience and psychology—would slot in between them. Similarly, molecular biology and its ilk deal with the implementation relationship between chemistry and biology and thus could slide in between these two disciplines in the hierarchy; and both chemical physics and physical chemistry fit between chemistry and physics.

It would be interesting in general to determine how many disciplines and subdisciplines could naturally be accommodated in a single implementation hierarchy, but that would take us too far away from our core focus on computing. If we do shift our focus to computing, however, it is easy to espy at least a small analogous hierarchy, where computer science (C), with its focus on software, is implemented by computer engineering, with its focus on hardware (C/P), which is in turn implemented

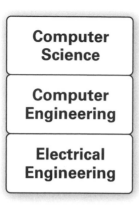

Figure 2.14
An implementation hierarchy for computing.

by electrical engineering (P), with its focus on electricity and electronics (figure 2.14). Other disciplines could be added to this hierarchy as well, with physics (P) for example extending the hierarchy downward to reflect its role in implementing electrical engineering.

One new facet of implementation hierarchies that is made evident by the addition of physics to this fragmentary computing hierarchy is that they cannot simply be linear if they strive to be inclusive. If we were to consolidate just the two hierarchies presented so far—with the computing hierarchy extended downward to include physics—the new combined hierarchy would need to branch upward from physics in order to denote that it directly implements both electrical engineering and chemistry. Similarly, downward branching will be required whenever one discipline is directly implemented by a combination of other disciplines. Such hierarchies must be lattices at least.

Can every great scientific domain implement every other great scientific domain? That is, is there a notion of universality here that is analogous to that of a universal Turing machine? The situation with respect to computing and the other domains involves a wide range of both implementation and simulation relationships. It is discussed in much more detail in chapter 3, with section 3.1 covering implementation of computing (C/Δ) and section 3.2 covering implementation by computing (Δ/C). From the traditional hierarchy of sciences, it should be obvious that the physical domain can implement the biological domain (L/P) and that the biological domain can implement the social domain (S/L). We do not yet completely understand how these particular implementation relationships work, but they are the basis for two of the most fundamental questions being asked: how life arose out of non-life (and how it operates at the mechanistic level), and how the brain thinks (resolving Cartesian dualism).

How about the inverse relationships? Life implementing the physical domain is difficult to conceptualize if the physical domain is by definition non-living, but life can at least simulate non-life—acting like a dead weight, behaving like a machine, and so forth—and perhaps truly implements it by dying. Individuals and groups of people may in turn act like a living organism that lacks the aspects of humanity normally the focus of the social domain. A mob on a rampage, for example, may not be fundamentally different from a stampeding bull. The physical domain clearly implements the social domain indirectly, through the intermediary of the domain of life. It is not clear if it could do it directly without one of the other domains as an intermediary, although there are proposals suggesting that the unique characteristics of thought arise from quantum phenomena.[36] Can the social domain implement the physical domain? Groups of people can join together to act as a physical object—such as a bridge—but such implementations involve the living body as much, if not more, than the social aspects.

Refocusing again on computing, can computing be fit into the traditional linear hierarchy of great scientific domains? Given that, as will be seen in chapter 3, computing can be implemented by all three of the other great scientific domains, an argument can be made for it to be at the top, just above the social sciences. However, if any of the hypothesized inverse implementation relationships—stemming from digital physics, alife, or AI—prove real, then an argument could be made that computing belongs below the domains that it implements. The result would be a mess rather than a hierarchy.

The problem is that a strict hierarchy must be defined in terms of an *antisymmetric* relationship; that is, a relationship that holds in at most one direction between any two distinct entities. Simulation is clearly not antisymmetric, so no reasonable hierarchy could be built based on which domains can simulate which other domains. Implementation may run into the same problem, but it is less clear whether or not it will at this point. If it does, there cannot be a single fundamental implementation hierarchy among the great scientific domains, despite the simplicity of the traditional hierarchy among the physical, life, and social domains. Instead, a domain hierarchy becomes simply an analysis tool that can be applied in understanding and explaining a particular combination of implementation relationships while possibly ignoring others that are less relevant for the

specific analysis. For example, we might use the domain of life to implement a computer that in turn implements a new form of life. The hierarchy
here would appropriately be described as L/C/L, involving an implementation loop for the domain of life while ignoring whatever sits below to
implement the bottom level of life. As long as this is merely a bit of analysis
rather than a statement about a fundamental relationship among the
domains, it should be fine.

Whereas implementation may yield a hierarchy, not all hierarchies are
based on implementation. The class hierarchy of the sciences in figure 2.1
provides one kind of alternative. Another kind of alternative is an organizational hierarchy. One form of organizational hierarchy relates smaller
organizations to larger ones. In the U.S. Army, for example, organizations
start at the level of squad, and proceed up through platoon, company, bat-
talion, brigade, division, corps, and army. Each higher level of organization
is implemented through a combination of the structures and processes at
the next lower level, implicating both (de)composition and implementation in the hierarchy. In contrast, the organization could instead be described
by a hierarchy of individuals in command relationships, starting with a
sergeant (squad), lieutenant (platoon), captain (company), and so on, up to
a lieutenant general (army). This is a hierarchy, but not based on either
implementation or decomposition. The relationships among individuals
are ones of interaction, albeit with asymmetries in power and control.

The full space of implementation relationships between computing and
the other great domains is rich and fertile. It covers both the plethora of
technologies that can implement computing—such as mechanical, chemical, biological, electrical, electronic, and quantum—and the potential to
implement/simulate everything that either exists or can be imagined.
What distinguishes these two flavors of *computational implementation* is the
directionality of the relationship. In the former, some other domain implements computation (C/Δ), whereas in the latter, computation implements
another domain: Δ/C. For example, standard hardware involves the physical implementation of computing (C/P), whereas computational science is
most often the computational simulation of physical phenomena (P/C).
Both of these types of computational implementation will be explored
further in chapter 3.

In contrast to implementation, interaction is a potentially symmetric
relationship among equals, in which two domains can be viewed as being
next to each other (figure 2.12), with some form of influence occurring
between them. Both brain–computer interfaces (L↔C) and human–
computer interaction (S↔C) involve symmetric interactions. If we focus on

pure dyadic computing, symmetric interactions (C↔C) arise for example when multiple processors are combined in parallel computers, when multiple computers are connected via networks, and when multiple dispersed computers collaborate in distributed, grid, and cloud computing. The notion that there may be something important in common across symmetric interactions in all great scientific domains has led to the nascent field of *network science*.[37]

Asymmetric interactions occur when information or influence exists in only one direction. Although human–computer interaction is fundamentally symmetric, many of the individual devices used in support of this overall bidirectional interaction provide only a single direction of interaction. A mouse all by itself only enables a human to influence a computer (S→C), whereas a monitor by itself only enables a computer to influence a human (S←C). These devices can of course be combined—as is typically done in a windows, icons, menus, and pointers (WIMP) interface—to provide bidirectional interaction, or a screen and pointing device can be combined into a single bidirectional interaction device, as in the touch-sensitive screens now used in most smart phones and tablets.

Although interactions are most simply conceived of as being among equals, the participants in an interaction need not be equal in all respects. There could, for example, be an asymmetric power, dominance, or control relationship among the interacting participants, as we just saw for the U.S. Army. For our purposes, the result would still be an interaction relationship, which it would make sense to visualize horizontally in contrast to the vertical direction of an implementation relationship. An asymmetric power relationship may modulate the resulting interaction, perhaps leading to a further elaboration of the relationship hierarchy under interaction, but such a modulation would not alter the fact that it is still an interaction and that it therefore corresponds logically to *next to* in this analysis. In a classical organizational chart, the vertical dimension represents a hierarchy of organizations, with the management of each organization listed at the corresponding node. Such a hierarchy of organizations implicitly reflects implementation relationships, in which each organization is implemented by a combination of the nodes linked below it plus the management at its node. However, the relationship between the management personnel at the two ends of a link would be an interaction relationship even though it too is normally shown vertically because of the asymmetry in power and control.

If we take interaction to the polyadic extreme, we can talk about interactions among all four great domains; that is, people (S), plants, animals,

Figure 2.15
A party of human-controlled avatars in the Second Life MMORPG.
From http://upload.wikimedia.org/wikipedia/commons/8/8e/SecondLife.png. Cre-
ative Commons Attribution-Share Alike 3.0 Unported license.

and human bodies (L), and computers (C) all interacting with each other
and the physical world (P). We start to reach this extreme in areas
such as massively multiplayer online role-playing games (MMORPGs),
where people interact with each other and with complex virtual/simulated
worlds over distributed networks (figure 2.15),[38] and ubiquitous computing, where computing interacts pervasively with the real world of
objects and organisms.[39] We will return to interaction in much greater
depth in chapter 4 and to some of these polyadic extremes in chapter 5
(section 5.1).

2.3   The Metascience Expression Language

Languages provide a means of communicating, recording, and formalizing content. *Programming languages*, such as C++ and Java, are for communication from people to computers. Attempts are made to facilitate their use in the reverse direction or to support sharing among multiple people, but these remain difficult open problems. Programming languages are by necessity formal. Interpreters and compilers assume a precise syntax (structure) and semantics (meaning) for programs they process, with any deviation being a bug that can lead to incorrect behavior or even complete failure. *Natural languages*,[40] such as English or Chinese, evolved to support communication among people, both synchronously (e.g., face-to-face speech) and asynchronously, where content is written by one person and later read by another (e.g., this book). Natural languages are more informal. Linguists identify rules of syntax and semantics, but they are routinely violated and may be influenced by the context in which the language use occurs.

Modeling languages—such as that used for describing atoms (e.g., Na^+, Cl^-), molecules (e.g., $NaCl$), and reactions (e.g., $Na^+ + Cl^- \rightarrow NaCl$) in chemistry—assist in capturing and communicating information about systems. With respect to formality, they can fall anywhere along the spectrum between programming and natural languages, generally depending on the subject matter and the intended uses of the models. Languages for expressing executable models of dynamic systems need the formality of programming languages, although they can be highly special-purpose—limited only to expressing particular classes of models—rather than general-purpose Turing-equivalent programming languages. Models intended to be used in proving properties of a domain are usually expressed in a *mathematical language*, where some parts are highly formal and precise and others are expressed in stylized natural language. Such languages are to be interpreted by people rather than machines, but in as unambiguous a fashion as possible. Models intended to facilitate understanding by people (e.g., in classroom learning) may be expressed informally in diagrams or natural language, although clarity and precision are always helpful.

The ME language is a modeling language whose predominant purpose is the understanding and shaping of the great scientific domains. It need not be executable, and it is unlikely—at least anytime in the near future—to be used in formal proofs. Thus, informality and ambiguity can be tolerated as long as they do not interfere with the goals of understanding and shaping. The language as it currently exists is semiformal. It is mathematical in form, yet it permits significant ambiguity. Sometimes this ambiguity will be reduced through accompanying text in natural language, and at other times it will simply be left as is.

Much of the ME language's notation has already been introduced in passing, in the course of this chapter up to the present point, so we can begin its unabridged exposition here with a review of these familiar aspects before adding in the few remaining concepts. Expressions in the ME language are built around five domain symbols: the four domain initials— P(hysical), L(ife), S(ocial), and C(omputing)—plus Δ to serve as a placeholder, or wildcard, that stands for any or all of the four domains. Five symbols are also used for relationships. Implementation is represented by the in-line division symbol (/), separating the domain being implemented from the domain doing the implementing, such as C/P for the physical implementation of computing via electronic circuits or quantum computing, and P/C for computing implementing/simulating the physical domain, such as in weather modeling and forecasting.

When we are not interested in distinguishing between full and approximate implementation (i.e., simulations, models, and representations), we will continue to use the standard notation for implementation, such as P/C for a model of the weather. When we do want to distinguish the two, we will lowercase the implemented domain to denote approximate implementation, as in p/C. When we want to denote simulation or representation of arbitrary domains, we will similarly use the lowercase Greek letter for Δ: δ. When discussing disciplines for which it is ambiguous whether or not there are true implementations or just simulations—such as AI (S/C or s/C) and alife (L/C or l/C)—we will feel free to use either uppercase or lowercase, depending on the situation and the point to be made. When we do not care about the difference or when talking about *strong* versions of these fields, uppercase is appropriate. When the emphasis is on simulation, lowercase is appropriate.

Implementation is not commutative, but it is associative and transitive. Reversing the order of the domains, such as was just done from C/P to P/C, changes the meaning dramatically, ruling out commutativity. In contrast, regrouping—say from (S/C)/P to S/(C/P)—may shift the emphasis, but both imply that P implements C, which implements S. Because of this associativity, the parentheses can safely be omitted from these expressions without introducing additional ambiguity, yielding S/C/P in both cases. Transitivity implies that P implements S in S/C/P; for example, when an AI system (S/C) is implemented on an electronic computer (C/P), intelligence is ultimately being implemented physically (S/P). The more intervening layers of implementation there are, the less interesting the transitively derived relationship may be, but it still technically holds. It is not like the *near* relation, where the probability of transitivity holding decreases as more and more instances of the relation intervene.

Interaction is denoted by one of three horizontal arrows, (↔,→, and ←), differentially signifying bidirectional interaction and the two possible unidirectional orientations. We can, for example, use S↔C for human–computer interaction, C↔C for computer networking, and C←P for computerized sensing of the physical world. The ↔ relation is commutative and associative but not transitive. S↔L is the same as L↔S; in both cases, there is a bidirectional interaction between the social and life domains. Similarly, (L↔S)↔C is the same as L↔(S↔C) because in both cases, all three domains interact. However, L↔S↔C implies that the social domain interacts directly with both the life and computing domains, while saying nothing about a direct interaction between life and computing. A single person (S), for example, may have both a dog (L) and a computer (C) but keep them completely compartmentalized with respect to their own activities. In principle, the interaction relationship could have been defined either way, as transitive or intransitive, but if it were defined to be transitive, then it would be difficult ever to express intransitivity of interaction. Whereas with an intransitive definition, transitivity can still be expressed via nested parentheses, as was seen above.

For the special case where there are an arbitrary number of instances of a single domain interacting symmetrically with each other—as, for example, in a large computer network—we can use a star notation, in analogy to how the Kleene star is used in regular expressions, to yield for example C* for computer networks.[41] When combined with a notation for a set of domains[42]—such as {L,S,C} for animals, people, and computers—the same * notation can denote interaction among an arbitrary number of elements of multiple domains: {L,S,C}*. Use of the star notation will not necessarily imply that every element directly interacts with every other one, but that in the aggregate all of these elements interact. Thus, it stakes out an indeterminate point in the space of mutual interactions, where some may be direct and some indirect.

The directional arrows, → and ←, represent one-sided interactions, with the domain at the arrow's head being influenced by the one at its tail. S→L might, for example, represent a human telling a dog to sit, and C←P might represent computerized sensing of ocean currents. Directional interaction is obviously not commutative, although C←P is of course identical to its mirror image P→C. Directional interaction, however, does share the other two attributes of bidirectional interaction in being associative and intransitive.

In addition to the symbols for implementation and interaction, we will also continue to use the addition symbol (+) to signify a generic overlap; that is, that two domains are related in some unspecified manner. It can be thought of as a wildcard for relationships, just as Δ is a wildcard for domains. Overlap is commutative—P+C is the same as C+P—and associative but not necessarily transitive.

Given these domain and relationship symbols, combinations of them can be used to denote the more complex expressions that are needed in the realm of compound relations and polyadic computing. For example, we can denote robotics simply as a form of dyadic computing, in which computing (C) interacts (↔) with the physical (P) world: C↔P. However, if we want to talk about intelligent robots, this gets elaborated to (S/C)↔P, a straightforward hybrid of robotics and AI. But we can also go beyond this if we want to represent that the robot is actually a physical (P) implementation (/) of life (L) that interacts (↔) independently with both a computational (C) implementation (/) of a mind (S) and the physical (P) world: (S/C)↔(L/P)↔P. Or we could represent that the computer (C) is also implemented (/) physically (P), yielding [(S/C↔L)/P]↔P, where square brackets are substituted for the outer pair of parentheses for ease of reading but without changing the meaning. Or we could consider a mind (S) interacting (↔) with a body (L), both of which are implemented (/) by interactions (↔) between the physical (P) and computational (C) domains: [(S↔L)/(C↔P)]↔P. We have gone here from a simple dyadic relationship to a range of complex tetradic forms, but all represented within the ME language.

All but the simplest expression in the previous paragraph could be simplified if we were to introduce a precedence ordering on the relations, as is generally found among operations in both mathematical and programming languages. The standard assumption will be that the star (*) has the highest precedence, followed by implementation (/) and then interaction (↔,→, and ←), so that C*/P↔S denotes a set of interacting (↔) elements from the computational (C) domain—such as a distributed computer (C*)—that is implemented (/) physically (P) and interacts (↔) with people (S). If we instead wanted to represent a situation where distributed computing (C*) is implemented (/) by the interaction (↔) between the physical (P) and social (S) domains, it would be expressed as C*/(P↔S). Exploiting this precedence ordering to simplify the intelligent robotics expressions in the previous paragraph, by eliminating extra parentheses or square brackets

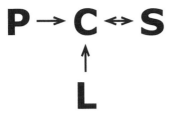

Figure 2.16
Two-dimensional representation of the expression for a computer sensing the physical and living worlds while interacting with a person.

around implementation relationships, yields S/C⟷P, S/C⟷L/P⟷P, (S/C⟷L)/ P⟷P, and (S⟷L)/(C⟷P)⟷P.

Earlier, the star notation was applied to the set of domains {L,S,C} to denote mutual bidirectional interactions among multiple instances. However, the same set representation can also be used to denote that a relationship applies to each of its elements, without necessarily implying any relationship among the elements of the set themselves. Consider a computer that senses the physical and living worlds around it and interacts bidirectionally with a human user. Representing this in the ME language without the set notation would require unidirectional arrows from P and L to C, plus a bidirectional arrow between C and S. Such an expression could be drawn as a graph in two dimensions—as in figure 2.16—but it could not be written linearly. The set notation lets us list P and L without asserting a relationship between them, so that the entire expression can be written on a single line as {P,L}→C⟷S. This expression denotes that both P and L individually affect C but says nothing about whether there is a relationship between P and L.

Just as the star notation was introduced to represent an arbitrary number of bidirectional interactions, we can introduce a new notation, °, to specify an arbitrary number of noninteracting domain instances; for example, C° represents an arbitrary number of unconnected computers, and {L,S}° represents an arbitrary number of noninteracting animals and people. A time-sharing computer that connects to an arbitrary number of people, who themselves are not directly connected, can thus be represented as C⟷S°.

The use of a precedence ordering plus parentheses in the ME language eliminates much ambiguity, but it cannot eliminate all of it. Because expressions in the ME language are abstract characterizations of world situations, there is often more than one way to interpret any particular expression, or equivalently, multiple distinct situations in the world that can be mapped onto a single expression. For example, the ME expression S→C can represent either a person actively typing on a keyboard or the same person passively being monitored by a vision system. Such ambiguities could be eliminated if we were to add more distinctions to the language, such as a modifier on the arrow that represents which participant controls the inter-action. Such a distinction might also be useful in modeling hierarchical organizations in which individuals interact bidirectionally, but where there are asymmetric power or control relationships. However, we will be content with our current set of distinctions in this work and leave the accumula-tion of additional distinctions to later efforts.

Beyond the ambiguity about the meaning of an ME expression, there may also be ambiguity in the other direction, where a single situation can be represented by multiple distinct expressions. This arose in spades with the five alternative expressions provided for the same intelligent robot interacting with the world (assuming that the initial dyadic form can also be used as an abstract characterization for an intelligent robot). As another example, we could consider modeling a neural prosthesis as either L/(L↔C) or L↔L/C. The first represents a brain being implemented by a combination of living and computational components, whereas the second represents part of a brain interacting with an implementation of a bit of life on a computer (the prosthesis). Although neither expression is inaccurate, they do provide differences in emphasis that might lead us to choose one versus the other in modeling a particular situation. In this particular case, the first seems more appropriate for modeling an embedded (biomimetic) prosthe-sis and the second for interaction with an external biomimetic device. Such representational choices can always crop up when modeling, and modelers have the freedom to choose those options they believe most appropriately capture the essence of what they are trying to express.

Beyond questions of emphasis, representational decisions may also be necessary about other aspects of a situation, such as the appropriate level of detail at which to specify the model. We saw this also in the intelligent robotics example, where at one point we decided to include the relevant aspects of the life and physical domains. Similarly in representing a neural prosthesis, we could model it as we have already done or drill down further and model it as L/(L*↔C)/P to incorporate the additional information that there are many interacting neurons and that both the neurons and the chip, along with their interactions, are implemented physically.

As a summary of the ME language, table 2.1 lists the notations that have been introduced and that will be used to structure, annotate, analyze, compare, and understand aspects of dyadic computing in the next two

Table 2.1
Notations used in the ME language

Symbol	Meaning
C, c	Computing domain
L, l	Life domain
P, p	Physical domain
S, s	Social domain
Δ, δ	Generic domain
/	Implementation relation
→, ←, ↔	Interaction relation
+	Generic relation
*	Indefinite number, interacting
°	Indefinite number, noninteracting
(), []	Precedence modification
{,}	Domain set

Lowercase letters denote simulation. Uppercase letters may denote either implementation or ambiguity between simulation and implementation.

chapters—implementation in chapter 3 and interaction in chapter 4. These notations will also be leveraged in creating, understanding, and applying forms of relational macrostructure in chapter 5 and in understanding polyadic computing inventions in chapter 6 (section 6.3).

3 Implementation

The previous chapter described implementation briefly (and at a high level) as *putting into effect* and described how one domain can implement another, as structures and processes in the first domain combine to yield the elementary structures and processes in the second domain. At its core, implementation involves the construction of something from pieces. The construction process could be a deliberate human-driven activity or it could be part of the natural order of things. A computer is deliberately constructed whereas a plant is not—unless you adhere to intelligent design—but they are both entities built out of a combination of pieces. In such a situation, we can talk about the domain(s) to which the pieces belong and the domain within which the constructed entity sits.

The most familiar instances of implementation in everyday life are constructed physical objects. Consider a chair. An all-metal chair may be implemented from metal sheets, bars, and screws. This is a pure dyadic physical example (P/P), where an object in the physical domain is implemented by a combination of other physical structures. There are no processes in this simple instance, unless the physical forces among the parts are considered.

An all-wood chair is one step more complicated. Now we would either need to talk about structures from the domain of life—pieces of wood—implementing the physical domain or we would need to understand how what was once alive is now no longer alive. We have had no reason to focus on death and decomposition in the context of computing, but they do play important roles in other domains. We could conceivably think of death itself as a process or as the termination of an organism's intrinsic processes, leaving only inert structure to remain. Among the processes that death terminates are those that maintain the organism's structures, enabling the extrinsic process of decomposition to take over. Decomposition then breaks down the structures into fragments.

In the physical domain, decomposition generally begins as soon as an object is constructed, whether by oxidation/rust, erosion, or other processes. There are many subtleties here, but the simplest way to think about a piece of wood for our purposes is probably as a physical object implemented by life (P/L), as it was a living process—and living components (cells)—that originally implemented the chunk of wood that is now an inanimate object. Thus, we can view our wooden chair as P/(P/L)* if we wish to emphasize that the chair is built out of multiple pieces of wood or simply as P/L if we wish simply to denote that the chair is implemented by (what was once) living matter. There is no temporal aspect to the metascience expression (ME) language, so we will make do without representing the distinction between what is living and what was once living.

A wooden chair with a leather surface (derived from dead animals) and plastic feet (derived from oil that is itself derived from dead plants and animals) is similar to the all-wood chair, only differing in the diversity of P/L components involved in the implementation. If we now add metal screws or support bars, we have a more complex instance of implementation, which can be characterized as P/(P↔P/L). Still, even these more complex instances of chairs are largely structural examples of implementation. There are minimal processes—loads due to gravity, as studied in physics within the subdiscipline of *statics*—but the full richness of process does not arise until there is motion, as studied in *dynamics*. A recliner brings in some amount of motion, although it requires either more physical implementation (a motor, etc.) or the addition of a human (S/L) to the system to make it actually move. A human–chair system can be viewed as an interaction between a human and a chair, involving the body as well as the mind: S/L↔P/(P↔P/L).

Cars are also familiar examples of the implementation of physical entities but are considerably more complex than chairs, comprising an intricate combination of structures and processes. Much of a car's structure derives from the physical domain—metal and glass most obviously—although, as with chairs, there may also be parts made out of leather, wood, and plastic. Processes move the vehicle and the individual parts of it (wheels, gears, windows, fuel, air, etc.), keep you warm or cold, defrost windows, play music, and protect you in an accident. As opposed to typical chairs, computing also plays a significant and ever increasing role in automobiles. Basic vehicles have at least thirty computers, and luxury models may have as many as one hundred.[1] In early 2010, considerable controversy swirled around computing in cars, with problems ranging from unintended acceleration to temporary brake failures and failed headlights being attributed to the complex nature of such systems.

A car has a driver, analogous to the person sitting in a chair. Is the driver, however, part of the car or merely interacting with it? Functionally, the person is *embedded* in the car; that is, the driver *interacts* with components of the car (the steering wheel, pedals, dials, etc.) in service of *implementing* an intelligent moving vehicle. Thus, both implementation and interaction are involved. Until cars are completely automated—as discussed in chapter 4 (section 4.4)—their full functionality is lacking unless a human driver is part of the system.

Computing is also composed of both structures and processes. It can both be implemented (C/Δ) and serve to implement (Δ/C). If you think of a simple dichotomy in computing between hardware and software, C/Δ is fundamentally about hardware, whereas Δ/C is the domain of software. The special case of C/C, where one form of computing implements another, is also worth acknowledging explicitly. It results in the kinds of layered architectures so familiar within computing. We will return to this topic again in chapter 5, but a few examples include: how microcode[2] implements a computer's architecture and basic instruction set; how compilers and interpreters implement one programming language on top of another; how operating systems implement high-level services on top of more primitive ones; how advanced distributed computing approaches, often now called grids[3] or clouds,[4] yield *metacomputers* (distributed computing resources that logically function as a single computer) on top of networks of computers; and how complex procedures and abstractions are implemented via combinations of simpler ones. When both instances of computing in the implementation relationship of C/C are identical (e.g., when a single programming language implements itself), metalevel or reflective processing is said to occur. In the extreme, this can lead to what is called the reflective tower,[5] where a language is interpreted by itself, which is itself interpreted by itself, and so on ad infinitum.

There are aspects of many of these topics that are monadic. For example, architectures, languages, and operating systems can be investigated independently of any possible implementations of them, but it isn't possible actually to realize them without implementations, and much of their study inherently concerns their implementations. Other aspects, such as compilers, are inherently dyadic. Because the computational implementation of computation is such a core topic within computing, it is needless to belabor it further here. As just mentioned, we will return to this topic in chapter 5 to discuss a standard layered systems architecture, but the remainder of this chapter focuses on implementation relationships between computing and the other great scientific domains. Section 3.1 considers how computing can be implemented by structures and processes from the physical, life, and social domains. Section 3.2 considers how computing can either simulate or truly implement structures and objects from these other domains.

The notion of implementation with which we are concerned here focuses on the relationship between an entity and the stuff out of which it is constructed, rather than on the relationship between the entity and whoever or whatever actually performed the construction. In computing, we frequently talk about a programmer implementing some functionality. For example, back in the early 1980s, I implemented a program that played the game Othello at a world championship level.[6] But this is precisely not the meaning of the term used here. Instead, this program was implemented in the language SAIL—the now defunct Stanford Artificial Intelligence Language[7]—so in our terms, the program I wrote (C) was implemented by computing (C), implying that the relationship was C/C rather than C/S.

According to the relational architecture, my implementation effort was instead an interaction with the computational implementation of computing: S→C/C. We could flesh this out further to include the fact that the code I wrote was an artificial intelligence (AI) program implemented on a computer that played interactively with people and other computers— S→S/C/C↔{S,C}—but the key point here would still be the distinction between *implementation* and *construction*, where the former refers to a material relationship between two domains and the latter to situations in which an interaction brings new entities into being. We will see some examples of construction as a form of interaction in chapter 4, but our focus here is on implementation.

3.1 Implementing Computing (C/Δ)

When a domain other than computing implements computing, we are largely talking about computer hardware. By far, the most familiar and well-explored forms of hardware are based on the physical sciences (C/P) with the standard these days being based on the electronic structures and processes studied in electrical engineering and solid-state physics. Computer hardware is currently so identified with electronics that computer engineering, the academic discipline most associated with the technologies for building computers, is frequently situated within electrical engineering, as it is at my own university. Yet, the physical domain—and electronics more particularly—provides just one of many routes to implementing computers. This section emphasizes the diversity, scope, and richness of the dyadic subspace concerned with the implementation of computing while highlighting some of the more interesting and obscure corners of it. But let's first start with some general background on the implementation of computing.

To be transformed, information must be instantiated in some *medium*. Natural forms of information (i.e., information not created deliberately by people) are instantiated all around us. Geologic strata (P), tree rings (L), and fossils (P/L) embody information about the history of Earth, its processes, and its occupants. Molecules (P) in bodies of water and the atmosphere convey information about human and natural activity. The size and skin texture of an individual (L) convey information about her or his age and possibly about her or his health and nutritional history. Facial expressions (S/L) embody information about mood and emotion. DNA (L) encodes information about how to construct a living organism. Antibodies encode information about diseases that an organism has experienced (L). The brain provides the pinnacle of natural means of encoding information and is the basis for all deliberate human instantiation of information (S/L).

There is also a long history of deliberate human construction of information (i.e., representations) in physical media, from rock carving (P) and painting (P, P/L), to the encoding of status in clothing (P/L) and jewelry (P), to writing on stone (P), wood (P/L), clay (P), papyrus (P/L), vellum (P/L), and paper (P/L). The abacus (P) is sometimes considered an early human-made computer, but it is actually just another means of representing information—numbers in this case—in a physical medium. In this way, it is like the use of fingers (L), pebbles (P), or a slide rule (P) in calculation. As with these other means of embodying numbers, an abacus facilitates calculations (transformations) of particular sorts by people, but it is the people who transform the information.

These early representations of numbers can all be considered as forms of *precomputing*. Where abaci differed from the other forms of precomputers was in their use of a positional, or Hindu–Arabic, representation for numbers. The others all used what might be called proto-Roman or analog—albeit discrete rather than continuous—numeric representations; they simply used object quantity to represent number. Still, computing in all of these cases had to be implemented by a hybrid human–physical system, C/(S↔P), although it might be better considered a human-life system, C/(S↔L), when fingers are used.

When people started building automated computing devices, the concern shifted from representations that are effective for use by people to forms of information instantiation that could be transformed automatically. Human representations could potentially be used by automated computers (e.g., by using a camera to read writing on paper and a robotic arm to alter it), but such information can be difficult to interpret, slow to use, and bulky in form. In consequence, information instantiation in computers has focused on simpler, less ambiguous, and ever smaller formats. In a digital computer, the basic unit for information is the *bit*—binary digit—an element that can be in one of two states, normally denoted 0 and 1, but which can also be thought of as true (T) and false (F). All information in a digital computer is thus represented as some structured sequence of bits.

Numbers are represented in computers by structuring a sequence of bits as a binary number. A typical human-oriented number, such as 35, is *decimal*, with each digit representing a number in the range of 0 to 9 (3 and 5 in this case). It is also Hindu–Arabic, in the sense that each digit further to the left is multiplied by a factor of 10 more than the previous one ($5 \times 1 = 5$ and $3 \times 10 = 30$, respectively). A binary number is similar, just with each position being limited to one of two values (0–1) rather than one of ten (0–9), so that each digit moving to the left is multiplied by 2 rather than 10: the binary number 101 is $1 \times 1 + 0 \times 2 + 1 \times 4 = 5$. The representation of number in computers gets more complex when there are negative numbers (e.g., –35) and very large numbers (e.g., 3.5×10^{20}), but the basic principles remain the same.

Beyond number, text is represented in computers by assigning a characteristic string of bits—a *byte*—to each letter and symbol in the language and then stringing together these bytes to represent the sequence of letters and symbols in the text. Similarly, images are represented by two-dimensional arrays of *pixels*, where each pixel is a string of bits. The number of distinct colors a pixel can take on is determined by the number of bits per pixel: *colors* = $2^{bits/pixel}$.

The fundamental approach to implementing information in digital computers is thus to devise technology for encoding bits that is unambiguous (i.e., for which it is easy to distinguish a 0 from a 1), fast to read and write, small in size, reliable, and requiring little power to use. Transformation then becomes the process of generating new patterns of bits from existing patterns. We can talk at a high level about transforming numbers (calculating), text (e.g., translating) and images (e.g., warping). We can also talk about transformation at its lowest level, in terms of a single bit or a small number of bits. Just as more complex forms of information are built up from the primitive notion of a bit, more complex forms of transformation can be built up from primitive transformations defined on a few bits.

Consider a light switch. If there is power to the switch and the switch is in the on position, then power will flow through the switch. The switch performs a computation/transformation known in Boolean logic—a system for elementary logic developed by the nineteenth-century mathematician and philosopher George Boole—as AND.[8] It takes two inputs—the state of power to the switch and the position of the switch—and generates power out of the switch if (and only if) both of the inputs are true/on/1, three terms that can be used interchangeably when talking about the use of Boolean logic in computers. If we assign symbols to the three parameters—A and B for the inputs and Y for the output—and use the logical symbol for AND ($\wedge$), we get the logical equation $A \wedge B = Y$ for the light switch. We can also represent this graphically as an *AND gate* (figure 3.1).

Beyond AND, the two other simple transformations in Boolean logic are OR ($\vee$), which produces a true output when either of the inputs are true, and NOT ($\neg$), which takes a single input and reverses its value, producing a true output when the input is false and a false output when the input is true. It is important to note that these logical operations need not precisely correspond to the everyday meanings of *and*, *or*, and *not*. In particular, OR is true when either input is true but also when both inputs are true. It does not capture the everyday notion of either one or the other being true but not both. This latter notion is formalized as an *exclusive or*—XOR ($\oplus$)— whose output is true when exactly one of the inputs is true and false when either both inputs are true or both are false.

Two other logical operations that arise in implementing computing are NAND (NOT AND) and NOR (NOT OR). These behave as implied by the parenthetical phrases: A NAND B is equivalent to $\neg(A \wedge B)$; and A NOR B is

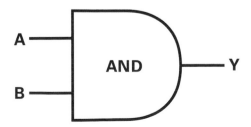

Figure 3.1
Diagram of an AND gate for the logical equation $A \wedge B = Y$.

equivalent to ¬(A∨B). Although NAND and NOR are a bit more complex conceptually, they are particularly convenient in implementing transformations because each one on its own is *functionally complete*, in the sense that every expression in Boolean logic can be re-expressed in a manner that only involves NAND (or NOR). Thus, as long as we can implement NAND (or NOR) gates, we can implement any computational transformation by combining enough of them. This is not true for the simpler operations.

Thus, if we can implement bits and NAND (or NOR) gates and combine multiple of them together into appropriate patterns, we can implement computing. Most of the technologies for this with which we are most familiar are from the physical domain—such as electromechanical switches, vacuum tubes, and transistors—but alternative technologies can also arise from the life, social, and computational domains, as can more exotic technologies from the physical domain.

Most implementations of computing focus on this traditional digital model of bits and logic gates. However, there are interesting variations that do not. *Analog computing* encodes information in continuous quantities and transforms these quantities via operations on them.[9] The first known analog computer was the *Antikythera mechanism*, an early *orrery*—dating from around 100 BC—that simulates astronomical positions.[10,11] Consider for illustration a simplified *liquid* analog computer for performing addition and subtraction (figure 3.2). It might consist of two containers (A and B) that can be filled to specifiable levels plus the ability to measure these levels. If containers A and B are filled with 2 and 3 ounces, respectively, and then container A is poured into container B, the sum of 2 and 3 (i.e., 5) can be determined by measuring the number of ounces now in container B. Then, if 1 ounce is poured back into container A, the difference between 5 and 1 (i.e., 4) can be determined by measuring the number of ounces

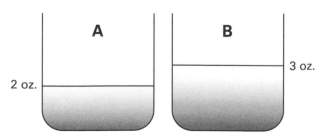

Figure 3.2
A liquid analog computer based on two containers.

now in container B. Electronic analog computers work in this manner but using such properties as electrical resistance and voltage rather than water volume. Analog computers are interesting in their own right but have primarily found application in the relatively narrow niche of simulating continuous systems, such as fluid flow. Within this niche, they may provide significant speed advantages over digital computers, but the narrowness of this niche falls far short of the impact of digital computers.

A second computing variant that commonly focuses on continuous quantities is *neural networks* (or *neural computing*).[12] According to one perspective, neural networks provide a model of the brain that is implemented on a computer (L/C). We will cover them from this perspective in section 3.2. However, they can also be viewed as providing a form of computing themselves that serves as an alternative to the conventional digital view (C/L or C/L/C). Rather than Boolean gates operating on bits, neural networks operate on continuous signals via *threshold logic units* that compute a weighted sum of their inputs followed by a nonlinear transformation on this sum (figure 3.3). *Perceptrons* use a linear threshold, yielding a 1 if the sum is above the threshold and a 0 otherwise.[13] It is trivial to see how perceptrons can simulate some of the varieties of Boolean gates; for example, with two inputs, an AND gate arises when the threshold is set to 1.5 and an OR gate when the threshold is set to 0.5. A NOT gate involves a negative weight on a single input. An individual perceptron cannot implement XOR, but a network of them can. In fact, a multilayer threshold logic unit can have the power of a universal Turing machine. Most modern neural networks actually transform the summed input via a differentiable function, such as the sigmoid in figure 3.3, rather than a simple linear threshold, to yield continuous outputs and to facilitate learning by enabling error signals to propagate backward through the network.

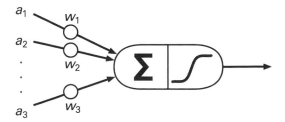

Figure 3.3
A threshold logic unit, as used in some neural networks.

A third computing paradigm that does not strictly follow the bit-and-Boolean-logic approach of digital computers is *quantum computing*.[14] Information in a quantum computer is instantiated in *quantum bits* (*qubits*). Rather than representing a single value at any point in time, whether binary or continuous, a qubit represents a type of mixture, called a *superposition*, of all possible values. A binary qubit at any point in time is both partly 0 and partly 1, with the degree of zeroness versus oneness specified by complex coefficients, such as $(1+i)/\sqrt{3}$ (where i is $\sqrt{-1}$). Multiple qubits can thus simultaneously represent an exponential set of possibilities in linear space, raising the possibility of polynomial algorithms for problems whose best conventional algorithms are exponential.[15] A recent survey of quantum algorithms identifies *quantum interference* as producing polynomial speedups over conventional algorithms and the *identification of hidden symmetries* as the key to exponential speedups.[16] It also mentions that the problems for which exponential speedups have been obtained are in both **NP** and **co-NP**; that is, of "Goldilock's [*sic*] complexity: not so hard as to revolutionize our notion of tractability by being **NP-complete**, but not so easy as to admit efficient classical solution." Although quantum computers may radically alter the complexity of solving a problem computationally, they do not fundamentally alter which functions are computable, as can be shown with the aid of quantum Turing machines.[17]

Beyond calculation, quantum phenomena are also beginning to have an impact on communications. *Quantum teleportation* uses *particle entanglement*—where two particles are so inseparable that one cannot be described without describing the other, even if they are physically far apart from each other—to enable quantum states accurately to be transferred over long distances, with the added benefit of enabling detection if any intermediary attempts to eavesdrop.[18] Quantum teleportation does not enable information to be transferred faster than light, nor does it enable the actual transfer of energy or mass, but it has definite potential for secure communication. Recent work has also shown the possibility of doing something that is actually akin to teleporting mass—where the quantum states of macroscopic objects are teleported—and energy.

As with analog computers, quantum computers can involve quite different implementation technologies from traditional digital computers, such as quantum dots and nuclear magnetic resonance (NMR). However, the remainder of this section focuses on implementation technologies, both traditional and nontraditional, for the standard model of digital computing. In the 1990s, NASA administrator Dan Goldin enunciated a philosophy for the agency that was summarized pithily as *faster, better, cheaper*. For much of the history of computing, the mantra has instead been *faster, smaller, cheaper*. However, with the heat dissipation limits currently being reached and the proliferation of small mobile devices with onboard computing, this is increasingly becoming *lower power, smaller, cheaper*. Other issues may also sometimes be factored in, such as the ability to work in hostile environments, where the environmental challenge may arise from heat, cold, radiation, impact, or liquids.

The material to come on digital computing is partitioned into subsections based on the domain that implements computing—P, L, or S—providing a top-level structure over the range of approaches. It is the obvious top-level choice given the relational architecture, but more structure is still needed to cope with the full complexity of implementing computing. One possibility for further structure is to continue following the ontology of scientific disciplines, as is partially shown in figure 2.1, on down to below the great scientific domains. Within the physical sciences, for example, implementation approaches could be further partitioned according to whether they are grounded in physics or chemistry, with even further subdisciplinary partitioning then occurring as necessary. Although this will prove useful in some cases as a third-level organizing principle, there is another principle that has proved more useful at the second level: *natural* versus *artificial*.

It may seem odd to exploit natural versus artificial as an organizing principle here, given the effort taken in chapter 1 to argue against this being a fundamental distinction in the sciences. The point there, however, was not that this could never be a useful distinction, but that it does not distinguish what is science from what is not; nor does it thus make sense as a top-level distinction among the sciences. The key is not to make too big a deal out of the dichotomy. But, as long as that is understood, differences in origins (i.e., whether or not the computing devices are constructed by people) may prove instructive at a subordinate level. Here its application is limited to within one form of dyadic computing, and even there it is used only as a second-level organizational principle.

Artificial computing is what we are most familiar with. It is the computers we as humans build and increasingly surround ourselves with. Our past lack of understanding of natural computing has been a key factor in the notion that computing is merely an engineering domain or a science of the artificial. But the increasing understanding of it, and of its preexisting presence all around us, is helping to break down the distinction between natural and artificial, at least within computing.

Further helping to break down this barrier is a third, hybrid form of computing that can be considered *naturally inspired*. Naturally inspired computing implements a form of computing that is constructed—and thus artificial by definition—but which functions in a manner that mimics, at some level of abstraction, natural structures and processes. The area of neural networks, for example, artificially implements a new form of computing (C) that mimics the computations performed by networks of real neurons (L or L*), and evolutionary computation works by mimicking other biological processes, such as genetic recombination and natural selection. Biologically inspired computing is a relatively hot topic in general right now, but forms of inspired computing can potentially be based on any of the great scientific domains. AI is, for example, a form of socially inspired computing, with the inspiration sometimes being quite direct and detailed and at other times more indirect and abstract.

The main argument for developing naturally inspired forms of computing is (1) that nature provides instances of computing that possess capabilities beyond what we know a priori how to contrive—consider, for example, how much better the human mind is at general intelligence—and (2) that by heuristically leveraging how the natural systems work, we will be able to apprehend sooner how to build such systems than if we start from scratch without such guidance. My own work on cognitive architecture has, for example, followed such a path, taking considerable inspiration from an understanding of the human mind that is due to cognitive psychology.

The typical counter to this argument takes as inspiration the history of human flight. In early years, attempts at naturally inspired human flight too often took the form of a set of wings that were covered with feathers and could flap. Yet we did not really make significant progress on flight until we ignored such biologically inspired attributes and focused on the fundamental principles, such as lift and thrust. This has never, however, seemed like a true counter to me, as the question is not whether you take inspiration from the natural system, but whether or not the inspiration you take focuses on the relevant aspects of the natural system, particularly given the differences that may exist in implementation technology. As much as possible, inspiration should arise from the fundamental principles underlying the natural system rather than from its surface features or its technology-specific attributes. The problem of course is that we often look for inspiration before it is completely clear what is fundamental and what is surface or technology specific.

Some researchers may respond to such a circumstance by shifting from a focus on naturally inspired computing to a better understanding of how the natural system works, hoping eventually to support a more fundamental level of inspiration. Others may push ahead on naturally inspired computing, using their best research judgment concerning which aspects matter and which do not and hoping that they get it sufficiently right to enable them to progress more quickly than if they ignored the natural systems.

Rather than C/Δ, naturally inspired computing is more appropriately expressed as C/δ, as it is based on a simulation of another domain rather than on the domain itself. Although naturally inspired computing can involve the creation of new hardware, yielding a situation in which some real domain implements a simulated domain that then implements computing ($C/\delta/\Delta$), more often the simulation is in software, yielding $C/\delta/C$. This is an important pattern that can be seen, for example, instantiated in both neural networks ($C/l/C$) and AI ($C/s/C$). It is also seen in other areas as well. In its full complexity, such a pattern implicates both this section and the next; and we will partition the material accordingly, with C/δ covered in this section and δ/C postponed until the next one.

Splitting the presentation of such topics across the two sections of this chapter helps clarify the two distinct aspects that they involve but also risks making too much of the split. This is a trap that the fields themselves unfortunately may fall into. For example, within AI, everyone in the field will acknowledge the importance of C/s in creating useful models of intelligent computation. But, whereas some in the field will then partner this with work on computational modeling of human cognition (s/C), others will consider it a peripheral activity that is more appropriately part of psychology (S) than computing (C). Thus, although it is an informative distinction to draw, it is important—at least in my view—not to promote it to the status of a boundary between scientific domains. More about how to deal with such boundary issues can also be found in the discussion of academic computing in chapter 5 (section 5.4).

With the addition of naturally inspired computing to the previous pair of natural and artificial computing, what we really have is a two-dimensional space in which only three cells are filled (table 3.1). The horizontal dimension distinguishes whether or not construction involves people—partitioning natural versus artificial—and the vertical dimension distinguishes whether or not the form of computation that is implemented aligns with one in nature. It makes no sense to have a type of natural computation that isn't aligned with nature, so that cell is empty. To

Table 3.1

The two dimensions underlying natural versus artificial implementations of computing

	Natural	Artificial
Aligned	Naturally occurring: C/Δ	Naturally inspired: S→C/δ
Nonaligned		Contrived: S→C/Δ

The horizontal dimension distinguishes whether computing occurs naturally or is constructed by people. The vertical dimension distinguishes whether or not the form of computing aligns with naturally occurring forms of computing.

distinguish the two variants of artificial computing, the nonaligned form is labeled as *contrived*, denoting that people invent the form of computing and construct it. Most of what we normally think of as computer hardware fits into the contrived cell, but there is a considerable amount of interesting work in the inspired cell as well.

The lone cell in the natural column has been labeled *naturally occurring* rather than *natural* to avoid a different source of confusion. Part of this is the need to distinguish between the individual cell and its column, but the bigger issue is that the discipline termed *natural computing* includes both naturally occurring and naturally inspired computing (i.e., the aligned row rather than the natural column) plus the use of computing to implement natural phenomena: Δ/C.[19] The term *natural* is just too useful and ambiguous all by itself.

The ME expressions for the three cells in the table denote that naturally occurring and contrived computing are based on a real domain, whereas naturally inspired computing is (almost always) based on a simulated domain. The expressions also represent that artificial computing is human constructed and omit any notion of construction for naturally occurring computing (although it could conceivably be denoted instead as Δ→C/Δ). What the expressions do not explicitly capture is what is in common between the two forms of naturally aligned computing: naturally occurring and naturally inspired. It isn't clear at this point whether an extension to the language should be sought to handle this kind of subtlety or whether it is a kind of detail that is just better off omitted.

The two overall organizational principles for the implementation of computing—domain and form of implementation—can be combined to form a 2×2 table, as in table 3.2. The domain dimension structures the remainder of this section into subsections, with the form-of-implementa-

Table 3.2
An organization over the approaches to implementing computing (C/Δ)

	Physical (P)	Life (L)	Social (S)
Naturally Occurring		Phylogenetic, ontogenetic, immunological, neural, collective/ swarm, biocomputing, biomolecular/DNA	Human cognition, mechanical Turks, Wizard of Oz, crowdsourcing
Naturally Inspired	Object oriented, simulated annealing, simulators, precomputing, analog	Evolutionary, cellular automata, developmental robotics, artificial immune systems, neural, autonomic, biomimetic robotics, swarm, Lindenmayer systems	Symbolic, probabilistic, intelligent agents, multi-agent systems
Contrived	Mechanical, electromechanical, electronic, optical/ photonic, chemical, quantum		

The top-level structuring into domains is across the horizontal dimension, and the second-level structuring according to the degree of naturalness versus artificiality is across the vertical dimension.

tion dimension used to organize the material more informally within these subsections. Below these two levels of organization—within particular cells, such as contrived physical computing—can be found distinctions among different source disciplines that are situated within the same scientific domain. This table is likely far from perfect, both in what approaches it includes and to where it sorts particular approaches. But it is at least a first attempt at categorizing the various approaches to the implementation of computing according to these two dimensions.

Three of the cells in the table have been left blank. For naturally occurring physical computing, plenty of varieties of naturally occurring information exist—as discussed earlier—but it is unclear whether any of the processes that normally operate on them can be considered as transforming information. Without this, I could not convince myself to include them even as aspects of naturally occurring computing. Perhaps as this area becomes better understood, just as naturally occurring life computing has become recently, this cell will be fleshed out. Without it, the core of physical computing is contrived, but with a smattering of items hypothesized as belonging to naturally inspired physical computing.

The other two empty cells are for contrived life and social computing. I would expect that at some point, approaches engendered by biologically and socially inspired computing will diverge sufficiently in form from those occurring naturally that it will make sense to refer to them as contrived rather than naturally inspired, but for the purposes of this table I did not assess any of those with which I am familiar as having gone quite this far. The remaining cells all have content—and will be discussed in the coming subsections—although the physically inspired cell also remains rather a stretch.

3.1.1   Physical Computing (C/P)

Today's computers are primarily physical in composition and at heart are contrived. They are based on silicon (for chips) and metal (for wires and other components), but components may also be made from plastic or other materials. The core processes in a computer are based on the movement and control of electrons. Photons are increasingly involved in communication (fiber-optic networks) and storage components (lasers in CD, DVD, and Blu-ray drives) and are starting to encroach more directly into computation itself. The alteration of magnetic fields is also important in hard drives. Together these structures and processes interact to yield computing, but they are still far from the only physical means of doing so.

The earliest forms of contrived computers were implemented mechanically. Data were encoded in non-living matter, and transformation involved physical movement. The earliest known attempt to move from the world of precomputers to an automated digital computer was taken by Charles Babbage—a nineteenth-century mathematician, philosopher, and engineer—with his *difference engine* (figure 3.4).[20] Although Babbage began work on the difference engine in 1822, the first full working implementation was not completed until 1991, based on Babbage's revised design from the 1840s. The figure shows the second completed difference engine, from 2008. It is composed of eight thousand parts, weighs 5 tons, and is 11 feet long. Although requiring a human to provide power—by turning a crank—this working difference engine performs computations automatically via gears, levers, cams, springs, rods, and wheels. It represents numbers via a positional, decimal approach, with one decimal digit per column. It is able

Figure 3.4
A working example at the Computer History Museum of Charles Babbage's difference engine that is capable of automatically performing numeric calculations.
From http://commons.wikimedia.org/wiki/File:Babbage_Difference_Engine_(Setting
_the_input_parameters).jpg. Creative Commons Attribution 2.0 Generic license.

to add digits represented by such columns, subtract numbers through the
addition of negative numbers, and perform multiplication indirectly
through the use of the method of *finite differences* (section 3.2).

Babbage also later designed the *analytical engine*,[21] which added to the
difference engine the ability to specify programs on punch cards. The
technology for punch cards was already in use for controlling looms, but
here it was adapted for specifying computations. Although Babbage first
described the analytical engine in 1837, he was unable to construct a
complete working version during his lifetime. Despite this, the first computer program was written for the analytical engine by the nineteenth-
century mathematician Lady Ada Lovelace, daughter of the poet Lord
Byron. Plans are now under way to build the first fully working version of
the analytical engine.[22]

New designs for mechanical computers are still being generated. Macroscopic proposals tend to be intended solely as thought experiments, however, because of the inutility of large, slow computers. The *billiard ball computer*, for example, is based on idealized billiard balls engaged in elastic collisions in a frictionless container.[23] It is similar to the notion of an ideal gas. In this case, a grid is imposed on the space within the container, and the presence of a ball at a location is interpreted as a 1, and absence as a 0. Computation occurs via collisions, which determine which locations will be 1 and which 0. The fixed structure of the computer—its hardware—is specified by the container's shape. The initial conditions of the balls specify the program and its input data.

Like a Turing machine, such an idealized computer cannot actually be built, but it does illustrate the principle of *reversible computation*.[24] A computation is reversible if it can just as well be run backward as forward. A NOT gate is reversible. Going forward, a 1 becomes a 0, and a 0 becomes a 1. Going backward, the same thing happens, so a NOT gate is not only reversible but also its own inverse. An AND gate is not reversible. If the two inputs are 1 and 0, the output of the gate will be 0. However, given the output of 0, the situation is ambiguous as to which input, if either, should be made 1. In mathematical terms, a function must be one-to-one for its computation to be reversible. Reversibility is interesting because its presence or absence makes a fundamental difference in the minimum amount of energy required to perform a computation—according to Landauer's principle, an irreversible computation must be accompanied by an increase in entropy[25]—and because of the role that reversible computation plays in some theories of the computational nature of the universe (section 3.2).

The other context in which mechanical computing remains of interest is at the nanoscale—of the order one billionth (10^{-9}) of a meter—where the movement of individual molecules forms the basis for computing. Figure 3.5 is a caricature of a *rotaxane switch*, essentially a ring that is trapped on a dumbbell and capable of changing position on the dumbbell.[26] The actual movement of the ring is triggered by nonmechanical means—such as chemical or photochemical processes—but the basic structure is mechanical.

Switches provide a core piece of technology out of which both memories for bits of information and logic gates that transform them are built. This is a subsidiary implementation relationship, where combinations of switches implement the elementary structures and processes most commonly seen in computers. Many of the implementation technologies we

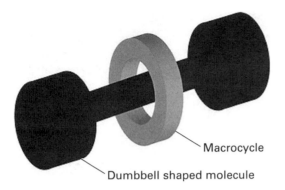

Macrocycle

Dumbbell shaped molecule

Figure 3.5
Caricature of a rotaxane molecular switch.
From http://commons.wikimedia.org/wiki/File:Rotaxane.jpg. Creative Commons Attribution ShareAlike 3.0 License.

will look at yield switches as a first step toward a full implementation of computing.

Eletromechanical computers were an intermediate development stage between mechanical and electronic computing. The *relay* is the core of such a computer (figure 3.6).[27] A relay uses an electromagnet to control whether another electrical circuit is open or closed. The flow of electricity in the electromagnet coil yields a magnetic field that moves an iron bar (the armature) to either connect or disconnect the other circuit (via the contacts). Thus, one electrical signal determines whether a second signal is flowing, implementing a switch. Konrad Zuse's Z3 computer, completed in 1941, was built from two thousand electromechanical relays.[28] It was the world's first programmable—via punched tape—fully automatic computer, given that the analytical engine was never completely built. It also pioneered the use of binary rather than decimal representations but operated at a rate of only five to ten computations per second, as opposed to billions of computations per second for current computers.

Electronic computers eliminated the mechanical aspect of the relay so that switches could be purely electrical. Originally, electronic computers were based on vacuum tubes—triodes—then discrete transistors, and then on integrated circuits (figure 3.7). All of these devices share the property that electrical activity at one port controls the flow of electricity between two others, but they have continually become smaller, faster, and cheaper.

Conventional integrated circuits are fabricated from silicon, but more exotic materials—such as gallium arsenide, germanium, and silicon

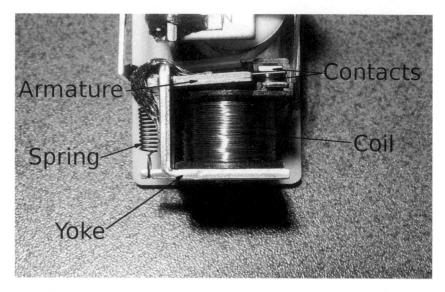

Figure 3.6
An electromechanical relay.

germanium—have also been used. As of March 2009, the world record for switching speed—of more than a terahertz (1000 gigahertz)—was held by transistors made from indium phosphide.[29] One general class of materials that currently is showing promise is the nitrides; that is, nitrogen-based semiconductors.[30] Nitrides have the advantages of allowing electrons to travel at four times the rate of electron travel for silicon while tolerating temperatures hundreds of degrees greater than those tolerated by silicon. They also enable tunable switching voltages, providing flexibility in designing electronic devices.

A significant amount of the effort in searching for physical materials that can go beyond silicon for everyday computing has focused on carbon. A *carbon nanotube* consists of a thin sheet of graphite rolled into a cylinder about 1 nanometer in diameter. Carbon nanotubes can conduct electricity and are being actively investigated as the basis for new transistors; for example, in 2005 a Y-shaped carbon nanotube was shown to be capable of functioning as a switch.[31] If the graphite sheet is only one atom thick, the result is *graphene*. Rather than being rolled up, flat sheets of graphene can be constructed on top of silicon carbide wafers to yield graphene transistors with switching rates up to 100 gigahertz.[32] Such investigations take us into the world of *molecular electronics*, in which the flow of electrons is

a) Triode

b) Transistor

c) Integrated circuit

Figure 3.7
Electronic switch technologies: (a) triode; (b) transistor; (c) integrated circuit.
From: (a) http://commons.wikimedia.org/wiki/File:Ibm-tube.jpg, Creative Commons
Attribution-Share Alike 3.0 Unported license; (b) http://en.wikipedia.org/wiki/File
:Transistorer_(croped).jpg, Creative Commons Attribution-Share Alike 3.0 Unported
license; (c) http://en.wikipedia.org/wiki/File:Diopsis.jpg, Creative Commons Attribution-
Share Alike 3.0 Unported license.

controlled within individual molecules.[33] The rotaxane-based molecular memory discussed earlier provides another such example, although it brings a mechanical aspect back into physical computing.

Optical, or photonic, computing provides another approach, in which computing is based on photons rather than electrons.[34] The particular appeal of optical computing arises from the speed with which light travels— nothing is faster—and its ability to represent many bits simultaneously across a spectrum of wavelengths. Light beams can also pass through each other without interference, simplifying the routing of many signals. Photons have already become central to computer networking through the use of fiber-optic cables for data communication. As of 2008, a single commercial fiber could embody up to eighty data channels—using the multiple wavelengths that are provided by wavelength-division multiplexing—each of which could transmit billions of bits (gigabits, or Gb) per second.[35] Fibers also suffer from less attenuation than electrical cables, enabling longer stretches between the repeaters that actively amplify the signals to counteract attenuation.

Photons are also central to long-term storage of data on optical disks, such as CDs, DVDs, and Blu-ray disks. Data is stored on such disks as pits that are written (burned) and read by lasers. The wavelength of the light determines how small the pits can be and thus is key to the density of data storage on the disk. CDs use 780-nanometer light, DVDs 650-nanometer light, and Blu-ray disks 405-nanometer light.[36] The amount of storage available on an optical disk is also affected by whether the disk is recorded on one side or both and whether recording occurs in one or multiple layers, but the core of a particular optical disk technology is in the wavelength of light used.

Optical computing becomes more futuristic when we talk about computing directly via photons or using them for holographic data storage. There exists a variety of technologies deployed for switching a light beam on and off, but these technologies have traditionally been non-photonic; for example, using microelectromechanical mirrors—tiny mirrors (mechanical) at the scale of micrometers (micro) that are controlled by electrical signals (electro)—to deflect light beams.[37] The first photonic transistor, which used one light beam to switch another on and off, was not invented until 1989.[38] Photonic computing is based on materials that exhibit nonlinear refraction; that is, the intensity of the light transmitted by a material is a nonlinear function of the intensity of the light coming in. The hope for optical computing technologies is that they will increase the speed of computing over electronic technologies while also dramatically decreasing the heat produced, a key issue limiting increases in performance in electronic computers.

Holographic data storage involves recording the interference pattern between two beams of light split from the same source: (1) an object beam, onto which is modulated the data to be stored, and (2) a reference beam.[39] The interference pattern ends up being spread across the storage medium rather than being localized in individual pits. Multiple patterns can be stored by varying properties of the reference beam, such as its orientation and wavelength. Reading the stored pattern involves shining an appropriate reference beam on it and detecting the light pattern that is produced. Because a pattern can be recorded across the entire medium at once and read from it at once, the hope is for increased speeds in reading and writing. The hope is also for increased data storage density, of up to 1 trillion bits (i.e., 1 terabit) per cubic centimeter.

Beyond the physical implementation technologies so far discussed are others that are mostly curiosities at this point. Chemical, or reaction-diffusion, computing is a good example. A chemical computer is based on a soup of chemicals of varying concentrations.[40] The chemicals react in such a way as to generate not just a stable equilibrium but an oscillatory state, yielding waves. Computation occurs via interactions among these waves. An analogy to optical computing might seem appropriate, but the inspiration for such a chemical computer actually came from an analogy between chemical waves and the billiard balls discussed earlier. Although technologies such as chemical computing may never yield a useful general-purpose computing device, they do help demonstrate the wide range of possible implementation technologies. There is also hope that such computers may one day provide the capability for controlling chemical processes while being directly embedded within these processes.

We will only consider the topic of physically inspired computing briefly, but a few illustrative examples will help make it more concrete. *Object-oriented programming* decomposes a problem to be programmed into objects, each of which contains some data (structures) and methods (processes).[41] The inspiration is obviously with the composition and behavior of physical (and living) objects. Object-oriented languages provide the ability to use a computational simulation of aspects of the physical domain (p/C) as a form of physically inspired computing (C/p), yielding an overall picture best characterized as C/p/C, or even C/p/C/P if we include the physical implementation of the original computer. *Simulated annealing* does not provide an entire computational system, but it uses a simulation of the physical process of annealing—heating a material to above its recrystallization temperature to improve its strength or hardness once it cools back down[42]—as inspiration for optimization algorithms used in neural networks and other applications.[43] Once again it yields C/p, but with a more complete characterization of C/p/C or C/p/C/P. However, if we want to talk about neurally inspired computational models that are themselves physically inspired by annealing—such as are provided by Boltzmann machines[44]—we end up with an implementation hierarchy over six domain instances, two of which are simulated: C/l/C/p/C/P.

Simulators, precomputing, and analog computing are also listed in the naturally inspired physical computing cell of table 3.2. Although simulation is a core topic in the next section, simulators are included here because languages that are constructed to simulate the physical world provide a form of physically inspired computation that can be distinguished on its own. To some extent, this can be thought of as a generalization of the approach taken to simulated annealing, toward more complete physically inspired computational systems. Precomputing is included because of the way in which naturally occurring numerosity information was converted into deliberately manipulated physical representations of number. Analog computing is included because its basic computing principle is to mimic physical processes.

3.1.2 Life Computing (C/L)

In contrast to the physical domain, where the implementation of computing dates back only to the nineteenth or twentieth century, computing has long been implemented by the domain of life. It is less familiar to us only because such computing is naturally occurring rather than man-made and in many cases has only recently been recognized as computing. In a recent book, the biologist Richard Dawkins states that:

Right up to the middle of the twentieth century, life was thought to be qualitatively beyond physics and chemistry. No longer. The difference between life and non-life is a matter not of substance but of *information*. Living things contain prodigious quantities of information.[45]

Dawkins goes on to list four different memories embodied by life: (1) the storage of "ancestral survival techniques" in the DNA of the reproductive system; (2) the record of "diseases and other insults to the body" in the antibodies of the immune system; (3) the history of "past experiences" in the nervous system; and (4) "collective memories inherited non-genetically from past generations, handed down by word of mouth, or in books or, nowadays on the internet," which are also maintained in the nervous system. If the focus is shifted from memories distinguished based on what they store to computers distinguished by their mode of computation, the picture becomes clearer for our purposes. The first memory bifurcates into *phylogenetic computing* and *ontogenetic computing*, with the former transforming gene pools to yield new species and the latter transforming individual genomes into fully formed organisms. The second memory underlies *immunological computing*, the third *neural computing*, and the fourth what can be called *collective computing*.

In everyday language, phylogenetic computing is simply evolution. It is a computational process through which the gene pools that embody information about species are transformed through processes such as mutation, lateral gene transfer—where genetic material is directly transferred from an organism of one species to that of another—and selection. Ontogenetic computing drives organismal development. Instructions encoded in the DNA of the genes are transcribed and interpreted to generate the proteins that drive the actual construction. Immunological computing, in a highly simplified form, uses antibodies as pattern recognizers for antigens, tagging them for later attack. The antibodies themselves arise within an organism from an evolutionary-like process, via random combinations of genes for detecting antigens and mutations, plus a transformation called *class switching* that alters the isotype of the antibody.[46]

Neural computing has been mentioned previously. The human brain is a massively parallel computational device with a hundred billion (10^{11}) neurons and up to a quadrillion (10^{15}) synapses at which processing can occur. Together these neurons and synapses implement a different computational device, the mind, which is at the heart of the social domain (S/L). Whether or not it makes sense to talk of other animals as being in possession of minds, they also still have brains of significant computational power, from the 302 neurons in the worm *Caenorhabditis elegans*—yes, it is exactly 302, as they have all been counted and are the same across individuals—up to the 10,000 in ants, the 1 million in cockroaches, the 300 million in octopi, and the 200 billion in elephants and whales.[47]

Collective computing occurs when a computation is performed jointly by a group of organisms. For example, figure 3.8 shows a mound built by a colony of termites. With humans, the group cognition required to build such a structure collaboratively would be considered part of the social sciences, but it is more ambiguous with other animals. If a mind, rather than just a brain, is required for the social sciences, social aspects of animals without minds would be part of the domain of life. In addition to termite colonies, other examples of collective computing include ant colonies, bird

Figure 3.8
Cathedral termite mound, Northern Territory, Australia.
From http://commons.wikimedia.org/wiki/File:Termite_Cathedral_DSC03570.jpg. Creative Commons Attribution ShareAlike 3.0 License.

flocking, and bacterial growth. One of the key concepts here is *stigmergy*, where communication among organisms occurs indirectly through the effects of their actions on the environment, such as the pheromone signals left by ants ($L° \leftrightarrow P$), rather than through direct organism-to-organism communication (L^*). Collective computing is one of the two pillars of the field of *swarm intelligence*,[48] with the other being a biologically inspired counterpart that will be discussed at the end of this subsection.

These five forms of biological computation—phylogenetic, ontogenetic, immunological, neural and collective—do not exhaust the repertoire of computational processes exhibited by living systems—the processes that occur in cell metabolism and at cellular membranes are other obvious candidates, for example—but they are enough for our purposes here. What may be more interesting and relevant instead is how natural forms of biological computation are being converted into human-controlled computational processes. In some cases, existing natural computational devices, such as molecules and cells, are being harnessed to perform computations of interest to people. Work in this area is usually called *biological computing* or *biocomputing*. Depending on how much human intervention is required to make this happen, biocomputing can be considered either a form of naturally occurring computing (C/L)—as it is in table 3.2—or contrived computing ($S \rightarrow C/L$). In both cases, however, it is grounded in real biological technology.

DNA computing, or *biomolecular computing*, is probably the most well known fragment of biological computing. It derives from ontogenetic computing, but with the goal of harnessing natural DNA transformations to perform useful work on demand. The earliest DNA computer solved the directed Hamiltonian path problem of finding a path between two nodes in a directed graph that visits each node in the graph exactly once while traveling along the links only in the directions indicated.[49] Nodes and links were represented as strings of *nucleotides*, the molecules that combine to form DNA and RNA, with the link nucleotides complementary to the node nucleotides (figure 3.9). When mixed together in large quantities, random paths through the graph became encoded in nucleotide sequences. Filtering steps, involving amplification and purification, then winnowed this large set of molecules down to those that were solutions to the problem. The initial step of generating random paths involved 10^{14} operations occurring in parallel, with the entire computation requiring seven days of laboratory work. Follow-on work has since extended this general approach to many other computational problems, including the creation of a single-molecule Turing machine,[50] a DNA computer that plays Tic-Tac-Toe,[51] RNA

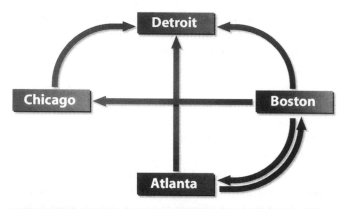

CITY	DNA NAME	COMPLEMENT
ATLANTA	ACTTGCAG	TGAACGTC
BOSTON	TCGGACTG	AGCCTGAC
CHICAGO	GGCTATGT	CCGATACA
DETROIT	CCGAGCAA	GGCTCGTT
FLIGHT	**DNA FLIGHT NUMBER**	
ATLANTA - BOSTON	GCAGTCGG	
ATLANTA - DETROIT	GCAGCCGA	
BOSTON - CHICAGO	ACTGGGCT	
BOSTON - DETROIT	ACTGCCGA	
BOSTON - ATLANTA	ACTGACTT	
CHICAGO - DETROIT	ATGTCCGA	

Figure 3.9
A Hamiltonian path problem of flying from Atlanta to Detroit while stopping in
each city exactly once. Cities are represented as nodes and flights as directed arcs.
The DNA sequence assigned to a flight is designed so that its first half matches—via
DNA complementarity—with the last half of the source city, and its last half matches
with the first half of the destination city.
Illustration by Slim Films.

computers that are embedded within living cells,[52] and DNA strands that
function as fiber-optic cables.[53]

As an offshoot of neural computing, a second significant area of biological computing uses networks of living neurons as computational elements
of a larger engineered system. For example, in 2005, 25,000 rat cortical
neurons were cultured on an array of sixty microelectrodes and then used
in stabilizing the flight of a simulated aircraft (figure 3.10).[54] The neurons
self-assembled into a living neural network and were trained to yield
appropriate weights for control of pitch and roll during flight.

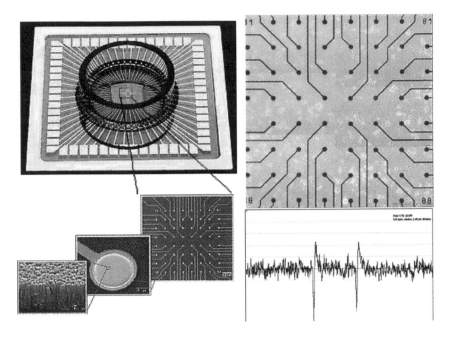

Figure 3.10
Neural flight control system based on rat cortical neurons (University of Florida).
Image courtesy of Thomas DeMarse, University of Florida. Figure 2 in Thomas B.
DeMarse and Karl P. Dockendorf, "Adaptive flight control with living neuronal
networks on microelectrode arrays," *Proceedings of the International Journal of Com-
putation and Neural Networks*, 3 (2005): 1548–1551.

There are even attempts at building useful computational devices
directly from the immune system. For example, there is a proposal to build
a *biomolecular immune-computer* as a device to control portions of the
natural immune system, much as chemical computers have been proposed
as a means for controlling chemical reactions in situ.[55]

What we have been referring to in this section as life-inspired computing
is more typically known as *biologically inspired computing*.[56] But, either way,
the key is using simulations of living structures and processes as the basis
for new approaches to computing (C/l). The simulation may be so approximate that the relationship to the biological system is at best metaphorical
or it can strive for as close a match as current understanding and technology
can enable. If we look at biologically inspired computing through the lens
of the five varieties of naturally occurring biological computing identified
earlier, the first topic of interest is *evolutionary computing*,[57] which takes its

inspiration from phylogenetic computing. Evolutionary computing focuses on searches, typically for optimal solutions to problems. The search maintains a population of candidate solutions, generating new members of this population by combining existing ones, and filtering population members based on a fitness function. Evolutionary computing is closely related to AI and optimization but differs from most traditional approaches to search and optimization through its focus on populations of candidates rather than individual candidates and in how it generates new candidates from combinations of existing ones rather than from individual ones. Within evolutionary computing, some of the work strives to follow the mechanisms of evolution found in the living world quite closely, whereas other work uses the idea only metaphorically.

No significant computational paradigms that I am aware of have been inspired by the details of ontogenetic computing, but several have been loosely motivated by it. *Cellular automata*[58] were invented by John von Neumann—a mathematician who also developed the concept of the stored-program computer (the foundation for all modern computers)—as a form of self-replicating computation. A cellular automaton consists of a grid of cells, each with a value, plus a set of local rules that determine how the cell values at any point in time are determined by a combination of their previous values and their immediate neighbors' previous values. Cellular automata embody aspects of both phylogenetic and ontogenetic computing, creating new full-grown instances from old ones. Like Turing machines, they provide a simple model of computation that occupies a central position in computing theory. They also underlie John Conway's *Game of Life*[59] and Stephen Wolfram's ambitious enterprise to reconstruct all of science on a computational basis.[60]

On a smaller scale, *developmental robotics*[61] is also loosely inspired by human development, but its focus is on robots that follow the developmental arc from human babies to adults—replacing explicit programming by experience—rather than on how a baby-like robot is automatically constructed from instructions encoded in something like DNA.

The area of *artificial immune systems*[62] is inspired by immunological computing. It appears to be tracking quite closely various aspects of learning and memory exhibited by the vertebrate immune system, but this work is still very much in its infancy.

Neural networks, as inspired by neural computing, have already been discussed. They tend to focus on central cognitive processing along with the peripheral processing implicated in perceptual and motor systems. There is also another form of peripheral nervous system, however, the autonomic nervous system, which controls internal processes central to life, such as breathing and blood circulation. Autonomic processing normally happens outside of consciousness, although some aspects, such as breathing, can be brought under conscious control at will. *Autonomic computing* is a form of biologically inspired computing that bears a metaphorical relationship to such biological control systems.[63] It implements a limited form of reflective processing in service of managing complex computer systems, enabling them to be self-configuring, self-optimizing, self-healing, and self-protecting. Whereas robotics was inspired by the manner in which living organisms interact with, and control, their external environment, autonomic computing was inspired by how such organisms control their internal environment.

In its full complexity, autonomic computing is not simply a dyadic relationship between computing and life. An appropriate ME expression for it would be something more like $C/(C{\leftrightarrow}l)$, representing that a simulated fragment of life is embedded within a computer; or, alternatively, that (traditional) computing plus a simulation of life interact to implement a new form of computing. This assumes we can gloss over the detail that the simulation of life (l) is itself computationally implemented (l/C). It also assumes that all of the *self-** activities are low-level enough that they can be considered as part of the life domain rather than intelligent processes requiring the social domain (S).

Robots also have all of these complexities, plus more, as the physical domain (P) plays a central role in both their implementation and interaction. An appropriate expression for an unintelligent, biologically inspired robot might be $P{\leftrightarrow}l/(P{\leftrightarrow}C)$, indicating that the physical and computing domains interact to implement a simulation of life that in turn interacts with the physical world. Typically, such work goes by the name of *biomimetic robotics*. Figure 3.11, for example, shows a biomimetic robot based on a penguin.[64]

The computational paradigm inspired by collective computing yields the second pillar of swarm intelligence, focused on decentralized, self-organized systems. As with evolutionary computing, swarm intelligence is frequently used as the basis for search and optimization algorithms. In the guise of swarm robotics it is also being investigated as a model for the control of large numbers of simple robots. It has even recently been argued that models of ant colonies provide a form of universal computation.[65] In one recently developed hybrid between swarm intelligence and biomolecular computing, single NOR gates are implemented within the DNA of individual *Escherichia coli* bacteria, with the inputs and outputs of the NOR

Figure 3.11
Conceptual drawing of the Festo AquaPenguin biomimetic robot.
Image courtesy of Walter Fogel, Fotodesign · BFF.

gates coding for different chemical signals across different strains of the bacteria. By arranging appropriate *E. coli* colonies spatially, multigate computations can be performed across chemically communicating populations of these bacteria.[66]

There are yet more forms of biologically inspired computing, such as Lindenmayer systems,[67] but we have seen enough by this point to indicate its overall richness.

3.1.3   Social Computing (C/S)

The idea of implementing computing via people may seem odd, but it has both a long history and an active present. People performed computation long before we built physical computers. In fact, the term *computer* was originally applied to people, at least as far back as the eighteenth century, referring to *one who computes*; that is, an individual who calculates.[68] Human computers (C/S) were employed, for example, in performing complex astronomical calculations. More generally, human cognition as a whole can be considered as implementing a significant form of naturally occurring social computing.

Employing people to simulate physical computers dates back to roughly the same time frame. Chapter 2 mentioned The Turk, an eighteenth-century automaton that embedded a person within a machine to simulate a mechanical computer. But not all uses of humans as computers are intended as frauds, nor are they necessarily all simulations. In The Turk, the human is performing a form of real computing, just not mechanical computing. He thus implemented computing (C/S) while simulating mechanical computing (C/p/S). In more modern times, within the domain of human–computer interaction, Wizard of Oz experiments use a human as the back end of a computer interface, performing tasks the computer either cannot yet or has not yet been programmed to perform. To a human subject in the experiment, it appears as if they are just interacting with a computer, as the front end is a computer interface. However, much of the action derives from the human who is hidden behind the interface, much as the wizard in the classic film *The Wizard of Oz*[69] manipulates an interface to his subjects from behind a curtain. The goal is to evaluate potential interfaces even when they cannot yet be built in reality or when they could be built but there is a desire to evaluate them before the effort is expended on their programming.

One of the most actively investigated forms of social computing at present is a variant of *crowdsourcing*, where a problem is outsourced to a community.[70] The particular variant of relevance here is where computational tasks are implemented by online communities. As mentioned in chapter 2, Amazon's Mechanical Turk is a prime example. Ideally, artificially intelligent computers would automatically perform the tasks crowdsourced—such as image interpretation—but these tasks are still too hard for computers, so we have people do them. Amazon calls this *artificial artificial intelligence* on their Web site[71]; it can be thought of as people simulating AI systems that do not yet exist (s/c/S). Someday, we might imagine a constantly functioning online version of the Turing test, where tasks are posed and solved by people or computers without the user ever knowing or caring which. Such a future of total piecework and human versus machine competition raises a variety of ethical issues, but it does seem to be a direction in which the world is heading. The company Mobile-Works has, for example, recently developed an Application Programming Interface (API) that enables the contributions of crowds to be directly incorporated into working software.[72]

Socially inspired computation (C/s/C) is the domain of AI. The discussion of the implementation (or simulation) of the social domain on computers (S/C or s/C) will be deferred until the next section, but the resulting implementation of new flavors of socially inspired computing (C/s) belongs here. Neural networks, to the extent that the mind as well as the brain inspires them, can fit here in addition to their earlier placement within biologically inspired computing. But the more characteristic form of socially inspired computing centers on the processing of *symbols*. Symbols are structures that denote other structures. For example, the string "Paul Rosenbloom" can be viewed as a symbol that denotes the author of this book.

Symbol processing as a form of socially inspired computing is grounded in the *physical symbol systems hypothesis*, first articulated by Allen Newell and Herbert Simon: "A physical symbol-system has the necessary and sufficient means for general and intelligent action."[73] The physical aspect here is that symbols must be "physical patterns" that can be combined into expressions and operated on by a collection of processes. Physical symbol systems are not simply to be a part of mathematics but full participants in computer science, leveraging its core computational paradigm of information transformation. Consistent with this, symbol processing formalizes to Turing machines and logic rather than to continuous mathematics. Within the language of first-order logic, for example, a symbol structure such as $\forall x\; Bird(x) \Rightarrow Fly(x)$ can represent the notion that all birds fly. This statement isn't of course strictly true, but it is a *heuristic rule*—or rule of thumb—that represents one aspect of what is generally, and usefully, considered as true.

Symbol processing has led to the creation of a diversity of computational languages, dating back to the late 1950s, with the early list processing languages IPL[74] and Lisp.[75] Rather than focusing on calculating with numeric expressions, these languages focused on reasoning with lists of symbols, such as (BALL1 COLOR RED), which might denote that a particular ball is red in color. They also brought to the fore such topics as recursion, functional programming, and garbage collection. Lisp eventually became the standard programming language within AI but has since become more of a niche language as it has been replaced for many applications by either standard programming languages such as C, C++, and Java that have incorporated various of its insights or by more specialized AI languages.

Specialized AI languages go beyond low-level support for symbol processing to provide formalisms for representing, and reasoning with, particular forms of symbolic knowledge. Logic programming languages, such as Prolog,[76] leverage the rich expressibility, formal nature, and well-defined inference algorithms provided by logic. Other languages have been based on constructs such as rules (*if–then* constructs),[77] cases (example problems and their solutions),[78] constraints (information about the mutual compatibility of values of different variables),[79] and agents (autonomous systems that interact with each other and their environment).[80] The expert systems boom of the 1980s was inspired by the realization that it was possible to capture much useful human expertise in such computational forms.

Probabilistic reasoning adds to symbol processing the concept of *probabilities*: real numbers between 0 and 1 that reflect the likelihood of a statement being true across a set of situations.[81] It deals with uncertainty in the truth of statements. If, for example, we add the probability 0.95 to the heuristic rule about birds, it implies that 95 percent of all birds fly, leaving room for ostriches, penguins, and any other birds that do not fly for whatever reason. Probabilistic reasoning is grounded in Bayes' law, relating the conditional probability of x given y to the inverse conditional probability of y given x and the prior probabilities of x and y: $P(x|y) = P(y|x) P(x)/P(y)$.[82] Some of the most interesting AI languages under development at this point—such as Alchemy[83] and BLOG[84]—combine general symbolic processing with Bayesian reasoning, often with a focus on automated learning from the vast quantities of data that are now available on the web and in databases.

Beyond languages, AI is also providing a range of useful but more specific algorithms and computational tools inspired by human capabilities. Some of these are still inferior to humans in their performance—such as systems for the understanding of speech and visual imagery and the translation of text among different natural languages—but others have matched or exceeded human performance in limited domains. Systems for planning large-scale activities,[85] learning regularities from massive data sets,[86] and playing complex games such as Chess[87] and Othello[88] fall into this latter class.

The last two topics listed in the socially inspired computing cell of table 3.2 are intelligent agents[89] and multi-agent systems.[90] Intelligent agents combine a set of capabilities necessary for intelligent behavior—such as the use of knowledge, decision making, learning, and interaction with external environments—into a single system capable of operating autonomously and appropriately in some environment. Agent languages provide the core around which such systems are built. The topic of cognitive architectures has already been mentioned several times over the previous chapters. What is important about them from the perspective of agents is that they provide one way of defining an agent language. However, they actually go beyond just providing a language, or a set of tools, to embody a theory of intelligence. Such a theory may be intended as a model of human cognition (s/C), as a socially inspired computational system (C/s), or as a combination of both (C/s/C). The two most mature architectures—Soar[91] and ACT-R[92]—mix both, although Soar is more of a computational system than a cognitive model, making it a natural fit for this section, whereas ACT-R is more of a cognitive model than a computational system, thus fitting better in the next section.

Figure 3.12 shows the latest version of the Soar architecture.[93] It is built around a working memory that holds the current state of the system and enables interchange among all of the other components. Connected to working memory are a perceptual system that provides input from the external environment and which includes both short-term and long-term perceptual memories; an action system that changes the environment; a

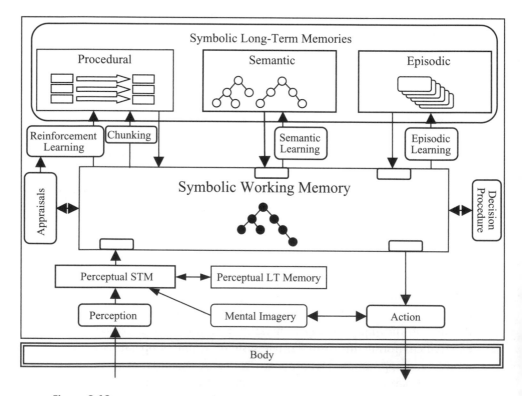

Figure 3.12
Structure of the Soar cognitive architecture (University of Michigan).
Image reprinted with permission from figure 1.4, John E. Laird, *The Soar Cognitive Architecture*, published by The MIT Press, © MIT 2012.

decision procedure that determines what to do next; three symbolic long-term memories, for procedural rule-based knowledge, semantic fact-based knowledge, and episodic history-based knowledge; four learning mechanisms, two for different aspects of procedural knowledge and one each for semantic and episodic knowledge; plus an appraisal mechanism that yields emotional evaluations of the current state. An intelligent system is implemented in Soar by adding some initial knowledge to its long-term memories and connecting it to some environment, whether the real world—through robotic sensors and effectors—or a virtual world of some sort. Over the roughly thirty years of Soar's development, it has been applied to a wide diversity of tasks, including control of the virtual humans in figure 1.3.

One of the intriguing possibilities for the future of cognitive architectures that I am pursuing in my own research is that a class of computational approaches known as *graphical models*[94,95] may yield a path toward integrating across neural, symbolic, and probabilistic approaches to intelligence, enabling the creation of broadly functional yet simple and elegant languages and architectures.[96] Major forms of graphical models have originated in, and shown significant promise for, such diverse areas as probabilistic reasoning, signal processing, and coding theory. Moreover, key forms of both symbol processing and neural networks[97] have been shown to map onto these models. The Alchemy and BLOG languages already mentioned leverage graphical models to blend general symbolic and probabilistic reasoning.

More on intelligent agents can be found in chapter 4, where the emphasis is on computational interaction. Multi-agent systems, which consist of multiple agents interacting with each other—(s/C)*—are also discussed there, although they also belong both here and in the next section because of how they implement new computational models (C/s*) and provide computational simulations of social groups (s*/C), respectively.

3.2   Computational Implementation (Δ/C)

Computational implementation in its broadest sense is what programming is all about. It deals with all aspects of using computational structures and processes to create new entities from one or more of the great scientific domains: Δ/C. When programmers are involved in this act of creation, as is most often the case, interaction is added between people (S) and computational implementation, yielding a form of construction that is appropriately characterized via the compound relationship S↔Δ/C. This expression obviously also covers software engineering as well. Although it is important to recognize that these topics do fall fully within the scope of this section, as discussed in the preface we will not spend much time on them here. A good chunk of these topics also falls within pure dyadic computing (C/C), where software is used to implement new forms of computing rather than aspects of other domains. This is another central subject in computing that we will not explore in detail here beyond what has already been mentioned in the chapter introduction.

What is less widely known, and thus worth more explicit focus here, is the full space of possibilities where computing implements one of the other three domains: P, L, or S. In the previous section, these domains provided the top-level principle for organizing approaches to implementing computing, with further organization then occurring via an artificial versus natural dimension that also included naturally inspired forms of computing. Here, a similar approach also turns out to be useful, albeit with the domain dimension now becoming a secondary organizational principle and a different dichotomy/trichotomy used as the top organizational level.

The artificial versus natural dimension from the past section isn't completely irrelevant here, but it is much less fruitful because nearly all computational implementations are artificial; that is, constructed by people. There are naturally occurring programs—such as DNA sequences and inborn reflexes—that we will hopefully continue to understand better over time, but I will not try to provide an overview of them here. Within the subspace of artificial implementations, most computational implementations are more appropriately described as naturally inspired rather than contrived, but the range is more of a continuum than a strict dichotomy. Consider AI for illustration. Even when bits of computational intelligence are built without the explicit goal of modeling human cognition, there is almost always some degree of inspiration from human capabilities. People do not strictly use first-order logic, so there is a contrived aspect to logical approaches to AI, but people certainly do reason in ways that maps well onto logic more abstractly, so that there is natural inspiration there as well. The field sometimes splits between those who tie themselves closely to the natural inspiration and those that take much more of a contrived perspective, but for our purposes here we will gloss over these subdisciplinary differences and instead maintain a focus on their common artificiality.

The dimension used instead to complement the division by domains is based on the distinction between *implementation* and *simulation* that was introduced in chapter 2. Simulation was characterized there as a form of implementation in which essential definitional aspects of the implemented thing are missing. It thus yields a form of approximate implementation. Representation and other forms of modeling were also likewise considered as forms of approximate, static implementation. True implementation, in contrast, fully meets the domain definition. In the remainder of this section, we will refer to all forms of approximate implementation as simulation, even when it is really just static representation, and we will narrow our use of the term *implementation* to refer to the subset that comprises true implementations. Simulation should still be considered part of implementation in the bigger picture, but when the focus is on the distinction between it and true implementation, it would be awkward constantly to use the longer phrase.

It is easy to conflate the implemented versus simulated dichotomy with the natural versus artificial one, but they are in truth distinct. The confusion arises because of the mistaken identification of simulation with artificial. All computational simulations are indeed artificial, but there are simulations in nature, mostly comprising *mimicry* for protective purposes—such as when the coloring of a nonpoisonous snake species mimics that of a poisonous species or a moth has eyespots on its wings to appear larger and more threatening. Similarly, although the world is full of natural non-computational implementation, the construction of artificial physical objects has long been a significant human activity. Fundamentally, implemented versus simulated comes down to whether or not a critical approximation is involved, whereas natural versus artificial concerns whether or not humans were involved in the construction.

Table 3.3 shows the two-dimensional space of ways in which computing implements other domains, with the domain being implemented shown horizontally and (true) implementation versus simulation vertically. The same qualifiers mentioned earlier with respect to table 3.2 should be kept in mind here. This table is a start, and it helps to organize the remainder of this section—with subsections on simulation and implementation that are in turn organized by domain—but it is likely far from perfect. It may seem odd to start with simulation rather than implementation, but the former has a deeper history in computing, much more is known about it, and it has had much more of an impact to date. Computational scientists and their predecessors have simulated natural phenomena since the earliest days of computing, and such simulations remain central in much of today's science (and entertainment). Mathematical representations of the physical sciences go back even further, originating thousands of years ago. In contrast, even the question of whether real computational implementations of the physical, life, and social domains are possible remains

Table 3.3
An organization over approaches to computing implementing other domains (Δ/C)

	Physical (P)	Life (L)	Social (S)
Simulation	Computational science, graphics, numerical analysis, virtual environments	Systems biology, virtual organs, virtual humans, neural networks, weak alife	Weak AI, cognitive science/ modeling, computational sociology, econometrics
Implementation	Digital physics	Strong alife	Strong AI

The top-level structuring according to simulation versus (true) implementation is across the vertical dimension, and the second-level structuring into domains is across the horizontal dimension.

contentious. Can we artificially create new universes, living creatures, or intelligent beings?

3.2.1 Computational Simulation (δ/C)

The roots of simulation, in the sense of approximate implementation, go far back into prehistory. The earliest cave paintings are representations, or approximate static implementations, via the physical domain: δ/P. The visual arts have maintained this tradition, with drawings, paintings, photographs, and sculptures all providing static simulations of real, and sometimes imagined, objects and entities. They have also developed various techniques to try to capture aspects of dynamic activity in a static snapshot, such as in figure 3.13. Comic strips extend this by affording a series of snapshots. Plays, television, and movies take activity simulation even further, using aspects of not just the physical domain (P) but also the social domain (S)—actors simulate other people (s/S), both real and imaginary, as they play roles—and even the domain of life, when the focus is on activity of the human body or when plants and animals participate: δ/(P↔S↔L). Computer graphics, along with various forms of digital media and games, are the computational descendants of this simulation tradition from the visual arts.

Mathematics, too, has a long tradition of representing natural structures and processes. This focused originally on the physical domain but eventually expanded to the other domains as well. Turning these representations into full simulations required not only mathematics but also either a physical machine (P)—such as the Antikythera—or a human (S) to provide the

Figure 3.13
Motion blur of London bus passing a telephone booth.
From http://en.wikipedia.org/wiki/File:London_bus_and_telephone_box_on_Hay market.jpg. Creative Commons Attribution-Share Alike 2.0 Generic License.

dynamics. Computational science, or scientific computing as it is also called, is the computational inheritor of this tradition, with computing (C) now filling the role that previously required either physical machines or people. In the beginning, just as with mathematics, the emphasis was on simulation of the physical world: p/C. ENIAC, the first general-purpose electronic computer, was originally designed to compute ballistic firing tables, although it was actually used instead for computations relevant to constructing the hydrogen bomb.[98] But the scope of simulation has since broadened to other domains.

The history of technologies for shaping the physical domain reveals that a long-term focus on the functional simulation of natural activity has been at the heart of the development of human civilization. By simulating aspects of both animals and humans, these living organisms can be replaced in work environments to reduce time, cost, and injury. Vehicles provide a canonical example through the ages. There are sledges, carts, carriages, cars, trucks, trains, boats, airplanes, and spacecraft. They are all different, but at the same time they are all effectively physical simulations of the mobility and carrying capacity of living creatures (l/P). Machines as a

whole—whether for agriculture, manufacturing, or whatever—are generically physical simulators of the ability of creatures to exert controlled forces
in their environment. AI and robotics—as well as all functional forms of
computational automation of activities that were previously within the
exclusive domain of the physical, life, or social sciences—are the computational inheritors of this tradition.

Computational simulation,[99] broadly, brings these threads together.
Work on data structures, databases, and programming languages is all
generically relevant. But two concerns that seem most characteristic of
simulation, particularly in the physical (p/C) and life (l/C) domains, are
(1) how continuous phenomena can be represented and processed on
discrete computers; and (2) how to cope with scale(s). We will briefly
examine both of these issues here, along with the use of computational
simulation across the physical, life, and social sciences.

Representing continuous quantities and phenomena on a digital computer is problematic, whether the continuity occurs in one dimension, as
with time and particular physical attributes such as color and hardness, or
it concerns two-dimensional surfaces or three-dimensional volumes. The
question is how to approximate, both finitely and discretely, these quantities in a manner that is computationally tractable yet sufficiently accurate
for the intended uses. Typically, this happens either by sampling a finite
number of points, each with a finite representation, from the underlying
continuous space or by tessellating the space via a decomposition into a
finite set of finitely described regions, as in figure 3.14.[100]

For one-dimensional attributes, the regions are simply line intervals. In
higher dimensions, there is more flexibility. In two dimensions, for
example, decomposition into an array of squares is one approach. Pixels—
picture elements—in two-dimensional images and displays can be considered as instances of such a representation, although they are actually
somewhat ambiguous as to whether they define a point-based or a region-
based representation. Triangular, rectangular, and polygonal two-
dimensional tessellations are also possible, as are more irregular coverings.
For two-dimensional surfaces embedded in three-dimensional spaces, triangular tessellations are common (figure 3.15). Texture images, such as
patches of ground or sky or face, are then mapped onto these triangles to
yield the full appearance, after issues such as visibility and lighting
are dealt with (figure 3.16). For full three-dimensional structures, the
concept of pixels can be extended to *voxels*; that is, *volume elements* or *volumetric pixels*. Structures in three dimensions are often represented by their

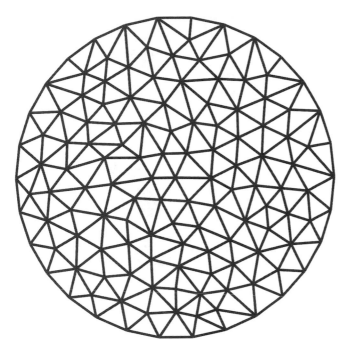

Figure 3.14
A triangular tessellation of a circular area on a two-dimensional surface.

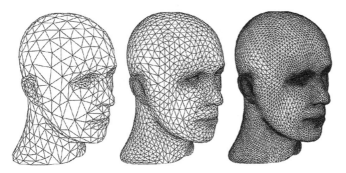

Figure 3.15
Three alternative triangular tessellations of a human head.
Image courtesy of Digital-Daily.com.

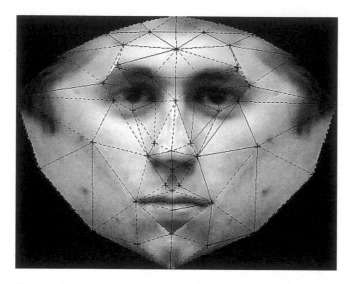

Figure 3.16
A triangularly tessellated texture map of a human face (California Institute of Technology).
Image courtesy of Douglas Lanman, Media Lab, Massachusetts Institute of Technology.

two-dimensional surfaces but sometimes also by a full three-dimensional volumetric representation.

Computational simulation of process brings in the notion of time, a continuous one-dimensional attribute. *Discrete-event simulation* uses a point-based approach for time. Each event is assumed to occur instantaneously, with time simply jumping over the interevent intervals. *Discrete-time simulation* instead takes an approach that is analogous to pixels, tessellating the time line into uniform time steps. *Real-time simulation* is then a variant of discrete-time simulation in which the computational time required for simulated time steps matches the passing of real time. It is essential for most human-in-the-loop simulations and real-time interactive games.

Computational simulations of physical phenomena typically are based on numerical approximation methods for differential equations that express relationships among values of variables and their derivatives. A differential equation might relate the position of an object, such as a car, to its velocity (the first derivative of position, representing the rate of change of position) and acceleration (the second derivative of position, representing the rate of change of velocity). Newton's second law of motion relates force to acceleration: $F=ma$ or $F=m(dv/dt)$ or $F=m(d^2p/dt^2)$. The Navier–Stokes equations, for example, arise when Newton's second law of motion is applied to fluid flow. They are used in modeling the flow of water in pipes, rivers, lakes, and oceans, as well as in modeling the movement of air in the atmosphere and over structures such as aircraft wings. Other important examples of differential equations in the physical sciences include the heat equation in thermodynamics, Hamilton's equations for classical mechanics, Maxwell's equations for electromagnetism, Schrödinger's equation for quantum mechanics, and Einstein's field equations for general relativity.[101]

Numerical approximation is required when the differential equations are too complex to be solved analytically; that is, when mathematical manipulations of the equations, either by humans or computers, cannot convert them into a form that enables direct calculation of the variable(s) of interest. Different approaches to discretizing the differential equations lead to different classes of methods, such as *finite difference*, *finite element*, and *finite volume*. Given that differential equations involve real numbers, any such approximation method will by necessity only deal with them up to some finite precision. The discipline of numerical analysis explores how to represent approximations of real numbers in computers via a finite precision floating-point representation.[102] It also investigates algorithms for computing with such numbers, along with how to deal with issues such as the occurrence, propagation, and growth of approximation errors.

Beyond the issue of continuity, the other major simulation issue that was listed is *scale(s)*. This includes at least three aspects: (1) the sheer number of structures and processes that need to be simulated for particular phenomena; (2) the resulting necessity for models that differ across time and length scales; and (3) the problem of integrating across these models both within and across scales. With respect to the first aspect of scale, military simulation provides a good example. It has traditionally represented forces as aggregate units; for example, an entire company of tanks may be considered as a single object. But more recent entity-level simulations provide greater fidelity in reproducing real phenomena while also enabling direct human participation—such as for a fighter pilot in a networked cockpit simulator—by explicitly representing individual vehicles, soldiers, and even missiles. The Defense Advanced Research Projects Agency (DARPA) project on virtual exercises mentioned in the preface was just such a simulation. It involved a few thousand entities, but more recent simulations have included millions.[103]

For such simulations, it has been essential to exploit the computational power of large-scale parallel and distributed computing, including grids and clouds. Modern massively multiplayer online role-playing games, such as World of Warcraft,[104] have comparable scale issues and have responded to them in a similar manner. Yet, parallel computation is not always the most desirable, or even a feasible, solution. Consider what would happen, for example, if you attempted to simulate a human by starting with atoms and implementing everything else veridically up from there. There are $\sim 10^{28}$ atoms in a single human.[105] For simplicity, let's assume that the computational cost is linear in the number of atoms and that it takes only one computational operation to simulate a single time step for an atom. Today's fastest supercomputers run at petaflop speeds—10^{15} operations per second. As there are approximately 10^7 seconds per year, this means it would take 1 million years on our fastest supercomputers to simulate a single time step for the entire human.

In the real world, successively higher scales are implemented via lower levels. For example, subatomic particles ($\sim 10^{-15}$ to 10^{-14} meter) implement atoms ($\sim 10^{-10}$ meter), atoms implement molecules ($\sim 10^{-9}$ to 10^{-6} meter), molecules implement cells ($\sim 10^{-5}$ to 10^{-4} meter), and cells implement animals ($\sim 10^{-4}$ to 10^2 meter). But, rather than always constructing complex simulations, such as of the human body, literally in this fashion—with each higher level implemented by a combination of structures and processes in the level below it—specialized scale-specific approximations and methods may be used to reduce simulation costs radically. This yields the second aspect mentioned earlier: the need for different models at different scales.

A coherent overview of many of these scale-specific approaches is obtainable by progressing through the sciences in what is essentially a scale-driven manner—not unlike how the hierarchy of sciences in figure 2.13 was created—starting with the physical sciences at the smallest scale, and progressing up from there through the life and social sciences. Although this is not guaranteed to hit all of the important simulation topics across the sciences, it yields a sufficiently broad treatment to illustrate this vital component of dyadic computing. We will then return to the overall issue of scale, with a discussion of its third and final aspect: integration.

Starting at the bottom of the physical sciences (p/C), Schrödinger's quantum mechanical equation may be used for a single atom or a small number of atoms. Density functional theory can then be used to scale up to more atoms in support of work in quantum chemistry and solid-state physics.[106] For larger numbers of atoms, statistical mechanics is leveraged to yield molecular dynamics simulations that have recently reached trillions of atoms.[107] Such simulations are particularly useful in materials science and in the understanding of biological molecules, such as proteins.[108] Continuing upward through the life sciences (l/C) reaches efforts to simulate the structures and processes within individual cells, yielding e-cells or virtual cells.[109,110] Specialized models of neural cells also exist, with the study of neural networks focusing on the interactions among multiple such simulated neurons.[111] Moving up further then yields models of individual organs (hearts, brains, etc.). The virtual heart, for example, simulates the electrical activity and contractions of the heart.[112]

At the level of organisms, the discipline of systems biology comes to the fore, with a focus on simulating the complex interactions among the various parts of the body. Several road maps exist for developing simulations of the entire *physiome*; that is, the function of the body and how it relates to its structure.[113,114] In computer graphics and games, more limited simulations of the external appearance and behavior of organisms are essential and in fact are quite far along. Typically, a surface model in the form of a texture-mapped mesh is generated either by scanning a real person or by designing an artificial person (figure 3.17).[115] Animation of this body surface can then proceed via a variety of different means, from adaptation of movement data derived from motion capture—where movements of real humans are recorded[116]—to physics-based models of the articulation of skeletons and the operation of muscles.[117]

For non-human organisms and societies, we then reach the domain of *artificial life (alife)*.[118] The goal of alife can be to simulate living organisms or truly to implement living organisms. Here we focus on the former, with the latter deferred until the discussion of strong alife in the next subsection. Soft alife simulates life via software, providing pure computational simulations of life (l/C). Hard alife incorporates hardware into the simulation. Theoretically, the hardware could be completely noncomputational, yielding l/P, but more likely there is an interacting combination of physical and computational structures and processes: l/(P↔C). Hard alife shades into biomimetic robotics—as in figure 3.11—with its focus on robots that borrow operational principles from, and may resemble quite closely, living organisms. Alife can also be based on biochemistry (i.e., wetware), but it is then a physical simulation of life: l/P.

Simulation in the social sciences (s/C) can be quite different in nature from what is seen in the physical and life sciences. In such disciplines as AI, cognitive psychology, cognitive science, and computational sociology, what is generally being simulated is thought processes: how knowledge is

Figure 3.17
A facial rendering of Digital Emily (Image Metrics and University of Southern California). The face has been rendered completely by computer and then fused with a photograph of the real Emily, containing her hair, body, and clothing.
Image courtesy of Image Metrics.

acquired, represented, and reasoned about; how skills are acquired and performed; how problems are solved and plans are made; how the mind perceives and controls the body's motor systems; the impact of emotions, personalities, and motivations; interaction through natural language and other means; and behavior in groups and organizations. The dominant simulation approaches are based on the three classes of techniques introduced in section 3.1: neural networks, symbol processing, and probabilistic modeling.

Neural networks straddle the boundary between the life and social sciences, focused as they are on computationally simulating how biology produces thought: s/l/C. It should not be surprising therefore that its techniques bear a close family resemblance to those used in simulating the domain of life and that they are formalized in terms of standard continuous mathematics. Symbol processing provides a strong contrast. Whereas neural networks directly model the brain, with the intent of indirectly producing mind-like phenomena through the interactions among simulated neural components, symbol systems bypass the brain, and biology in general, to model the mind directly: s/C. They are formalized in terms of logic and other discrete computational models, such as finite state machines,[119] that provide finite analogs of Turing machines. The directness of symbolic modeling makes it easier to simulate complex thought processes while simultaneously making it harder to tie such models to the brain and thus often to model subtle or lower-level cognitive phenomena.

Probabilistic modeling builds on symbol processing, although most often of simplified propositional forms, by introducing probabilities to enable representing and reasoning about uncertainty in a mind's understanding of the world.[120] In so doing, it combines the discrete representational and reasoning capabilities of symbol processing with continuous statistical processing. Statistics is used across science in service of data analysis. It is also commonly used in simulation, in the form of *stochastic simulation*, to reflect uncertainty on the part of scientists about the processes they are modeling. The use here, however, is different from either of these. Probabilities in cognitive modeling represent uncertainty in the mind of the person being modeled rather than in the mind of the person doing the modeling.

As with the physical and life sciences, multiple levels of simulation are possible within the social sciences. Newell, with his characteristic knack for identifying and exploring foundational concepts, laid out a first pass of how scale counts in cognition.[121] He stratified human action into four bands—biological, cognitive, rational, and social—and then further partitioned each band into a hierarchy of levels by their temporal orders of magnitude, from 100 microseconds for activity in organelles within the brain, on up level-by-level to months for social behavior. In humans, the biological band was the home of neural processing and the cognitive band of symbol processing, but the assumption was that the cognitive band could also be implemented on top of other technologies, such as conventional computers. The relationship between adjacent levels—such as neurons at 1 millisecond and neural circuits at 10 milliseconds—as well as between adjacent bands, is clearly one of implementation. This overall stratification of human action is analogous to earlier diagrams of abstraction levels in complex computational systems, such as operating systems,[122] and in fact was likely inspired by them.

The task of simulating complete minds falls under the domain of *unified theories of cognition*.[123] Such theories are analogous to the *theory of everything* sought in the physical sciences and to the ultimate goals of both systems biology and alife within the life sciences. A unified theory of cognition is generally composed of a cognitive architecture that defines the fixed structure of cognition plus the knowledge and skills that are acquired, either through learning or programming, and then processed by the architecture.[124,125] ACT-R, as mentioned in section 3.1.3, is by far the dominant basis for such theorizing. Its various mechanisms have even recently been mapped onto regions of the human brain, yielding an important milestone in theoretical cognitive neuropsychology.

Beyond simulation of individual minds, these same techniques can apply to the simulation of groups of individuals and the interactions among them. However, for large groups this becomes computationally infeasible. One alternative is to use less computationally intensive techniques for simulating individuals that are more akin to those from alife. Alternatively, it is possible to move up a level to focus on populations as units, using either statistical techniques or differential equations to drive the simulations. Economics, and particularly econometrics, leverages such an approach to modeling human populations, with *Black–Scholes* being a particularly influential example of a model of financial markets based on partial differential equations.[126] Traditional unit-level military simulation has also exploited such an approach, with force-on-force attrition computed from Lanchestrian differential equations.[127]

The problem of integration among simulations was mentioned earlier as the third aspect of scale. This can involve combining simulations across scales, scientific domains, or just heterogeneous structures and processes at a single level. Integration across scales presents a constant challenge. Is it, for example, possible to nest lower level, higher resolution simulations within higher level, lower resolution simulations just where more accuracy is needed? Also, is it possible to shift dynamically the level of simulation over time, as components require or can dispense with additional resolution? Some successes with this do exist; for example, in materials science, where a combination of semiempirical tight binding is used in modeling quantum mechanics, molecular dynamics models are used for simulating atoms, and finite element models are used for continuum mechanics.[128] This remains, however, a hard problem in general.

When successfully taken to the extreme, integration across domains can yield comprehensive models of entire worlds: {p,l,s}*/C. This clearly goes considerably beyond strictly dyadic computing—involving simulation of multiple domains plus the interactions among them—but it provides an appropriate capstone for simulation. The U.S. military was an early leader in developing such simulations, such as those that have already been mentioned. They have also put significant effort into developing the *high-level architecture* to federate multiple independently developed simulations.[129] This provides a structural framework for integrating both across domains and across heterogeneous entities within a domain. The military likewise early on started to explore how to embed people as participants in these simulations, {p,l,s}*/(C↔S), an important and interesting topic in its own right, but one that will be discussed more thoroughly in chapter 5 (section 5.1).

Today, such integrated simulations are central in applications of computing to science, training, education, and entertainment and show increasing penetration into manufacturing, sales, and other areas. An international group of scientists, for example, has recently announced the Living Earth Simulator (LES) initiative, with the ambitious goal of simulating everything on Earth.[130] In our work at the Information Sciences Institute (ISI) on responding to unexpected events, we also looked at the concept of using a simulator of an entire city to support a range of planning and analysis activities.[131] The entertainment industry in particular has become a major producer and consumer of such simulations, with games such as World of Warcraft focusing on real-time, low-cost simulation and movies such as *Avatar*[132] focusing on very high quality, but non-real-time, simulation. The military now frequently tries to leverage what is coming out of the entertainment industry, rather than always leading the development of new such technologies.

The University of Southern California's Institute for Creative Technologies (ICT)—which I helped to found while leading new directions activities at ISI, where I am pursuing my latest research on cognitive architecture, and which is analyzed in chapter 5 (section 5.3)—was set up jointly by the University of Southern California and the U.S. Army specifically to further these simulation (and social embedding) technologies for military training, with a particular focus on the human element. A significant fraction of the work at ICT concerns simulations of virtual humans, covering the body and the mind working together: (s↔l)/C (or s/l/C if the simulated mind is implemented by the simulated body, rather than being implemented separately and then interfaced to the simulated body).[133] The focus at ICT is not on battlefield training, but on training to handle the more social aspects of the Army's mission, such as negotiation with local populations and treatment of psychologically traumatized soldiers. The image in figure 1.3, for example, is from a prototype system for training multiparty cross-cultural negotiations. The term *Creative* in ICT's name stems from its charter to combine computing technology with expertise from the entertainment industry in developing new technologies and systems for the Army.

3.2.2   (True) Computational Implementation (Δ/C)

Computational simulation of the physical, life, and social domains is a long-standing and well-developed area within computing. In contrast, computational implementation of these domains—in the true sense of implementation described at the beginning of this section—although not new in concept, mostly continues to occupy a netherworld. Simulations can get by with reproducing any useful aspect of a phenomenon and still be helpful. An implementation must reproduce the real phenomenon in its entirety, raising definitional issues concerning what distinguishes the real phenomenon from any approximation to it, as well as scientific and pragmatic issues concerning how to create something that meets the definition.

For each of the traditional great scientific domains, we thus need to begin with a definition that discriminates real from approximate phenomena—including identifying which are the essential aspects of the phenomena—before we can say anything concrete about the possibility of computationally implementing them. Well accepted such definitions don't exist, but reasonable starting points are within reach. Although these definitions are unlikely to be universally accepted, it is impossible to proceed without such a beginning. In the remainder of this subsection, we will therefore propose a definition for what it means for something to be part of each domain and then discuss what is known about meeting the definition. We will, however, do this in the reverse domain order from that used so far in this book, starting with the social domain, where the topic seems to have seen the most development—or at least the one with which I am most familiar—before then proceeding through the life and physical domains.

Within the social domain, the concern has traditionally been whether a computational implementation of intelligence (S/C) is possible or whether intelligence can only be simulated computationally (s/C). This presupposes that intelligence is the only trait of a system required for it to be accepted as a full member of the social domain, ignoring for example the emotional, or affective, aspect of people. But even with this limitation, deriving a crisp definition and meeting the definition remain difficult problems. We must first decide whether we are asking specifically about human intelligence or about some broader and more abstract notion of intelligence in general. We could conceivably consider either, but the focus here will be on the latter, at least partly because it is easier to define intelligence in the abstract than to define human intelligence in particular. Given a computational implementation of intelligence in the abstract, it may be possible to use it as a simulation of human intelligence—just as an orrery is a real physical system that can be used to simulate a different physical system (the solar system)—but that would not necessarily make it an implementation of human intelligence.

Because AI is the discipline within which most such implementations are attempted, the distinction between implementing and simulating intelligence has become known as *strong AI* versus *weak AI*. The philosopher John Searle, for example, denies the possibility of strong AI based on a claim that consciousness is inherently a biological phenomenon. As I understand this, it goes beyond the traditional notion of materialism, where the brain is understood to implement the mind, to a notion that the mind is inseparable from the brain.[134] I have never been able to quite understand what it is he thinks is unique to biology in producing intelligence, but if it were true, any computational implementation of intelligence would have as a prerequisite a computational implementation of a person—S/(L/C)—should that itself be possible.

In one attempt to show that even when symbol processing is simulating intelligent behavior it cannot be said to understand truly, Searle has put forth the *Chinese room argument*:

Imagine a native English speaker who knows no Chinese locked in a room full of boxes of Chinese symbols (a data base) together with a book of instructions for manipulating the symbols (the program). Imagine that people outside the room send in other Chinese symbols which, unknown to the person in the room, are questions in Chinese (the input). And imagine that by following the instructions in the program the man in the room is able to pass out Chinese symbols which are correct answers to the questions (the output). The program enables the person in the room to pass the Turing Test for understanding Chinese but he does not understand a word of Chinese.[135]

Overall, the Chinese room argument has led to a lively debate, with a variety of responses from the AI community and counters by Searle,[136] but, from what I can tell, no movement toward consensus.

The physicist Roger Penrose goes a step beyond Searle in proposing that quantum phenomena in living systems may underlie what is missing in computers.[137] This need not imply the impossibility of nonbiological intelligence but is intended at least to support a claim that conventional computers are incapable of yielding strong AI. His argument begins with the claim that there are uncomputable results discernible by people and that therefore computers must be incapable of the kind of intelligence embodied in human beings. He then proposes quantum phenomena as the difference maker. The two biggest questions about such an argument would appear to be (1) whether people are actually doing anything uncomputable; and (2) even if they were, whether quantum mechanics would really make up the difference. If he is wrong with respect to the first argument, the whole thesis collapses. If he is correct with respect to both, quantum AI, based on quantum computing, might be the answer.

Fundamentally, the question of whether or not strong AI is possible has yet to be resolved by such arguments. Many AI researchers actually do not care whether or not strong AI is possible, as long as they can build suitably useful simulations of intelligence. For those who do care, a general definition of intelligence—as opposed to definitions of either human or artificial intelligence—is ultimately necessary to enable determining whether intelligence is actually implemented. Unfortunately, there is no generally accepted definition of intelligence.[138] What does exist is a space of attempts at definitions of intelligence that all ultimately derive from human capability, the principal reference point for what it means to be intelligent. We will review four classes of such definitions before settling on one for now.

One class of definitions is based on tests or standards. A circular form of this, apparently stated at least partly out of desperation, is that "Intelligence is what is measured by intelligence tests."[139] The *Turing test* provides a more appropriate variant that focuses on humans as the standard of intelligence and maintains that any thought processes—as revealed in overt behavior—are intelligent if they are indistinguishable from what a human would produce at some level of abstraction.[140] As originally proposed, irrelevant human aspects, such as visual and auditory appearance, are abstracted away. Both the computers and the humans who are used as points of comparison are placed behind walls, with a textual interface—a Teletype in those days—providing the only means of interaction. In what is now referred to as the unrestricted Turing test, if human examiners cannot accurately determine which is a computer and which is a human based on interactions through the Teletype, the computer must be deemed intelligent. Annual competitions have been held for the Loebner prize since 1991, based on restricted versions of the Turing test, but they are far from central to evaluating progress in developing intelligent systems.

The Turing test has the benefit of obviating the need to refer to anything inside of an entity in deciding if it is intelligent, although in doing so it has also ceded the ability to provide guidance as to how to implement, or even simulate, intelligence. More importantly, by defining what can legitimately be abstracted away in the interactions, it provides an implicit definition of what is irrelevant to intelligence in human behavior and appearance. It has several fatal flaws, however, over and above its lack of provision of research guidance. First, people are very poor judges in such tests. They tend to anthropomorphize anything that acts in any way human. An early example within AI was ELIZA, a program that could simulate a Rogerian psychotherapist.[141] The facility with which people accepted it as a substitute for a real psychotherapist, when it was really only a simple script-based system that had no true understanding of or care for the people with whom it interacted, so disturbed its developer that he turned into one of the earliest critics of AI.[142] The second, and bigger, issue is that although people are our original source for the notion of intelligence, they are much more than just intelligent organisms—they are caring, behaving organisms with particular experiences in particular environments—and simultaneously quite possibly much less than perfectly intelligent. Any definition of intelligence based on uncritical indistinguishability from humans may therefore require both too much and too little. As with naturally inspired work, it is critical to distinguish here what is essential in the source of inspiration versus what is surface or technology (or evolutionary) specific.

A second class of approaches to defining intelligence focuses on a specific capability as comprising its essence, such as the "capacity to acquire and apply knowledge,"[143] "the ability of an organism to solve new problems,"[144] "the capacity for abstraction,"[145] and "the ability to use optimally limited resources – including time – to achieve goals."[146] Such approaches go beyond the direct standards-and-tests approaches by proposing an actual content definition of intelligence while still suggesting straightforward ways of testing it. But they often seem too limiting. Even the best of them, such as the last one, leaves things out. Is a thermostat, which can be considered to have the single goal of maintaining a constant temperature, perfectly intelligent if it does this job perfectly? If not, do we need to add a second criterion for the scope of goals over which such optimality can be achieved? Likewise, does the lack of learning from presented opportunities not reflect a lack of intelligence if the information is irrelevant to the current goals? If not, do we need to add a third criterion that requires anticipating future goals?

Such considerations have led some to take the opposite extreme of defining intelligence in terms of a laundry list of capabilities, such as the "general mental ability involved in calculating, reasoning, perceiving relationships and analogies, learning quickly, storing and retrieving information, using language fluently, classifying, generalizing, and adjusting to new situations"[147] and "a very general mental capability that, among other things, involves the ability to reason, plan, solve problems, think abstractly, comprehend complex ideas, learn quickly and learn from experience."[148] Such definitions strive for comprehensiveness but lack coherence and make testing intelligence a difficult endeavor. Still, most of the actual work in AI is driven implicitly by some form of a laundry-list definition of intelligence and explores how to implement one or more items on the list.

The fourth and final class of definitions arises out of general constraints on mind. Allen Newell was again the pioneer here with his 1980 list that included[149]:

1. Behave as an (almost) arbitrary function of the environment (universality).
2. Operate in real time.
3. Exhibit rational, i.e., effective adaptive, behavior.
4. Use vast amounts of knowledge about the environment.
5. Behave robustly in the face of error, the unexpected, and the unknown.
6. Use symbols (and abstractions).
7. Use (natural) language.
8. Exhibit self-awareness and a sense of self.
9. Learn from its environment.
10. Acquire its capabilities through development.
11. Arise through evolution.
12. Be realizable within the brain as a physical system.
13. Be realizable as a physical system.

As can be seen from a number of the items in this list, the focus here is not on intelligence in the abstract but on human intelligence. A follow-on list was, for example, later used as the basis for evaluating the leading psychological cognitive architecture, ACT-R.[150] Although in form this may appear to be just a variant of the laundry-list approach, the items in such a list are constraints on any complete implementation of mind—or, alternatively, properties that must be exhibited by any such implementation—

rather than a list of distinct capabilities. It leaves open which combinations of lower level capabilities satisfy each constraint or yield each property. These constraints thus can serve as subgoals for the researcher interested in implementing intelligence.

When I teach introductory AI, I use a definition that fits into this last class and that owes a great debt to these earlier lists, but it is focused specifically on defining intelligence in the abstract. It amounts to *the common underlying capabilities that enable a system to be general, literate, rational, autonomous, and collaborative*. Generality concerns the scope of problems the system can reasonably attempt. Is it limited to just maintaining a constant temperature, or playing chess, or is the space much more open, as it is for people? Literacy concerns the extent of knowledge available to the system. This is not intended to equate ignorance with stupidity, but intelligence is concerned with enabling systems to acquire, maintain, and effectively use large bodies of diverse knowledge. Rationality concerns making the best decisions given the system's goals, knowledge, and capabilities. It is not about producing optimal behavior but about doing the *right thing*[151] given what it wants to accomplish, what it knows, and what actions it can perform. Autonomy concerns operating without assistance. People are not completely autonomous—most of us need others to survive and thrive—but neither are they *hothouse plants* requiring constant attendance, which is how Allen Newell used to characterize computing systems. Collaboration concerns working well with others

Attempts to put it all together, to implement a fully functional intelligence, go by names such as integrated intelligence, intelligent agents, artificial general intelligence, universal artificial intelligence, virtual humans, and intelligent robots. The most complete working systems to date are embodied in some form—whether in a physical robot, an intelligent agent, or a virtual human body—and are usually based on the combination of a cognitive architecture and knowledge about the environment in which the system is to operate. Such a system necessarily incorporates some significant subset of the laundry lists of capabilities for: interacting with the environment through its body, representing and reasoning with knowledge, making decisions, planning for the future, solving novel problems, learning from experience, reflecting on its own behavior and thought processes, using language, experiencing emotions, and existing in a social context. Work on the Soar architecture, for example, has demonstrated versions of all of these capabilities, with important segments of the effort then going into exploring and evaluating the extent to which such a system can meet the articulated constraints on mind.[152]

Such approaches to strong AI have not yet yielded results so compelling as to convince the skeptics, but in my admittedly quite biased judgment, they are making significant progress. In particular, I see no showstoppers and fail to find the arguments for impossibility at all compelling. Of course, we do not know what we have yet to uncover, so it is still possible that an insurmountable problem may turn up around any corner. The philosopher Hubert Dreyfus early on used the metaphor of climbing a tree to reach the moon.[153] You may make steady progress, but you will eventually reach a gap that is insurmountable by the approach being taken. Of course, this at most only works as a critique of a particular approach—in this case Dreyfus was arguing against the symbolic paradigm within AI—rather than as an argument for the impossibility of the goal itself. My fundamental faith in the possibility of strong AI stems from the belief that there is nothing special about biological implementation. If something, such as intelligence, is implementable in one form of technology, then once we understand it well enough, other implementation technologies will also often prove sufficient. Such an assumption is now known as *substrate independence*.[154]

Before we leave the social domain and the possibility of strong AI, it is worth a brief look at one intriguingly different approach to this question. *Universal artificial intelligence* focuses on the creation of systems that can behave optimally—with respect to a set of goals or utilities—in any computable environment.[155] It provides a single mathematical equation for a system that learns to make sequential decisions in all such environments and argues that it is "the most intelligent agent" possible. Unfortunately, the equation is uncomputable. If it were thus to be used as a defining characteristic for membership in the social domain, then nothing could meet it, even people, unless Penrose were right in his assumption of people being capable of the uncomputable. Still, formulating the problem in this way at least suggests a novel research path that explores computable approximations to this uncomputable ideal, perhaps providing a path to satisfying directly the generality and rationality constraints on mind while showing that the others are merely indirect consequences of these two rather than independent constraints.

For the life sciences, we need to ask the equivalent question as to whether it is possible to actually implement life computationally (L/C) or only simulate it (l/C). Because the effort to implement life largely occurs within the discipline of alife, this distinction has become known as *strong alife* versus *weak alife*, in direct analogy to the distinction in AI. Continuing the analogy, it is also possible to consider whether what is being implemented artificially is an instance of a natural kind, such as a dog, or an instance of the abstract category of living things that may not fit within any preexisting species. As with our discussion of intelligence, we will focus here on the implementation of life in the abstract, rather than implementation of new instances of particular species.

As in the earlier discussion of alife-based simulations of life, we are concerned here only with soft alife (L/C) and those parts of hard alife that include computation: L/(P↔C). But, as with intelligence, we need to start with a definition that will enable us to distinguish whether something is simply a program (soft) or a robot (hard) that simulates life versus a corresponding implementation of life. And, as also with intelligence, life is difficult to define. Of the definitions I have examined, the basic dictionary definition that it is "the condition that distinguishes organisms from inorganic objects and dead organisms, being manifested by growth through metabolism, reproduction, and the power of adaptation to environment through changes originating internally"[156] seems to be as good as any (although ones that focus on the local ability to decrease entropy provide intriguing alternatives). The one question I would raise about this definition, however, is whether growth is essential to life. Metabolism—which concerns how organisms autonomously power, maintain, and reconstruct themselves over time—is clearly necessary, but the need for growth appears to be a side effect of how natural organisms reproduce rather than being an inherent necessity for life. If reproduction yielded full-grown individuals, no growth would be necessary, although life would certainly seem to exist. We will therefore focus on metabolism independent of concerns about growth. We will also consider reproduction, the self-creation of new organisms. Adaptation, although important, is primarily a neural function. Artificial adaptation thus overlaps strongly with AI, and in particular with the neural network approach to AI. Given that this topic has already been covered, we will not attend to it further here.

Of the requirements listed under metabolism, the need for power is the simplest. Most software entities, whether arbitrary programs or virtual characters, exist in computational environments in which power is not a relevant issue; the energy required to power the hardware that executes the software is a given as far as the software is concerned. There have, however, been alife systems that were forced to compete for computational cycles (and space in main memory).[157] This can be considered as one form of struggle for the energy that supports life. Even if we go beyond soft alife to hard alife, it is not difficult to construct a robot that can find power outlets that will enable it to recharge its batteries. The idea goes back at least to Walter's Turtle from 1950[158] and is common in some form in today's robotic vacuum cleaners.

Much more difficult is building of computational systems that can maintain and reconstruct themselves. As with growth, it isn't completely clear that this is inherently necessary for life to exist, but it is required if lifetimes are to extend beyond when initial components start to break down. Although natural systems have limits on the extent to which they can maintain and reconstruct themselves, within these limits the abilities they do have here are both remarkable and essential. The simplest forms of this in computational systems can once again be found in software. What is required is software that can monitor software ($C \leftarrow C$) to detect and diagnose existing and potential issues in it and alter the monitored software ($C \rightarrow C$) as necessary to fix the problems, yielding in toto a form of pure dyadic interaction: $C \leftrightarrow C$.

If the monitoring software is the same as the software being monitored, we have reflective software that monitors and repairs itself. Otherwise, we have two distinct programs and the additional issue of how to monitor the monitoring software. This second level of monitoring can also be done either reflectively or by a third bit of code. But at some point this recursion must terminate in either reflective code or code that is so simple that it need not be monitored and repaired to continue functioning over the system's lifetime.

The Soar cognitive architecture provides one example of such a capability.[159] When there is insufficient knowledge to make a decision, rather than simply halting with failure the architecture itself detects such *impasses* in decision making and reflects, enabling it to bring its full capabilities to bear on the problem of resolving the impasse. One of its procedural learning mechanisms, *chunking*, then compiles the results of this processing into new rules that will enable the system to make comparable decisions directly in the future without reflecting. Although these capabilities do not enable Soar to detect and fix all problems that occur in its own processing, they do take a significant step in that direction.

Within hard alife, the problem again gets tougher in general, although even here there are some cases that are relatively simple and others that are much harder. The simpler subclass occurs when there is software that can monitor both software and hardware and can perform software workarounds for not only problems in the software but also for at least some problems in the hardware. Autonomic computing concerns itself with this kind of activity in general, in service of making computers more robustly autonomous. NASA's Deep Space 1 was a spacecraft developed to test a range of advanced technologies, including the Remote Agent,[160] which planned aspects of spacecraft operations while also monitoring, diagnosing, and working around problems that occurred during flight. The Remote Agent was successful enough at these activities for it to co-win NASA's 1999 Software of the Year Award.

Reconfigurable robots, as are discussed in chapter 4 (section 4.3), may also engage in a more complex form of this, with nonworking hardware automatically being jettisoned and dramatic alterations possibly then being required in the coordination of the remaining parts; shifting, for example, from four-legged locomotion to slithering like a snake. Beyond this, when no form of reconfiguration is adequate, we find the most difficult class of problems in maintaining and reconstructing hard alife, which require hardware addition or replacement. One step toward this might be implementing the ability automatically to replace broken parts from a stock of spares. A much bigger step would be systems that could construct their own replacement parts. One possible path to such a capability might be based on *rapid prototyping* technologies that can create arbitrary three-dimensional objects from a generic feedstock such as plastic or concrete, as was illustrated in figure 1.4 and as will be discussed further in chapter 4 (section 4.3). But even such state-of-the-art automated production capabilities currently fall far short of being able to reconstruct the full range of replacement parts needed by a living organism.

Reproduction goes beyond reconstruction of existing organisms to the self-construction of new organisms. Within soft alife, computer viruses are notorious examples of programs that clone themselves through a form of asexual reproduction. Evolutionary computation, which was mentioned in section 3.1.2 as a form of biologically inspired computation, provides a form of sexual reproduction. Although the primary goal of evolutionary computation is implementation of a new form of computing, it nonetheless computationally implements a real aspect of life, reproduction, as an enabling step. Demonstrations of *irreducible complexity*—where removing any one component of a system makes the entire system nonfunctional—in evolutionarily designed systems has contributed to the refutation of the claim that its presence in natural organisms must derive from intelligent design rather than evolution.[161] Within hard alife, the problem of reproduction is much like the hardest case of maintenance and reconstruction, but now whole organisms must be self-constructed from raw materials rather than just individual pieces.

In summary, as with strong AI, there is progress toward strong alife. Soft alife appears to be closer to fulfilling the full definition at this point than hard alife, with computer viruses perhaps on the borderline of providing simple but true computational implementations of life. Much further progress still seems to be required, however, before full instances of hard alife will be among us.

When we get to the physical domain and the question of implementing (P/C) versus simulating (p/C) physical structures and processes, it may be puzzling at first what is being discussed. We are not talking about robotic construction, such as in figure 1.4. Construction provides the other sense of implementation mentioned at the beginning of this chapter, mapping to an interaction relationship between the computational and physical domains rather than to an implementation relationship. Such activities are more the focus of the next chapter (section 4.3). What we are instead concerned with here is the actual creation of physical structures and processes out of information and its transformation.

Standard definitions of *physical* in the context of the physical sciences take the form of "noting or pertaining to the properties of matter and energy other than those peculiar to living matter."[162] A computational implementation of the physical domain thus requires using information to implement matter or energy, but it need not cope with the additional complexities just discussed for life. At the macro level of human experience, this is hard to imagine. How after all could information implement a rock or a drop of water? Yet, at the smallest scales, such a notion is taken seriously within the discipline of *digital physics*.[163] The core hypothesis behind digital physics is that if you dig down deeply enough into the basic elements and laws of the universe, you will discover information and computation staring back up at you. Quantum mechanics is, after all, based on the notion that energy is found in discrete packets. The broader concept of *physical information* also seeks to understand the information embodied in physical systems, whether or not the whole universe is assumed to be informational.[164] The specific idea for digital physics goes back at least to a 1967 article by Konrad Zuse, the computer pioneer mentioned earlier.[165] John Archibald Wheeler, a noted theoretical physicist later captured the idea succinctly in the catchphrase *it from bit*, stating that:

It from bit symbolizes the idea that every item of the physical world has at bottom—at a very deep bottom, in most instances—an immaterial source and explanation; that which we call reality arises in the last analysis from the posing of yes-no questions and the registering of equipment-evoked responses; in short, that all things physical are information-theoretic in origin...[166]

A number of approaches to digital physics have been developed based on cellular automata,[167,168] and more recent work includes approaches based on quantum computers.[169]

The philosopher Nick Bostrom goes beyond considering whether it is possible to computationally implement a universe to argue that most likely we are living in a computationally implemented (or simulated) universe.[170] Part of his argument is based on the notion of substrate independence, a term that he coined in this context, but which is really a flavor of the strong AI assumption. The rest is based on the assumption that any civilization that lasts long enough will generate many simulations of its past. Minds embedded in such simulations would not be able to tell that they were in simulations, much as in the *Matrix* movies.[171] If these two assumptions hold, there would only be one reality but many simulations, making it more likely that we abide in one of these simulations than within the single thread of reality. Were the true universe implemented computationally, you would likely not be able to distinguish reality from a simulation in the first place. But, if not, and if Bostrom's arguments prove correct, then we are probably part of one of the simulations.

3.3 Implementation Summary

This chapter has provided an extended, yet still far from complete, overview of the implementation relationship as it applies within the computing sciences. The focus here has been on the multidisciplinary aspects of computing; in particular, the segments of mixed dyadic computing (C+Δ) that concern how it can be implemented by the three other domains (C/Δ) as well as how it can implement (Δ/C) or simulate (δ/C) them. The implementation of computing by itself (C/C)—a form of pure dyadic computing (C+C) that includes, for example, compilers and operating systems—is also relevant here but has mostly been skipped over, as has been most conventional work on programming and software engineering, whether or not it concerns the implementation by computing of computing (C/C) or other domains (Δ/C). Many of the more complex polyadic forms of implementation have also been ignored, although some of these will be picked back up in chapter 5.

The intent behind this focus has been to illustrate and make concrete the implementation side of the relational approach while highlighting and providing an organization over often obscured multidisciplinary aspects of computing, many of which yield intriguing potential for the future of the computing sciences, the other sciences when in combination with computing, and the world in which we live. New kinds of computers with novel properties always raise such a possibility, but we have only begun to witness the impact of the pervasive development, integration, and deployment of simulations. True computational implementation of other domains is further in the future but potentially even more revolutionary, raising the possibility of new—and new kinds of—organisms, intelligences, and worlds.

4 Interaction

Interaction, as defined in chapter 2, is "reciprocal action, effect, or influence." Without interaction, computing would be much like the old notion of a brain in a vat, perhaps performing wonderful calculations in its own isolated world—C—but of little value to anything or anyone else. Interaction connects the structures and processes of a domain with their surroundings. Within the physical domain (P↔P or P*), interaction is about forces. Within the life domain (L↔L or L*), interaction is mediated by physical forces, but building on these forces yields additional forms that are unique to this domain. One organism may, for example, observe, injure, caress, feed, or consume another. It may also communicate, fight, or mate with another. Within the social domain (S↔S or S*), physical and living forms of interaction are available, but people may also converse, collaborate, argue, negotiate, trade, and party with each other, and even educate each other.

In contrast to implementation, interaction is fundamentally a symmetric relationship: ↔. Yet, in many circumstances only one direction may be active, → or ←, at least at the level of analysis used. For example, when one person says something to another, influence only goes from the speaker to the listener: S→S. Like implementation, interaction frequently crosses domain boundaries. If a person, such as Fred, throws a rock at a coyote, Fred (S) interacts with the rock (P), yielding S→P; and the rock interacts with the coyote, yielding P→L. The overall result is S→P→L. Of course, Newton's third law states that *for every action there is an equal and opposite reaction*, so technically both of these interactions do implicate the reverse direction as well, but these reverse influences are second-order details at this level of discussion and are thus omitted from the analysis and the ME expression. If it were actually desirable to represent these reactions, they could be included in the expression, yielding S↔P↔L, but this would obscure the primary influences.

A bit more thought will show that a variety of other details are also missing from the original expression for this situation; for example, that Fred's act of throwing is mediated through his implementation as a form of life (S/L), which is itself implemented by the physical domain (L/P). Likewise, the coyote's being hit is also mediated by its physical implementation (L/P). So, the original expression could be elaborated as S/L/P→P→L/P or even as (S/L→P→L)/P if we wanted to model that the whole set of interactions is implemented by the physical domain, including the rock (via molecules, for example). These are kinds of modeling choices that we will often need to make when exploring computing and its interactions. But, when focused specifically on interactions, this will generally mean attending to the primary domains that are interacting and the principal directions of influence among these domains. Here, this simply yields S→P→L.

As an example of across-domain interaction that comes more directly from the sciences, consider photosynthesis, where a plant combines carbon dioxide and water in the presence of sunlight to create a sugar molecule plus water.[1] In chemical notation this becomes $6CO_2 + 6H_2O \rightarrow C_6H_{12}O_6 + 6O_2$, with light perhaps used as an annotation on the reaction arrow. In the ME language, this would be represented as L⟷P if all of the chemicals involved are assumed to be part of the physical domain and as L⟷(P⟷L) if the organic chemicals are assumed to be part of the domain of life, leaving only water, light, and oxygen as part of the physical domain.

The focus of this chapter is on interactions involving computing, first where computing is influenced by another domain, C←Δ, then where computing influences another domain, C→Δ, and finally where there are bidirectional influences between computing and another domain, C⟷Δ. In deciding which direction the arrow will go in any particular case, it is important to understand that it aligns with the direction of influence, not necessarily the direction of activity. Consider if Fred now puts away his rocks and reads a book. Fred is the active participant in this interaction, and he has to be so because the book is a passive object. Fred does exert a physical influence on the book when he picks it up, turns its pages, and puts it down, and, depending on how much we want to represent Fred's human, animal, and physical nature in these physical interactions with the book, this could be expressed as S→P, S/L→P, S/L/P→P, S/P→P, L→P, L/P→P, or even P→P. But, whichever of these options is chosen, the arrow of interaction goes from Fred to the book, aligning with the direction of activity. In contrast, if the desire is instead to represent how the contents of the book influence Fred, the arrow goes counter to the direction of

activity: S←P, or S←δ/P if we want to emphasize it is the book's contents
(i.e., what it represents) that does the influencing in this case.

The question of which partner(s) in an interaction are active, although
not definitional for the direction of interaction, can yield a useful additional organizational principle over the space of interactions, particularly
when the distinction concerns whether computing itself is an active or
passive participant. This can then be combined with the direction(s) of
interaction and the domain with which computing interacts to structure
the dyadic space of computer interaction, as shown in table 4.1. The horizontal dimension concerns whether computing plays an active or passive
role in the interaction. In cases where both participants are computing,
presence in the passive column implies that one of them is active—the one
substituting for the Δ on the right—and the other is passive. If both were
passive, no interaction could occur. If both were active, the topic would
belong in the active column.

When computing is a passive participant in an interaction, the only
kinds of active participants we will consider are people and other computers, as to date I have been unable to come up with any interesting examples
where the physical or life domain interacts with passive computing. But
even for the cases of humans and computers, the variety of topics is sparse
enough that we will cover all of them in a single section (section 4.1). The
space of possibilities is considerably richer when computing plays an active
role. The three choices of directionality for active computing will be the
subject of the three following sections. If the interaction arrow points
toward computing (Δ→C), we find a set of topics ranging from computational sensing at the lower end to computational understanding at the
upper end (section 4.2). If the arrow points away from computing (Δ←C),
the topics stretch up from computational acting to computational shaping
(section 4.3). For bidirectional interaction, when it is across domain (C↔Δ),
informatics and robotics come to the fore, along with various other means
of interacting with the human body and mind. Within-domain bidirectional interaction (C↔C or C*) leads to parallel and distributed computing
systems of all sorts. Both of these bidirectional topics will be covered in
section 4.4 but with more of a focus on across-domain interaction.

4.1   Passive Computing Interactions

As mentioned in the introduction, the focus in this section is on active
elements of the social and computing domains as they interact with a
passive instance of computing. When the influence flows from the social

Table 4.1

The space of dyadic computer interactions

		Passive	Active
C←Δ	P		Sensors, scanners, computer vision, optical character recognition, localization
	L		Eye, gesture, expression and movement tracking, biosensors
	S	IT industry	Input devices, learning, authorization, language and speech understanding
	C	Automatic programming	
C↔Δ	P		Robotics, informatics
	L		Brain–computer interfaces, assistive robotics, bio/medical informatics
	S	Computer and software engineering	Human–computer interaction, full immersion, games, natural language, social robotics
	C	Automated debugging, autonomic computing	Networks and security, parallel and distributed computing, grids, clouds, multirobot and multiagent systems
C→Δ	P		Computational acting and shaping, effectors
	L		Bioeffectors, haptics, sensory immersion
	S	Computational thinking, critical code studies	Presentation, screens, printers, graphics, speech generation, cognitive augmentation
	C	Self-monitoring	

The vertical dimension is structured according to the direction of the flow influence, and within this according to the domain that interacts with computing. The horizontal dimension is structured according to whether computing plays a passive or active role in the interaction, although when computing also provides the other domain, that instance of computing is always active.

domain to passive computing (C←S), people are doing something to computers. The information technology (IT) industry, with its human development of computing systems, is an obvious piece here. If, for example, we follow the lead from chapter 3 and represent hardware and software as C/Δ and Δ/C, respectively, we get C/Δ←S for the hardware industry and Δ/C←S for the software (programming) industry. The former has people constructing new computers by implementing them out of structures and processes from some other domain. The latter has people programming computers by constructing aspects of other domains out of computational structures and processes. Both can loosely be referred to as implementation but according to the relational model are fundamentally constructive interactions that yield implementations, rather than implementations themselves.

Characterizing the IT industry in this way captures its essence but still does it a disservice in at least two ways. First, it implies that there is no influence back from computing to the people who construct the hardware and software. To say that the computer industry does not learn from what it builds would be ludicrous—so the expression really ought to be C↔S to be complete—but this reverse form of interaction is a subsidiary relationship that can be abstracted out to yield a useful caricature of the industry that distinguishes it from other related activities. Still, it is important to note that IT does actually extend into symmetric interactions as well.

Second, it abstracts away the reality that computing can itself play an active role in the IT industry. Computing can be active within IT on the left side of the expression, when used for example in experimentation, or it can be added in a second role that is active on the right side of the expression. Computers can, for example, participate in the development of their own programs through integrated development environments,[2] Δ/C←(S↔C), or even take over completely the act of programming in automatic programming,[3] Δ/C←s/C. In each of these topics, there is an instance of computing that plays a passive role (Δ/C←) as the recipient of programs, but there is also an active instance of computing that is involved via human–computer interaction (S↔C) or artificial intelligence (s/C). Thus the former hybridizes software development with human–computer interaction, whereas the latter hybridizes it with artificial intelligence (AI). The latter variant can also be seen as shifting the focus from C←S to the next row down in the table, C←C, as we now have a real computer actively performing the programming, with only a simulated social component. Integrated development environments are too complex to fit directly into this table unless they are abstracted to yield a single bidirectional interaction between a human and an active instance of computing by combining both C's in the original expression to yield something more akin to human–computer interaction: C↔S.

Beyond the IT industry, all forms of human invention of computing technology can reasonably be represented as C←S. We are seeing a range of such inventions throughout this book. An explicit compendium of recent polyadic inventions—from *Time* magazine's lists of best of inventions of the year—can also be found in chapter 6 (section 6.3). As has been emphasized recently, however, inventions by themselves are insufficient to accomplish all of the shaping that is desired of the world. *Innovation*, which is frequently confounded with *invention*, but which concerns the adoption rather than the creation of change,[4] is also crucial. The distinction between invention and innovation in computing can be succinctly captured in the ME language as C←S versus (S←C)←S, with the former indicating how people influence, or shape, computing and the latter how people shape the impact of computing on society.

If we now shift from how the social domain influences passive computing to the passive influences of computing on the social domain (C→S), we primarily reach how the concepts of computing influence people. *Computational thinking*, where ideas from computing influence how people mentally solve problems, can be thought of as one significant component of this.[5] A manager might for example break up a difficult task into multiple parts (decomposition), assign the individual parts to different subordinates (parallel processing), and provide procedures for each to follow (algorithm design and coding). But computational thinking also comprises people thinking like, or mentally simulating, an abstract form of computing that is itself solving the problem in question; so a more complete expression might replace the S with δ/c/S. And further, these internal thought processes are in service of actually performing the task by some mixture of humans and computers, so a term like Δ/{C,S} or Δ/(C↔S) also seems relevant. The full expression for computational thinking is thus something like C→δ/c/S→Δ/(C↔S). Computation passively influences how a person thinks about a problem, leading to a human–computer solution to it.

In reading about computational thinking, I have occasionally struggled to understand what the full meaning is that is intended by the phrase, assuming generally that something like C→S or C→c/S was the right way to think about it, but recent articles also include as part of it key aspects of programming and computational science.[6] The second interaction relationship in the full expression presented here explains how such activities fit in, with $\delta/c/S\rightarrow\Delta/(C\leftrightarrow S)$ covering the human thought processes involved in programming and the implementation of scientific simulations. Still, it is the first interaction relationship that seems most central to computational thinking, and thus why in its most basic form it can be thought of simply as $C\rightarrow S$.

Beyond computational thinking is the idea of computers as a metaphor for how things work. Prior to computers, clocks or other forms of machines often filled this role. So we would talk, for example, about a clockwork or mechanistic universe. What this actually means is that a human is mentally representing the metaphorical phenomenon as implementing the world: $\delta/p/S$ for machines and $\delta/c/S$ for computers. However, the metaphor arises from the passive influence of the metaphorical domain on people: $P\rightarrow S$ and $C\rightarrow S$, respectively.

One last example of the passive influence of computing on people is the relatively new area of critical code studies, a subarea of the digital humanities concerned with understanding computer programs, just as if they were books or other cultural artifacts.[7] In critical code studies, a scholar reads the computer code—and reads between the lines of code—searching for hidden meanings and cultural connections. Chapter 6 will propose that the humanities are part of a broad conception of the social sciences as a great scientific domain (S), which then makes the digital humanities part of the dyadic relationship between the social and computing domains (S+C), and critical code studies becomes $\Delta/C\rightarrow S$.

When there are bidirectional interactions between people and passive computing ($C\leftrightarrow S$), we get the academic disciplines of computer and software engineering. These are the academic analogues of the hardware and software industries, respectively, but with bidirectional interactions ($C/\Delta\leftrightarrow S$ and $\Delta/C\leftrightarrow S$) emphasizing the combination of understanding and shaping. As was mentioned earlier, the IT industry also overlaps with these expressions, but learning from computing is a much more explicit part of the mission of the academic disciplines. Other primarily unidirectional activities, such as critical code studies, might also eventually overlap with this form of bidirectional interaction if they were to have an impact back on computing at some point.

The discussion to this point of interactions with passive computing has largely focused on people as the active participant, with the exception of automatic programming's inclusion of an active instance of computing that influences a passive instance: $C\leftarrow C$. In the reverse direction we get forms of self-monitoring, where an active computer monitors another computer: $C\rightarrow C$. The monitored computer could be active in this relationship, but nominally it can be thought of as passive. When there are bidirectional interactions between passive and active forms of computing, we see the combination of automatic programming and self-monitoring in areas such as automatic debugging: C↔C. We can also conceive of autonomic computing as fitting here as well. In chapter 3, the discussion of autonomic computing focused on the role of a computational simulation of life (l/C) in an interaction with computing (C↔l/C). But, as with the discussion above of automatic programming, we can abstract the right side of this expression to C, yielding C↔C as an alternative (abstract) expression for autonomic computing in which the C on the left side can be passive.

4.2   Influencing Active Computing (C←Δ)

When computing plays an active role in its own influence, the focus shifts to computational sensing, the perceptual processes that convert raw sensations into interpretable forms and the understanding processes that convert perceived forms into knowledge about the world. Computational sensing of the physical, life, and social domains occurs via a pathway such as that outlined in figure 4.1.

It begins with a correlate of some aspect of P, L, or S being transported to a sensor, such as when light reflecting off of a scene reaches a camera. The electromagnetic energy conveyed by this transmission is then sensed, first by a sensor that transduces it to an electrical signal and then by an analog-to-digital (A/D) converter that transforms this analog signal to bits. Perception then interprets combinations of these bits as recognizable structures. If the perception is of more than just a static scene, there may also be a process of activity recognition, in which the dynamics of the situation

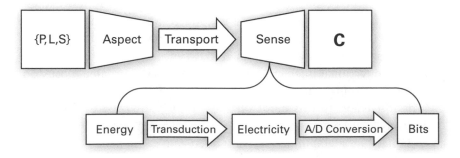

Figure 4.1
Schematic pathway for computational sensing.

are interpreted as one of a class of known activities, such as playing tennis. If there are teleological (goal-oriented) entities involved in the activity, then theory of mind—where mental states are attributed to others—also becomes involved,[8] with processes of goal and plan recognition for both individuals and groups. If more than one variety of signal is sensed, the separate information streams must be fused somewhere along this pathway. If it happens early, it is generally referred to as *sensor fusion*.[9] If it happens late, it is more appropriately considered part of an integrative understanding process.

The early aspects of sensing fall within the domain of electrical engineering, although other engineering disciplines may also be involved in sensors for specific kinds of phenomena. The overall space of sensors is large. A partial list for the physical domain, grouped according to the type of energy to which the sensors are attuned, includes thermal (temperature, heat); electrical (resistance, current, voltage, power, magnetism); mechanical (pressure, flow, position, strain, orientation, motion, acceleration); chemical (proportion); optical (intensity, time of flight, proximity, color, interference, disturbances); ionizing radiation (radiation, subatomic particles); and acoustic (sound, time of flight).[10] Global Positioning System (GPS) sensors—as are central to location-based computing—do not show up explicitly in this list but are based on time of flight, in this case for signals from satellites.

Sensors can also be built for the life, social, and computing domains as well. Such sensors generally start with physical measurements but then interpret them in terms of structures and processes in their domains. Much of this focuses on sensing aspects of the human body, sometimes for biomedical (L) purposes and other times for sociocognitive purposes (S). A heart rate monitor, for example, measures electrical changes in the skin (P) but interprets these changes in terms of heartbeats (L). Body sensors may also measure such things as heart rate, blood pressure, blood oxygenation, blood sugar, galvanic skin response, and body temperature. Automated DNA analysis actually enables sensing the genetic makeup of a body.

X-rays, computerized axial tomography (CAT) scans, and magnetic resonance imaging (MRI) all provide noninvasive means of sensing structures inside of bodies. Ultrasound, electroencephalography (EEG), positron emission tomography (PET), and functional MRI (fMRI) go beyond sensing of internal structure to sensing of internal activity. An fMRI machine, for example, measures photons produced by the decay of electromagnetic fields to determine blood oxygenation and flow in the brain.[11] Such techniques can form the basis for noninvasive brain–computer interfaces, but when very high resolution sensing of the brain is required, invasive interfaces that connect to individual neurons or small groups of neurons, such as the one shown in figure 2.7, become necessary.

Both laser scanners and stereo cameras can determine the three-dimensional surface of a body. Cameras can also go beyond just sensing body geometry to sense other surface properties, such as color, texture, and reflectance. Such techniques enable the biometric approach to computer security, where fingerprints, retinal or iris patterns, palm prints, or faces are used to identify people and thus help to determine whether a person is authorized to perform whatever action he or she is attempting.[12] They can also be deployed for many other kinds of applications.

Many body-sensing technologies go beyond measuring static structure to tracking dynamic behavior. Physiologic sensors, such as heart rate monitors, may continuously discern aspects of the body's functioning over time. Video cameras can observe movement of body parts and thus sense behavior. This all gets even more interesting when interpretation of this behavior moves up to the social domain (S), such as when attempts are made to determine a person's intent from their behavior. Such work falls within the domain of human–computer interaction—specifically, *user modeling* when the human is actively interacting with the computer[13]—which may also bring in concerns from psychology, human factors, and design to craft a hardware-and-software pathway that is particularly attuned to the needs of humans interacting with computers.

The people involved in such interactions may play a passive role, being sensed but not otherwise engaging with the computer, or may deliberately make movements—such as pressing keys or pointing at objects—that are known to have certain effects on what the computer does. Many of the types of body sensors discussed so far are potentially deployable for either form of interaction. This can mean sensing eye movements, head nods, finger movements, hand configurations, arm gestures, leg movements, facial expressions, configurations and movements of whole bodies, or even thoughts.

By monitoring the blood oxygenation levels in a person's brain over time (L), an fMRI machine may, for example, effectively read their mind (S). Figure 4.2 illustrates how one such system was able to learn to predict fMRI patterns for concrete nouns, with the aid of semantic features extracted from a large online text corpus.[14] Such capabilities are limited at present but are growing apace. There is nothing fundamental stopping the same kind of technology from eventually being deployed in recognizing deliberate mental commands or in recognizing lies. EEG devices—such as

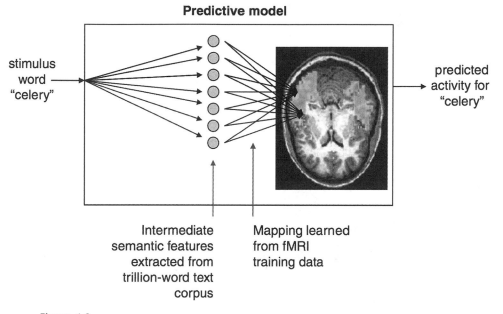

Figure 4.2
Learning to predict fMRI patterns for concrete nouns (Carnegie Mellon University, University of South Carolina, and University of California San Diego).
From Thomas M. Mitchell, Svetlana V. Shinkareva, Andrew Carlson, Kai-Min Chang, Vicente L. Malave, Robert A. Mason, and Marcel A. Just, "Predicting human brain activity associated with the meanings of nouns," *Science* 320 (May 2008): 1191–1195. Reprinted with permission from AAAS.

the one in figure 2.8—are already being used for deliberate control. Although such devices yield coarser signals than fMRI machines, they are cheaper and more portable. More invasive brain–computer interfaces, including implanted electrodes that interface directly with neurons, also provide other possibilities.

Traditional devices for human input to computers—such as keyboards, buttons, mice, drawing tablets, track pads, joysticks, and game controllers— depend on active human participation to eliminate ambiguity in the signal. They all sense human movements but have predetermined ways in which they interpret them. Keyboards recognize pressure on buttons in terms of characters to be entered or as triggers for specific computational activities. Other devices recognize acts of pointing at particular locations on a screen or pathways of movement—such as a sideswipe with multiple fingers—that can then be interpreted in various ways.

Figure 4.3
The CyberWalk omnidirectional treadmill.
From   http://en.wikipedia.org/wiki/File:Cyberwalk1.jpg.   Creative   Commons
Attribution-Share Alike 3.0 Unported, 2.5 Generic, 2.0 Generic and 1.0 Generic
license.

Typically such devices focus on the movements of fingers. But research
is increasingly focused on sensing and understanding much broader classes
of human gesture. Sometimes this still takes the form of special-purpose
devices with which people can interact, such as multitouch screens for
sensing patterns of finger movements, instrumented gloves, accelerome-
ters, or an omnidirectional treadmill for sensing the speed and direction
of walking (figure 4.3). But machine vision is now well-enough understood
to enable much of this sensing to occur through a single general sensor—a
camera—in combination with the appropriate recognition software. Microsoft's Kinect bar, for example, combines a camera, a depth sensor, a micro-
phone array, and appropriate software to capture a range of both passive
and active information from human game players.[15]

When we move beyond sensing human movement to sensing how
people interact with the environment around them, the interface possibili-

Figure 4.4
Tangible computer programming (Northwestern University). Each block controls an action, and they can be strong together to execute controlled sequences of actions. Image courtesy of Michael Horn, Computer Science and Learning Sciences, Northwestern University.

ties grow even further. Tangible user interfaces sense how people interact with their physical environment—$C \leftarrow (S/L \leftrightarrow P)$—to determine how to control computational activity. For example, tangible programming enables kids to program computers by arranging blocks whose identities and configuration can be sensed by the computer (figure 4.4).[16]

Electrical engineering covers sensory processes up through the generation of bits by A/D conversion. Once there are bits, electrical engineering, computer engineering, and computer science overlap through their shared interests in areas such as device drivers and machine perception. Device drivers provide the low-level interfaces between hardware devices on one side and operating systems and applications on the other side. Machine perception then focuses on, for example, recognizing objects in visual images[17] and extracting sentences from human speech,[18] but every distinct flavor of sensor yields its own recognition problems. Various forms of graphical models, as mentioned at the end of section 3.1, often provide the leading techniques for these recognition problems, with, for example, Markov and conditional random fields handling vision[19] and hidden Markov models handling speech.[20] Various forms of neural networks may be competitive as well.[21,22]

The higher-level aspects of sensing and understanding, where meaning is extracted and knowledge is brought to bear, fall primarily within the domain of AI, but other disciplines are also involved for particular types of understanding, such as computational linguistics in the understanding of textual material. Understanding the meaning of words, sentences, paragraphs, and even whole books—whether heard, seen, or felt (e.g., via Braille)—requires knowledge about language but also about the world described by the material. It also requires algorithms that can reason effectively and efficiently about these combinations of knowledge. The Defense Advanced Research Projects Agency (DARPA) *Machine Reading Program*, for example, has the goal of automatically reading large bodies of text—such as are present on the Web and in other computationally accessible places—and understanding these masses of text well enough to convert the knowledge they contain into a more formal representation with which AI systems can easily reason.

In the early days of the field, language understanding was treated as largely a symbolic problem of representation and reasoning. But the growing availability of large bodies of textual material on the Web has enabled learning techniques to substitute vast quantities of automatically extracted, shallow, statistical regularities for the earlier small amounts of hand-coded deep knowledge, while actually improving average performance in the process. For example, a system that translates between English and French may be built largely automatically by extracting regularities from parallel texts provided in profusion by the government of Quebec. Combining the differential strengths of the statistical and symbolic approaches to language understanding is one of today's outstanding research problems.

Computational understanding in general depends strongly on the AI specialties of machine learning and automated reasoning. It can span everything from just understanding the identities, positions, and movements of whatever objects are currently being sensed; to a more integrative understanding of the surrounding world that relates what is currently perceived to what has come before, which may also be useful in predicting what is likely to come next; or even to something more akin to scientific discovery of novel properties, regularities, and laws—the classic *Bacon* system could, for example, rediscover basic physical laws from data.[23] Understanding can focus, with increasing complexity, on inanimate objects, living creatures, or people. With respect to people in particular, it can implicate understanding of not only their current activities but also their broader beliefs, desires, and intents, as well as their motivations, personalities, and emotional states.

When the breadth of what is to be sensed grows, either increasingly functional single sensors can be developed or multiple sensors can be deployed. The contrast between Nintendo's Wiimote and Microsoft's Kinect is illustrative. The Wiimote has two special-purpose sensors, an optical sensor to detect position—by locating infrared dots on the sensor bar—and an accelerometer to detect motion.[24] Together, these two simple sensors enable unambiguous monitoring of the motion of a single point over time but are essentially useless for anything else. The Kinect instead uses a single unambiguous depth sensor plus two general-purpose sensors, one for visible light and the other for sound. Although the interpretation of the signals from the two general-purpose sensors is much more ambiguous and computationally complex, they are potentially usable for recognizing a much broader range of phenomena, from the position and motion of all visible body parts of multiple people to facial expressions and what is being said.

Similar issues occur when the spatial scope of what is to be sensed grows. One approach to sensing over a large spatial extent is to make individual sensors larger and position them further away—such as in space—leading to *remote sensing*.[25] A second approach is to make the sensors mobile, leveraging some of the robotic mobility characteristics to be described in the next section. Particularly high profile examples of *mobile sensing* are unmanned aerial vehicles (UAVs), such as Predators and Global Hawks, which are increasingly playing an important surveillance role in military operations. A third approach is to replicate and distribute the individual sensors, with computer networks tying them together, yielding *distributed sensor networks*.[26] Such a distributed sensor network may range in scale from a nation-wide ecological sensor network, such as the National Ecological Observatory Network (which "will collect data across the United States on the impacts of climate change, land use change and invasive species on natural resources and biodiversity"),[27] to monitoring of a more limited spatial region, such as a single volcano (figure 4.5), down to a *body area network* that monitors the health of an individual human body.[28]

As more and more different varieties of sensors come online, covering ever broader scopes, it would seem that the logical end point would be sensing and understanding—plus likely storing—of everything at all times: $C \leftarrow \{P,L,S,C\}^*$. But even if not possible to this extreme, the world— and particularly human presence within it—will increasingly be sensed,

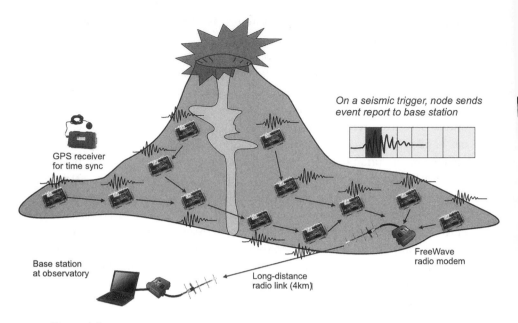

On a seismic trigger, node sends
event report to base station

GPS receiver
for time sync

FreeWave
radio modem

Base station
at observatory

Long-distance
radio link (4km)

Figure 4.5
Schematic of a sensor network for monitoring volcanic eruptions (Harvard University).
Image Courtesy of Matt Welsh, Google.

recorded, and automatically interpreted. Such forms of comprehensive computational awareness will provide extraordinary power, pervasively affecting our lives and the future of everything on our planet. Mostly, such a capability is ethically neutral in and of itself, but it raises major questions about how it will be used and to what extent it will lead to a utopian versus a dystopian future.

On the positive side, such capabilities should enable us to detect automatically, and even to anticipate, when things are going wrong, so as to be able to intervene before too much damage is done. Both ecological and biomedical monitoring are prime instances where such a capability would be of great value. Such capabilities should also help to improve efficiency and decrease waste, moving to more optimal use of limited resources, and to enable better decisions in general, whether human or computational. They may also help enrich human experience by providing veridical access to the past and instantaneous access to what is transpiring all over our world. Potential applications include personal and group memories—such as the MyLifeBits project, which has been recording many aspects of the personal life of one computer scientist (Gordon Bell)[29]—and virtual travel and tourism.

On the negative side, it may mean the end of all privacy for both action and thought, going far beyond the privacy concerns of today that have been spurred by the Internet and social networking. The goal of achieving *total information awareness*, proposed by DARPA in 2002, is one example.[30] In service of counterterrorism, the idea was to gather and integrate across vast quantities of information of all sorts. Concerns about the implications of this ultimately led the U.S. Congress to defund the effort in 2003, but such systems will continue to become easier to build. Even without the specter of government knowing everything about us, and the resulting possibility of forms of oppression beyond even the nightmare scenarios from classic speculative novels such as *1984*,[31] devices all around us plus those we carry on us continue to provide more and more information about us and our activities to a range of commercial organizations.[32]

4.3   Computing Actively Influencing (C→Δ)

Computational acting and shaping occurs via a pathway that is roughly the inverse of that shown in the previous section for sensing and understanding. At the highest level, it might start with a goal of accomplishing something in the world. This intention leads to generating a plan composed of some combination of actions that will achieve the goal. The actions must then be converted into signals for effectors that can alter some aspect of the domain of interest. Although the term *effector* is derived from robotics, it can be used—and will be used here—as a generic for any form of computer-controlled mechanism capable of manipulating the external environment, including even such mundane output devices as liquid crystal display (LCD) screens and inkjet printers. The early stages of this pathway are studied by AI and user interfaces, the middle stages by robotics (plus also, as with sensing by the area of device drivers, although we won't focus on this here), and the latter stages by electrical engineering, mechanical engineering, and other disciplines.

Computational/robotic action can be partitioned roughly into three realms: mobility, manipulation, and presentation. Mobility concerns how a system changes its location within its environment (C→P). Manipulation focuses on shaping the surrounding physical (C→P) and living (C→L) world. Presentation provides information for a human cognitive system (C→S).

The most conventional forms of robotic mobility co-opt techniques from preexisting noncomputational vehicles, often beginning with direct automation of existing vehicles and then moving on to specially designed robotic vehicles that retain the same basic motive force. On the ground this usually means wheels, but tracked robots are not uncommon for rugged outdoor terrain (figure 4.6a). Airborne robots, such as UAVs, may be based on propeller or jet aircraft (figure 4.6b), or on helicopters (figure 4.6c), or on other (combinations of) mechanisms that yield both lift and thrust, such as fans. Propellers drive robotic boats and submarines, and rocket engines generally drive robotic spacecraft.

Robotic mobility may alternatively be biomimetic, imitating how animals locomote rather than adopting preexisting mechanistic approaches. This can be considered as an aspect of hard artificial life, including flying like a bird or an insect (figure 4.7a), swimming with fins or flippers (figure 3.11), walking with legs (figure 4.7b), or slithering like a snake or caterpillar (figure 4.7c). Beyond biomimetic locomotion is the actual computational control of the movement of living organisms ($C{\rightarrow}L{\rightarrow}P$). For example, the flight of a beetle has been remotely controlled by a computer chip interfaced with its nervous system (figure 4.8). Not surprisingly, such capabilities will raise serious ethical issues as they are extended to higher organisms.

It is conceivable that completely novel modes of mobility will be developed for robots as well. One intriguing idea that was briefly mentioned in chapter 3 (section 3.2.2) concerns reconfigurable robots that are composed of an arbitrary number of identical modules.[33] Each module has onboard computation and communication, the ability to connect with some number of other modules and to disconnect from them, and an ability to flex in some dimensions. Such robots can take on a wide variety of configurations—such as wheels, snakes, or legged structures—and exhibit the appropriate mobility pattern for each such configuration (figure 4.9). They may also have the ability automatically to reconfigure themselves to work around a broken module or to change how they locomote; shifting, for example, from a wheel used for rapid long-distance travel to a snake for working their way through a small opening. If the modules are small enough, and there are enough of them, this starts to reach the domain of programmable matter[34] and amorphous robots,[35] as made famous in the movie *Terminator 2: Judgment Day*.[36] Mobility shades into manipulation when it becomes difficult to tell a leg from a hand, as can be the case with both reconfigurable and amorphous robots.

If we now shift to straight manipulation of the physical and living worlds, we enter the world of effectors. General-purpose effectors often mimic the human hand at some level of abstraction. The simplest are two-fingered grippers, but quite sophisticated five-fingered hands also now exist (see figure 5.4). Special-purpose effectors can comprise any form of tool or machine controllable by a computer. Welding robots provide a prime example of long-term success based on a special-purpose tool, in this case an arc welder. Not nearly as far along, but with great potential for the future, are surgical robots (figure 4.10). Although still primarily controlled by humans, surgical robots enable precise manipulation of tiny biological tissues and structures.[37] Computational control of special-purpose machines has developed under the heading of computer numerically controlled (CNC) machines[38] rather than robotics, but it is clearly just another form of computational shaping. So also are straightforward output devices for computers, such as screens and printers.

Computational action, whether normally considered robotic or not, can occur over a wide range of spatial scales. At the very smallest are nanorobots,[39] where just achieving mobility or manipulation at the scale of 10^{-9} meters can be extremely challenging. Moving up a level we find microelectromechanical systems (MEMS), which operate at spatial scales of 10^{-6} to 10^{-4} meters. They have been applied to, among other things, control airbags in cars and guide optical signals in projectors and switches.[40] Robots and other computationally controlled machines that interact with people tend to be on a human scale. This includes typical computer output devices, service robots—such as robot vacuum cleaners—and surgical robots, although the latter can be capable of much finer scale manipulation of living tissue. Manufacturing robots may be built to operate on scales from the very small to the very large, depending on the size of the objects to be fabricated. Other large-scale computationally controlled systems may likewise perform tasks in areas such as transportation and construction.

One of the most exciting recent developments in computational shaping has been the invention of techniques for rapid prototyping, solid free form fabrication, and three-dimensional printing (figure 4.11).[41] A rapid prototyping machine can create complex three-dimensional objects using only a single special-purpose effector capable of controlled deposition of a formable material—such as plastic, water/ice, papier mâché, metallic powder, or concrete—in a layer-by-layer fashion. As each layer is deposited, it hardens into a solid mass that bonds to the previous layer and helps to support later layers. Depending on the materials used, rapid prototyping

(a)

(b)

Figure 4.6
Varieties of robot locomotion. (a) iRobot PackBot. (b) General Atomics MQ-9 Reaper
unmanned combat air vehicle. (c) Northrop Grumman MQ-8B Fire Scout.
(a) Image courtesy of iRobot Corp. (c) from http://en.wikipedia.org/wiki/File:MQ-8B
_Fire_Scout.jpeg, Creative Commons Attribution-Share Alike 2.5 Netherlands license.

(c)

Figure 4.6
(continued)

can yield models (i.e., physical simulations of real physical objects) such as plastic scale models of buildings or it can yield real functioning objects such as metal gears. Recent work has even explored fabrication of living tissue and organs[42] as well as various forms of food. CandyFab, for example, forms complexly shaped pieces of candy out of a sugar-based feedstock.[43]

One effort that seems to have tremendous potential, and with which I was involved for a number of years, seeks automatically to construct buildings (figure 1.4). *Contour Crafting* is based on controlled extrusion of a paste-like material, such as concrete, to build up structures layer by layer; a robotic trowel to smooth and shape the material as it is extruded; and more conventional manipulators to install utilities into the walls as the structural layers are completed.[44] The technology can be viewed as a scaling up of traditional rapid prototyping techniques to building-sized objects, based on large-scale robotics and the deposition of thick (~1-inch) layers. One grand challenge for Contour Crafting is to construct a high-quality 2000-ft^2 house automatically in a single day, at a quarter of the cost of a conventional building. But the technology can potentially apply to even

(a)

(b)

Figure 4.7
Forms of biomimetic robot locomotion. (a) Cornell flapping-wing hovering insect.
(b) Boston Dynamics BigDog. (c) Carnegie Mellon Snake Bot.
(a) Image courtesy of Charles Richter, Cornell University. (b) BigDog image courtesy
of Boston Dynamics. (c) Image courtesy of Howie Choset.

(c)

Figure 4.7
(continued)

Figure 4.8
A cyborg beetle, remotely controlled via a brain–computer interface (University of California Berkeley).
Image courtesy of Hirotaka Sato, Nanyang Technical University.

larger structures, such as high rises and various kinds of towers. Should it succeed, Contour Crafting could revolutionize emergency and low-cost housing while also enabling walls to be based on organic curves as easily as straight lines. Existing systems can build wall segments, but there is still much to be done to get to full buildings.

Whereas robotics focuses on shaping the physical ($\rightarrow$P) and the biological ($\rightarrow$L) worlds, computational presentation focuses on shaping the social world ($\rightarrow$S). It seeks in particular to influence human minds by providing information perceptible to the senses. In its simplest form, presentation can be represented in ME as C$\rightarrow$S, but various elaborations on this expression are possible to emphasize additional aspects of the relationship, such as C$\rightarrow$S/L to indicate the biological nature of human sensing or that presentation may be intended indirectly to influence noncognitive aspects of people, such as their emotional state; Δ/C$\rightarrow$$\Delta$/S to signify that it is content on the computer that is being conveyed to the human mind; or C$\rightarrow$P$\rightarrow$S to denote that the physical environment always mediates between computers and human senses. Combinations of these elaborations are also possible.

Figure 4.9
Some of the possible configurations of the SuperBot modular reconfigurable robot (University of Southern California).
Image courtesy of Wei-Min Shen, Information Sciences Institute, University of Southern California.

At its most general, presentation involves determining what effect is desired on whom, determining what sensory experiences to provide in order to achieve the desired effect, and developing the algorithms and technologies necessary for providing these experiences. The focus may be on visual techniques for helping people interpret static scientific or business data, as in Tufte's well-known books,[45] or on a broader set of techniques for understanding dynamic processes. Simulations may play a key role in presenting such processes, but simulation can also serve as its own vertically integrated paradigm for presentation. The appeal of this paradigm comes from the general utility of simulations in motivating and explaining content, and the manner in which they support active engagement by people in the experience. It also comes from the opportunity of leveraging how people evolved to interact with other people—through such means as language, expression, and gesture—by populating simulations with virtual humans functioning as participants, interfaces, guides,

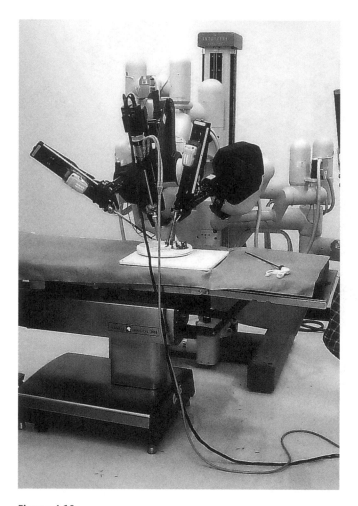

Figure 4.10
Intuitive Surgical's da Vinci surgical robot.
From http://en.wikipedia.org/wiki/File:Laproscopic_Surgery_Robot.jpg, Creative Commons Attribution-Share Alike 3.0 Unported license.

Figure 4.11
Reproduction (right) of a gargoyle figure (left) by 3D scanning and printing.
From http://commons.wikimedia.org/wiki/File:3D_scanning_and_printing.jpg. Creative Commons Attribution-Share Alike 3.0 Unported license.

and instructors. Figure 4.12, for example, shows a pair of virtual human twins acting as exhibit guides at the Boston Museum of Science.[46]

Computational research within this paradigm involves development of the kinds of simulation technologies discussed in the previous section, technologies for immersing people—sensorially, intellectually, and emotionally—in the simulations, and approaches for creating experiences in such environments. There are reasoning aspects that fall within artificial intelligence, modeling aspects that focus on understanding the capabilities and limitations of human perception and understanding, engineering and graphics aspects concerned with inventing devices and algorithms that can take maximal advantage of human perceptual abilities, and experience

Figure 4.12
Ada and Grace, virtual twins acting as tour guides at the Boston Museum of Science
(University of Southern California).
Image courtesy of the USC Institute for Creative Technologies.

design aspects from areas such as education and entertainment that seek
fully to leverage human understanding capabilities. AI and graphics have
already been sufficiently discussed in the context of simulation. The modeling of human perception and understanding is grounded in biology and
psychology, and thus mostly outside of computing (except for their computational aspects). Experience design is an active focus in such areas as
human–computer interaction, scientific visualization, education, entertainment, and the creative arts.[47] It is an increasing crucible of interaction
between computing and the humanities, particularly within the simulation paradigm, where issues of story and character can come to the fore.
The twins in figure 4.12 provide a good example. They are provided with
personalities and back stories more effectively to engage with, and guide,
human visitors.

Perhaps the most visible source of progress in presentation is in the
invention of new device technologies for stimulating the five senses:
sound, sight, touch, smell, and taste. Sound consists of vibrations in matter
perceived by the ear. How it is perceived is a function of both its nature as
waves and the cues provided concerning the directions from which these
waves arrive. Sound presentation devices thus primarily focus on how to
reproduce wave properties and location cues. Early hi-fi systems focused
on high-fidelity production of wave properties, with accurate frequency
response and a minimum of noise and distortion, while ignoring the location aspect. Stereo extended this to one-dimensional localization; surround
sound to two-dimensional localization; and recent work has focused on

three-dimensional (spatial) sound. Localization of sound can be relatively simple when individualized though a single set of headphones or when directed to a single individual in a known location in space, but it requires complex combinations of speakers and signal processing when it is to be provided to multiple individuals over a region of space.[48]

Research on visual presentation devices focuses on displays and projectors. Early approaches used technologies quite limited in what they can represent, such as the off-or-on status of an individual light or the limited numeric or alphanumeric capability of mechanical displays, printers, and nixie tubes. Improvements occurred with the development of alphanumeric and vector graphics terminals based on cathode ray tubes (CRTs). The advent of displays capable of accurately representing colors across a two-dimensional array of picture elements (pixels) revolutionized the field of visual display, enabling arbitrary two-dimensional scenes to be represented on ever-larger screens at increasingly finer resolutions. Since then, much of the focus has been on flattening the three-dimensional devices required to generate two-dimensional images—moving from CRTs to plasmas, LCDs, and organic light emitting diodes (OLEDs)—and expanding the images themselves from two-dimensional to three-dimensional. Techniques for three-dimensional presentation focus on either generating pairs of images that can be directed differentially to the two eyes—with the aid of special glasses to separate the two images or autostereoscopically without the glasses—or on synthesizing true three-dimensional images, such as in figure 4.13, where images from multiple perspectives are reflected off a rapidly rotating mirror.[49]

Another trend in visual presentation has been to expand the varieties of surfaces that can act as displays. One aspect of this is flexible displays that can be bent or folded.[50] Such a display might eventually fit more easily in one's pocket when not in use yet still provide a large display surface when in use; or it may conform to arbitrary object surfaces to enable chameleon-like appearance properties; or, if it were capable of the structural flexibility of a reconfigurable or amorphous robot, it could physically mimic both the structure and surface of arbitrary objects of interest. Electronic paper (e-paper) might ultimately take on the flexibility of real paper, but at present its focus is on replicating the ability of text on paper to be read via ambient rather than display-provided lighting and on requiring negligible energy to remain visible as long as its contents are not being changed.

Two other approaches to expanding the set of possible display surfaces include embedding fragmentary display capabilities within other materials,

Figure 4.13
Three-dimensional teleconferencing system (University of Southern California).
Image courtesy of Steve Cohn / Steven Cohn Photography.

such as fabric, and using projectors to convert arbitrary non-display surfaces into displays. The area of *computational fabric*, for example, looks to
combine computing, power, and displays directly into fabric to yield everything from adaptive camouflage for uniforms and tents to radically new
forms of designer outfits (figure 4.14).[51] Projectors have the advantage of
potentially being quite small—witness today's latest generation of pico
projectors that are tiny enough to be embedded in or attached to smart
phones—while displaying large images on a wide range of surfaces, such
as walls, desktops, and skin. Projectors may also eventually even bypass
external display surfaces by projecting images directly onto the retina.[52]

Presentation for the three other senses—touch, smell, and taste—is
much more primitive in form and more limited in deployment. Haptics—
which focuses on the sense of touch, usually via vibrations or the exertion
of some counterforce—is the best developed of the three.[53] A simple form
of vibrational haptics has been incorporated into touchscreen buttons on
some smart phones to provide sensory feedback that is otherwise lacking
in such interactions, and haptic gloves and vests can provide a variety of
tactile sensations over wider regions of the body. Robotic arms may also
be used to provide controlled forces that can simulate the presence of

Figure 4.14
Philips SKIN displays a wearer's emotional state via dress pattern and color change.
Image © Philips Design—SKIN Project, emotion dress. Reprinted by permission.

physical objects with particular surface properties. Presentation of odors is based on dynamically combining chemicals that are released into the atmosphere.[54] Presentation of flavors is only just beginning to occur, through such means as the nascent technologies mentioned earlier for the rapid prototyping of food.

Beyond the five basic senses are other sensory modalities, for things like motion, balance, temperature, and pain. Whatever people can sense can potentially form the basis for a presentation modality, and, in fact, some of these—such as motion—are already well developed in amusement park rides.

When the simulation paradigm within computational presentation becomes immersive, the human plus the simulation effectively implement a new world that is divorced from the original one, $\delta/(\delta/C{\rightarrow}S)$, yielding the perceptual side of virtual reality. This often requires presentation devices that engross the corresponding sensory systems, completely blocking out the real world and only allowing perception of the virtual world. For vision, this can be based on head-mounted displays that take up the full visual field of an individual at a short distance (figure 4.15a) or spaces totally enclosed in presentation hardware, what are known as CAVEs[55] (figure 4.15b).

4.4   Bidirectional Active Influence (C↔Δ)

The full sense of interaction is only reached once understanding/sensing and shaping/acting combine to yield full interactivity. As noted in the chapter introduction, this amounts to informatics and robotics (C↔Δ), plus more specialized forms of interaction with bodies and minds—in particular brain–computer interfaces (C↔L) and human–computer interfaces (C↔S)—and distributed systems when the interaction is with itself (C↔C or C*). We will not focus on informatics in this chapter. In Europe, *informatics* has a meaning that is synonymous with the American usage of the term *computer science*,[56] whereas in the United States informatics focuses more narrowly on issues concerning data, particularly the management and analysis of data across the sciences. Chapter 5 (section 5.2) describes the pursuit of science and the use of computing to assist in this pursuit. Further discussion of informatics will therefore be postponed until then.

The term *robot* is sometimes applied to any implementation of an effector that is human-like or animal-like. The robot arms that have been used for many years in manufacturing provide a prototypical example. Such robot manipulators were discussed in the previous section and are not the

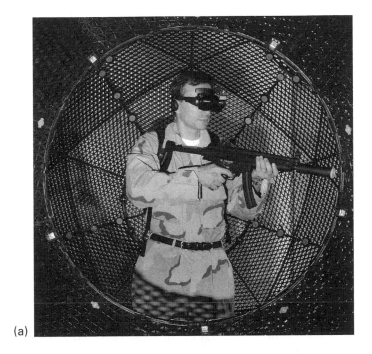

(a)

(b)

Figure 4.15
Immersive display technologies. (a) Using a head mounted display at the Naval
Research Laboratory. (b) CAVE automatic virtual environment with a floor display
plus multiple wall displays (Copyright UTBM and Antycip Simulation).
(b) Image courtesy of UTBM and Antycip Simulation.

focus here. To be capable of bidirectional interaction, a robot must have both effectors and sensors. Adding perception is critical in environments that are not completely predictable. Robotic arms without perception are only usable when a factory is engineered to provide precisely regimented location and timing of part presentation. Without this, perception is required for effective action. It is also required for mobility in dynamic worlds. In analogy to how we used the term *effector* as the generic term for computational action in the past section, here the term *robot* is used as the generic term for computational systems that both receive input from their environment and affect it in turn.

Although it is useful to characterize robotics as comprising a dyadic interaction between computing and another domain ($C \leftrightarrow \Delta$), this does require a considerable amount of abstraction. A basic robot, independent of any concerns with interaction, is more accurately considered a simulation of life—if not an actual implementation of life—that is constructed out of an interaction between the physical and computational domains: l/($C \leftrightarrow P$). When the interactions with the external physical and life domains are included, this then becomes $\{P,L\} \leftrightarrow l/(C \leftrightarrow P)$. When minds are added to the robots, we get intelligent robots that are more accurately described as $\{P,L\} \leftrightarrow (s \leftrightarrow l)/(C \leftrightarrow P)$, assuming that the social simulation isn't implemented by the life simulation. This expression can be rearranged to emphasize that the mind is simulated solely by computing technologies (s/C)—denoting more directly how intelligent robotics is at the intersection of robotics and AI—whereas the body is simulated either by the physical domain alone (l/P) or by a combination of the physical and computing domains l/($C \leftrightarrow P$). But, either way, we see how the full richness of intelligent robots is thoroughly polyadic, implicating as it does all four great scientific domains. This section, although nominally dyadic, will therefore delve more deeply into the polyadic than have the other sections in this survey.

One set of recent notable successes in robotics was the DARPA Grand Challenge (2004 and 2005)[57] and Urban Challenge (2007).[58] DARPA's focus was not on effectors but on autonomous mobility, with a significant emphasis on the requisite sensing and understanding (figure 4.16). In particular, could automated vehicles be developed capable of negotiating long distances on their own over difficult unpaved terrain or in complex urban environments? The answer in 2004 was no, but by 2005 success was achieved with difficult unpaved terrain and by 2007 in complex urban environments. Although not providing complete solutions to the problem, particularly for coping with all of the complexities of real urban environments, these successes provided a landmark for autonomous ground vehi-

Figure 4.16
DARPA's 2007 urban challenge for automated vehicles.

cles that is comparable to Deep Blue's success in chess and Watson's in Jeopardy.

When multiple robots interact, we are in the world of distributed and reconfigurable robotics. The former involves teams of robots, usually intelligent, that are collaboratively working toward common goals: $\{P,L\}\leftrightarrow[(s\leftrightarrow l)/(C\leftrightarrow P)]^*$. Robot soccer (aka football), as practiced for example in the annual RoboCup competition (figure 4.17), pits teams of robots against each other in a soccer match.[59] Teams of robots may also work together on more pragmatic tasks, such as building construction and military engagements. The U.S. Army's Future Combat Systems (FCS) program, for example, was an ambitious effort to build combat forces out of cooperating unattended ground sensors (UGSs), unmanned ground vehicles (UGVs), and UAVs, together with manned combat vehicles. This program was canceled in 2009, but parts of it were rolled into a new program on Brigade Combat Team Modernization.[60]

As described in the previous section, reconfigurable robots are constructed out of the interactions among multiple relatively simple robotic modules, each endowed with its own power, computing, communication, and ability to move (or flex). Such robots are analogous to multicellular organisms, where the modules (or cells) are physically connected, and

Figure 4.17
RoboCup soccer played by teams of Sony AIBO robot dogs.
From http://commons.wikimedia.org/wiki/File:Aibos_playing_football_at_Robocup _2005.jpg, Creative Commons Attribution-Share Alike 2.0 Generic license.

must therefore work together in a tightly coupled fashion. Just as we can think of a dog either as a single instance of life (L) or as an interaction among many living things (L*)—or even as a single complex instance of life implemented by interactions among many simpler living things (L/L*)—we can also consider a reconfigurable robot as not only a single complex robot, l/(C↔P), but also as an interaction among many simpler robots, [l/(C↔P)]*, or even as the implementation of a complex robot via interactions among simpler robots: l/[l/(C↔P)]*.

Agents are the analogue of robots in the world of software.[61] They are software simulations of life that interact with the broader world of software systems: l/C↔C or l/C↔Δ/C. There is clearly an intersection with soft artificial life (l/C), but the focus here is less on the simulation of life itself than on the bidirectional interactions such a simulation enables with the computational world. A search engine such as Google is an agent in this sense. It constantly probes the Web for new content to index. *Intelligent agents* are then the software analogues of intelligent robots, combining agents with AI (s/C) to provide autonomous programs that can behave appropriately in complex computational worlds: (s↔l)/C↔C.[62]

Agent teams, and *multiagent systems* more broadly, enable groups of agents to work together on common problems: [(s↔l)/C]*↔C.[63] One project I helped start in this area at the Information Sciences Institute (ISI) was entitled *Electric Elves*.[64] It provided teams of intelligent agents that facilitated the workings of a research group by "rescheduling meetings, selecting presenters for research meetings, tracking people's locations, organizing lunch meetings, etc." The elves would even order food for meetings via fax, leading one local restaurant owner to state that ". . . more and more computers are getting to order food . . . so we might have to think about marketing [to them]!!" Descendants of this kind of technology, although in the form of single intelligent agents—rather than agent teams—that act as virtual personal assistants are available commercially these days via, for example, *Siri* on the iPhone 4S.

There is a strong intersection here with distributed systems (C↔C or C*) in general, a topic that we will get to shortly, and more specifically with new software approaches such as *service-oriented architecture* (SOA).[65] In an SOA, each software component—here called a service rather than an agent—is capable of performing actions in the online environment, such as filling out a form or making a request for information. Orchestrating combinations of these services then yields full systems.

Despite so far characterizing robots as interacting with the physical and life domains and agents as interacting with the computational domain, both can also interact with people. Assistive robotics provides one flavor of this, where robots provide physical and mental assistance to people: (s↔l)/(C↔P)↔S/L. Such caregiver robots might, for example, lift people from a bath to a wheelchair, as in figure 4.18, or remind them to take their medicine. If caregiving is limited to mental assistance, we are in the domain of socially assistive robotics,[66] (s↔l)/(C↔P)↔S, which shares its ME expression with, and is part of, the broader domains of social robotics[67] and human-robot interaction.[68] From this ME expression, it should be clear how all forms of social interaction with robots lie at the intersection between robotics and human–computer interaction. Abstracting away the interaction relationship yields intelligent robots, (s↔l)/(C↔P), whereas abstracting away that computing is part of a complex implementation relationship yields human–computer interaction: C↔S.

Robotic interaction centers on a perception–action cycle, where the robot perceives its environment and generates an action appropriate to the situation. Human–computer interaction, in contrast, often involves a

Figure 4.18
RIBA (Robot for Interactive Body Assistance) is intended as a caregiver robot for lift-and-carry activities (RIKEN).
Imagery courtesy of the RIKEN-TRI Collaboration Center for Human-Interactive Robot Research.

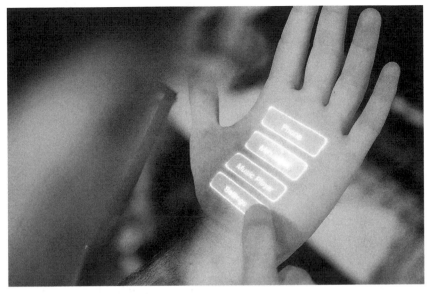

Figure 4.19
"Skinput" combines a pico projector and an acoustic sensor on the skin to turn the palm into a virtual keyboard (Carnegie Mellon University).
Image courtesy of Chris Harrison, Desney Tan, Dan Morris—Microsoft Research & Carnegie Mellon University.

perception–action cycle on the human side of the interaction but an action–perception cycle on the computational side. The computer prompts the human via a communication action to set up a subsequent need on its part of perceiving, and understanding, the human response. In such circumstances, the computer is in charge, as it drives the interaction. This is true even in newer and more exotic approaches to human–computer interaction, such as when a pico projector presents a virtual keyboard on a person's arm, and a camera or acoustic sensor on the skin is used to determine what keys are pressed (figure 4.19). Allowing computing to drive interaction generally yields systems that are simpler computationally because it limits the human responses that the computer will need to perceive and understand to those that make sense in the context of the computer's communicative prompt, but it can be both frustrating and dehumanizing for the human participant.

More symmetric interactions involve human–computer dialogues, where there is turn taking and each of the participants are in control at different times. Such forms of interaction leverage insights from interactions among people and may scale better to many mutually interacting participants than can the computer-driven techniques. Extending computers for symmetric interactions with people leads in the direction of intelligent user interfaces, s/C↔S, and agent–human interaction, C↔(s↔l)/C↔S.[69] Taken to the extreme, such an approach can lead to the development of virtual humans that support natural varieties of human–computer interaction that are inspired by traditional forms of human–human interaction: (s↔l)/C↔S/L. Not only the minds of the real and virtual humans are involved in these interactions but also their bodies. Features such as facial expressions, gestures, and body positioning all become part of the language of interaction.

Augmented cognition[70] moves the human–computer interaction paradigm more strongly in the direction of polyadic computing, combining sensing of the state of the brain, usually through a noninvasive brain–computer interface, with a form of presentation that is adapted according to this perceived state: C↔S/L or L→C→S. For example, if measurements via EEG show that the brain is overloaded, presentation of information can be reduced to lower the overall cognitive burden.

This form of augmented cognition senses the brain directly but then affects the mind indirectly through normal human sensory mechanisms. In section 4.3, we also saw an example where the brain of a beetle was remotely controlled by computer. A full development of bidirectional brain–computer interfaces (C↔L) will yield one of the most dramatic changes imaginable to our human existence. It will not only bring us into intimate contact with the exterior world of information and computation, but it could also enable a range of other scenarios that have previously been limited to the worlds of fantasy and science fiction. Examples include erasing and implanting memories into people, as in the movie *Total Recall*[71]; human control of the thoughts and actions of other people, S→C↔S/L; and brain-to-brain communication capabilities—mediated through computers and networks—that may be indistinguishable from the heretofore pseudo-scientific concept of telepathy, (S/L)°↔C*.

But computational telepathy is not the only manner in which computers can facilitate interactions among people. Much less exotic approaches exist. Online social networks, such as Facebook, use human–computer interaction plus computer networks to mediate social intercourse among large numbers of humans.[72] Social networks provide communication, storage, and sharing of wide varieties of information—such as text, photographs, videos, and opinions—within a community. At the most abstract level of description, a social network is simply S*, so we need to dig deeper to understand the role of computing in online social networks. In the old time-sharing context, where one computer would serve—and mediate the interactions among—many human users, this became $C \leftrightarrow S°$, but in the modern era of networked distributed computing it becomes $(C \leftrightarrow S)^*$ or $C^* \leftrightarrow S°$.

When computing implements part or all of a world—either real or simulated—with which people interact, we are in the space of virtual/ mixed reality, prosthetics, and ubiquitous computing. Discussion of these topics will be postponed until chapter 5 (section 5.1).

Telepresence provides a computational interface to a person analogous to that used in virtual reality, but where the world with which the person interacts is a remote segment of the real world rather than a virtual world.[73] Think of the progression from voice calls to video calls, then to three-dimensional calls—as in figure 4.13—and finally immersive calls. Such interactions can even go beyond observing a remote location and chatting with people there if some form of embodiment—a robotic *avatar* (figure 4.20) or a human telemediator[74]—can be provided for the human effectively to locomote in, and possibly even physically interact with, the remote location. When telepresence becomes good enough, it could end the need for much, though not likely all, of business and leisure travel.

When the focus shifts to interaction among multiple active instances of computing—generically, distributed systems[75]—the concern is mostly with large numbers of interacting systems (C^*) rather than with pairwise interaction ($C \leftrightarrow C$). At its broadest, when the interacting elements can be from any domain, this area of study is now termed *network science*: Δ^*. Distributed computing can be viewed as a subdiscipline of network science that is specialized to the domain of computing, but the field of distributed computing predates network science by many years and has served as one of the main motivations for the development of the broader field. The foundational 2005 National Research Council report on network science makes the case that the key word to describe the essence of the twenty-first century is *connected* and motivates this through a discussion of the Internet and all that it has enabled.[76] Oddly enough, though, it then decomposes the world of networks according to the three traditional great scientific domains—yielding physical, biological, and social networks—with the Internet included as just one variety of physical network. There is certainly a physical aspect to the Internet—which can be characterized as C^*/P whether the focus is on the implementation of wired or wireless networks— just as there are physical aspects to biological and social networks, but to consider the Internet as primarily a physical network rather than as a

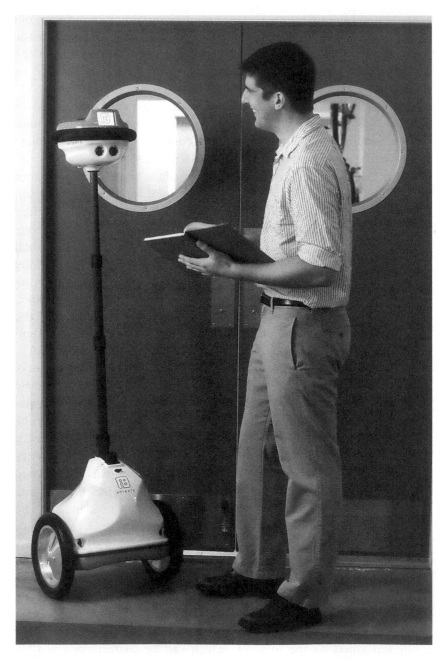

Figure 4.20
Interacting with the Anybot QB telepresence robotic avatar.
Image courtesy of Anybots.

computational or informational network is a truly bizarre instance of what can happen when the status of computing as a distinct great scientific domain is ignored.

Within the area of distributed computing systems are found such computing disciplines as parallel[77] and distributed computing and networking.[78] In their simplest forms, distributed systems can be considered as pure dyadic—reflecting the interaction between two elements of the computational domain (C↔C)—or pure polyadic if the desire is to emphasize the number of elements involved from the computational domain (C*). However, as we dig deeper into the topic, other domains almost always also loom into sight.

Parallel and distributed computing concerns the hardware and software involved in performing multiple computations at once. Such parallelism can occur at multiple levels in the computational hierarchy. If we start down at the level of transistors, complex chips such as Intel's latest Itanium and Xeon microprocessor chips now have more than two billion transistors operating in concert.[79] At one level up, groups of these transistors can be organized into functional units that execute instructions. A scalar processor then executes one instruction on one set of data at a time (single instruction, single data; SISD), a vector processor executes one instruction on multiple sets of data at a time (single instruction, multiple data; SIMD), and a superscalar processor executes multiple instructions, each on their own data set, at a time (multiple instruction, multiple data; MIMD).

When multiple processors are combined on a single chip, they are referred to as *cores*. The number of cores that can be placed on a single chip depends on both the complexity of the individual cores and the chip technology used. Today's multicore chips may embody anywhere from two to a few hundred cores. Multiple such chips may then be combined to yield multiprocessors. When multiple conventional computers are combined via a local area network, a cluster computer results.[80] As of November 2010, the world's fastest supercomputer was the Chinese Tianhe-1A.[81] It was built from 14,336 6-core Xeon processors (for a total of 86,016 cores) plus 7168 graphics processing units (GPUs) that are specialized for fast floating point computation.[82] It runs at more than 2.5 petaflops (i.e., 2.5 quadrillion floating point operations per second).[83]

One of today's hottest topics, *cloud computing*, takes this all yet another step further up the hierarchy, combining networks of commodity parallel computers (servers) into a single virtual computer.[84] *Grid computing* is much like cloud computing, although it comes out of the world of scientific computing, where the focus is on sharing cycles, data, and specialized experimental equipment.[85] The ALICE detector at CERN—essentially a large expensive physical sensor for heavy ion collisions—generates 1.25 GB of data per second from the Large Hadron Collider (figure 1.6). This data is processed by a collaboration of 130 organizations across 34 countries using more than 100,000 processors.[86]

In its most trivial sense, what are called *embarrassingly parallel problems* enable multiple computations to proceed with little to no interaction: $C°$. SETI@home is a canonical example, in which the goal is to analyze data from radio telescopes scanning the heavens in search of signals from extraterrestrial civilizations.[87] Rather than using expensive supercomputers, the independent chunks of calculation are parceled out to screen savers on millions of computers around the world whose owners have volunteered their computers' downtime. There is, however, still interaction with a central computational server, yielding a more accurate representation as $C \leftrightarrow C°$. Furthermore, it is the interactions that make parallel and distributed computing a difficult intellectual and computational problem, whether we are talking about the kinds of parallel and distributed hardware just described or parallel software: $(\Delta/C)^*$ or Δ/C^*. Developing parallel and distributed operating systems, programming languages, and algorithms—and writing parallel programs—remains a particularly challenging enterprise.

Networking, in conjunction with the Web, has revolutionized the world over the past few decades. Digital communication has enabled global sharing of both information and computational services, along with the creation of new kinds of online communities. It isn't just the raw computing technologies by themselves, however, that has brought about this revolution. For the Web and peer-to-peer file sharing, the key addition is human interpretable content, embodied in text, images, audio, and video: $\delta/C^* \rightarrow S$. The *Semantic Web* incorporates AI knowledge representation techniques to enable computers to understand and use Web content: $\delta/s/C^* \rightarrow C$.[88] For social networks, it has been critical that the network interact with whole communities of people, $C^* \leftrightarrow S°$ or $(C \leftrightarrow S)^*$, whereas for sensor networks, the network must interact with a distributed environment, $C^* \leftrightarrow \Delta°$ or $(C \leftarrow \Delta)^*$. One concept I advocated during my earlier years of leading new directions at ISI was that of *physically coupled webs*, which blends concepts from sensor networks and distributed robotics to yield networks of sensors and effectors. The idea was for the network to form the backbone of a worldwide-distributed robot: $1/(C \leftrightarrow P)^* \leftrightarrow \Delta$. Such extensions add a variety of domains and relationships to the pure dyadic or polyadic notion of networking, making the discipline as a whole mixed polyadic.

The most typical means of adding complexity to distributed systems is by scaling up the number of entities, but it may also be increased by introducing heterogeneity in the entities that are interacting. Generally, there is a tension between scale and heterogeneity, as scaling almost always implies replication and thus homogeneity. Living populations combine scale with heterogeneity through reproductive strategies that foster variety. In computing, the variety is usually much more limited, with a large-scale heterogeneous distributed system—such as the Tianhe-1a supercomputer—generally composed of large numbers of replicas of a small number of types of entities. Still, such combinations only provide heterogeneity within the domain of computing. It is also interesting to explore systems that combine multiple entities from different domains. For example, the concept of robot–agent–person (RAP) teams[89]—{(s↔l)/(C↔P), s/C, S/L}*—was developed as part of a DARPA study I led back in 2001. The idea was to take advantage of the individual strengths of each of these three types of participants while offsetting each other's weaknesses.

4.5   Interaction Summary

As with the previous chapter on implementation, the focus in this chapter has been primarily on a single mixed dyadic relationship between computing and one other domain, C+Δ, although here the relationship has been one of interaction (C→, C← or C↔) rather than implementation (/). However, some polyadic examples have been included as well—particularly in the context of bidirectional interaction—along with some discussion of both symmetric and asymmetric pure dyadic interactions (C↔C and C→C) where computing interacts with itself. This overview of interaction complements the earlier one for implementation, illustrating and making concrete the other side of the relational approach while highlighting and providing an organization over even more multidisciplinary aspects of computing. The potential of computational interaction to connect everything intimately with information and computation, as well as to provide pervasive computational understanding and shaping of everything, is truly revolutionary; not to mention how all of these direct connections should also enable indirectly linking everything with everything else. We have only begun to see what is possible here.

5   Relational Macrostructures and Analyses

The previous three chapters began the process of understanding the relational approach to computing. They have introduced the relational architecture and the metascience expression (ME) language and surveyed at various levels of detail much of monadic and dyadic computing, along with bits of polyadic computing. Mostly, this has involved examining a wide variety of individual topics in computing. Yet the structure of the survey has, in the process, also yielded a novel taxonomy over much of the computing sciences. Dyadic computing, along with several bits of polyadic computing that could usefully be abstracted to dyadic, have been organized according to the scientific domains they involve and the relationships implicated among them. Several supplementary dichotomies—natural versus artificial, (true) implementation versus simulation, and active versus passive—have also been used to aid in structuring this taxonomy.

Such a taxonomy provides one form of macrostructure over the computing sciences that can help in organizing and understanding them. In this chapter, we examine three such macrostructures: one directly based on this taxonomy, a second based on systematic usage of the ME language, and the last based on a second form of hierarchical structuring that can also be interpreted in terms of the ME language. These three forms of macrostructure are then applied in analyzing four large-scale aspects of computing science: *mixed worlds* that combine people, computing, and usually at least one other domain (section 5.1); the pursuit of science, with a particular emphasis on the use of computing in this pursuit (section 5.2); university-based computing research institutions (section 5.3); and academic computing departments and schools (section 5.4). The overall goal for these four analyses is to understand the respective aspects of computing better while examining the utility yielded for them by the three relational macrostructures. The analyses also yield general feedback on the relational approach, in terms of the utility provided by these more indirect implications of it, and illustrate additional aspects of polyadic computing beyond what has already been presented in chapters 3 and 4. Because a systematic traversal of polyadic computing is infeasible, we will just see a further smattering of this larger space here. We will also see some additional bits in chapter 6 (section 6.3).

The first form of relational macrostructure is derived from abstracting away the supplementary dichotomies used in the surveys of implementation and interaction to yield a compact two-dimensional map of dyadic computing. Table 5.1 embodies the most complete version of this map published to date, having benefitted from the systematic surveys in the previous two chapters.[1] When the first version of this table emerged some years ago, it surprised me with the novel yet coherent organization it suggested over much of conventional computing. This result inspired me to look deeper into the relational approach and was thus a major factor in making this book happen. I keep returning to refresh the table because it is the best big-picture view of the computing sciences of which I am aware and because it provides a simple yet comprehensive tool for understanding much about their structure.

As shown in the table, the space of dyadic computing can be charted in two dimensions as the cross product of four points along the (horizontal) domain dimension (for C+P, C+S, C+L, and C+C) and five points along the (vertical) relationship dimension: C/Δ, Δ/C, $C\leftarrow\Delta$, $C\leftrightarrow\Delta$, and $C\rightarrow\Delta$ (although this reduces to just two relationships, C/C and $C\leftrightarrow C$, in the rightmost column because of the symmetry implied by pure dyadic computing). Computing (C) is one of the two domains in every relationship row, with the other being denoted by the domain wildcard (Δ), signifying that it can be any one of P, L, S, or C. The body of the table has a cell for each combination of values along the two dimensions, with the generic symbol in each dimension, + for relationships and Δ for domains, filled in by the content in the other. For example, the top left cell covers the physical implementation of computing (C/P), whereas the bottom right cell concerns interactions between computing and itself ($C\leftrightarrow C$ and C*).

This overview can be viewed as arising from combining abstractions of tables 3.2, 3.3, and 4.1 with the items needed to flesh out the cell for pure dyadic implementation. The initial three cells in the first row of table 5.1 derive from compressing the three rows in table 3.2 and then eliminating some of the less critical elements. Similarly, the initial three cells in the second row derive from table 3.3. The passive and active columns in table 4.1 are merged, and the itemization of domains is rotated

Table 5.1
Two-dimensional map of dyadic computing

	C+P	C+L	C+S	C+C
C/Δ	Mechanical, electromechanical, electronic, optical, quantum, chemical, precomputing, analog	Phylogenetic, ontogenetic, immunological, neural, collective, biomolecular, biomimetic, evolutionary, autonomic, swarm, biomimetics	Human cognition, mechanical Turks, Wizard of Oz, crowd-sourcing, artificial intelligence	Compilers, OS, emulation, reflection, abstractions, procedures, architectures, languages, databases
Δ/C	Computational science, graphics, numerical analysis, virtual environments, digital physics	Artificial life, systems biology, neural networks, virtual humans	Artificial intelligence, cognitive modeling, computational sociology, econometrics	
C←Δ	Sensors, scanners, computer vision, optical character recognition, localization	Eye, gesture, expression and movement tracking, biosensors	Information technology industry (hardware and software), input devices, learning, authorization, speech understanding	Networking, security, parallel and distributed computing, grids, clouds, multirobot and multiagent systems, automated programming and debugging, self-monitoring
C⇔Δ	Robots, informatics	Brain–computer interfaces, assistive robotics, bio/medical informatics	Computer and software engineering, human–computer interaction, full immersion, games, natural language, social robotics	
C→Δ	Locomotion, fabrication, manipulation	Bioeffectors, haptics, sensory immersion	Presentation, screens, printers, graphics, speech generation, cognitive augmentation, computational thinking	

Each column characterizes the overlap between computing and one other domain, which may be computing itself. Each row focuses on one type of relationship and on one direction within a type. The first two rows cover *implementation* and the final three cover *interaction*.

from the vertical to the horizontal to yield the final three rows in table 5.1. With the merger of the passive and active columns, the unidirectional aspect of automatic programming and self-monitoring is of less import, and they are simply merged into the cell for bidirectional pure dyadic interaction.

Secondary domains and relationships that might apply to particular topics—such as the physical (P) and social (S) aspects involved in brain–computer interfaces (C↔L)—have also generally been abstracted away to enable inclusion in the table of any area that involves a single dominant relationship and domain pair. Thus, within each cell of the table are listed computing topics that naturally sort to that location based on their dominant relationship and (noncomputing) domain. Quantum computing, for example, is a particular approach to using the physical domain in implementing new types of computers (C/P), whereas a computer network involves computers interacting with each other (C↔C or C*). The table covers only dyadic computing, albeit including polyadic topics that are usefully abstracted to their dominant dyadic relationships; however, in exchange, it is simple to use and can be exhaustive in its coverage. It provides a tool that will be exploited in this chapter to analyze university-based computing research institutes (section 5.3) and academic computing organizations (section 5.4).

The ME language goes beyond the dyadic table to enable characterization of arbitrary combinations of domains and relationships—whether monadic, dyadic, or polyadic—providing insight into the relationships implicated in each participating domain overlap. In exchange, it adds complexity and sacrifices the ability explicitly to map out the entire space. It does, however, embody an implicit definition of the space of computing topics—all ME expressions that contain at least one C—making it possible, at least in theory, incrementally to generate the space implicitly defined by the language. The idea is to start with the simplest computing expression, C, and systematically add domains and relationships. From monadic computing, this would first generate all of dyadic computing, as one-step additions to C, and then increasingly complex forms of polyadic computing. Although such an approach is unwieldy when what is wanted is an overview of computing, in more limited usage it could enable identification of new subdisciplines of computing that are potentially interesting yet still largely unarticulated and unexplored. It also points the way toward the second form of relational macrostructure, which is based on systematic synthesis, decomposition, and comparison of ME expressions within a constrained subdomain of computing. This form of macrostructure is

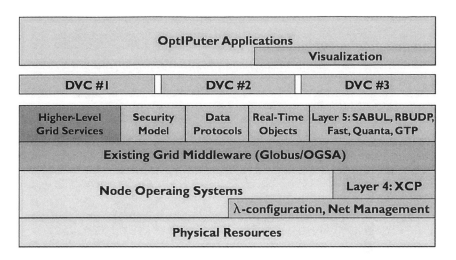

Figure 5.1

Layered architecture of the OptIPuter metacomputer (University of California, San Diego, and University of Illinois at Chicago).

From Larry L. Smarr, Andrew A. Chien, Tom DeFanti, Jason Leigh, and Philip M. Papadopoulos, "The OptIPuter," *Communications of the ACM* 46, no. 11 (November 2003): 58–67, © 2003 Association for Computing Machinery, Inc. Reprinted by permission.

central to analyzing, in section 5.1, the space of *mixed worlds* that combine people, computing, and usually at least one other domain. It also plays an important role in understanding the pursuit of science and the use of computing within it (section 5.2) and the structure of academic computing organizations (section 5.4).

The third form of relational macrostructure is a hierarchical *systems architecture*. Systems architectures are familiar in computing as a means of structuring, understanding, and explaining complex computing systems. Figure 5.1, for example, shows the architecture of a virtual metacomputer called the OptIPuter,[2] and figure 5.2 shows the architecture of the Aura ubiquitous computing environment.[3] The focus here is on a more generic systems architecture that can be instantiated in a variety of specific ways, whether it is to understand metacomputers, ubiquitous computing environments, virtual environments/worlds, biomedical informatics, computing infrastructure (what is often now termed *cyberinfrastructure*), or large research institutions. Although the systems architecture has been applied to all of these topics, we will limit ourselves here to this last application— in section 5.3—where it will supplement use of the dyadic map. The

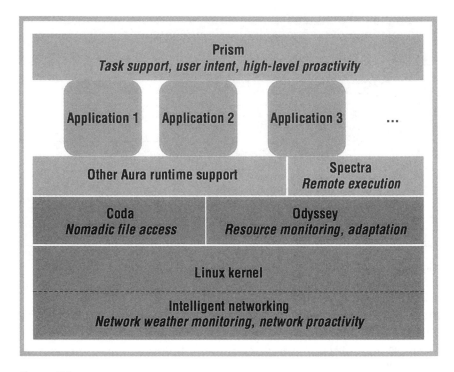

Figure 5.2
Layered architecture of the Aura ubiquitous computing environment (Carnegie Mellon University).
© IEEE. Reprinted with permission, from David Garlan, Dan Siewiorek, Asim Smailagic, and Peter Steenkiste, "Project Aura: Toward distraction-free pervasive computing," *IEEE Pervasive Computing* 1, no. 2 (April 2002): 22–31.

systems architecture will also crop up briefly in the discussion of academic computing organizations in section 5.4.

Table 5.2 depicts the latest version of the systems architecture, comprising a hierarchy of six layers. As with many other aspects of this work, this architecture has evolved considerably since it was first described in print.[4] Many of these changes have resulted from attempts to reconcile it with the relational architecture. Originally, the two architectures were conceived of as yielding two independent perspectives on computing, with the relational architecture more targeted toward the research enterprise (focused on understanding) and the systems architecture more targeted toward the development enterprise (focused on shaping). Attempts to apply the ME language to early versions of the systems architecture too often ended up messy or incoherent. Gradual revisions of the systems architecture over a

Table 5.2
The hierarchical systems architecture of six layers, divided into two bands with three layers each

Band	Layer	Isolated	Contextual
(Applications) **Software**	Organization	$\Delta/\Delta*$	
	Environment	$\Delta*$	
	Entity	Δ/C	$\Delta/(C\leftrightarrow\Delta)$
(Systems Software &) **Hardware**	Cloud	$C/C*$	$\Delta\leftrightarrow C/(C\leftrightarrow\Delta)*$
	Network	$C*$	$(C\leftrightarrow\Delta)*$
	Platform	$C/\{\Delta,C\}$	$\Delta\leftrightarrow C/\{\Delta,C\}$

period of years have finally yielded a version that articulates better with the relational architecture and the ME language and is more coherent as a result.

Each layer in the table specifies a class of technology, with vertically adjacent layers alternately being related by implementation or interaction. The band of three layers at the bottom of the hierarchy roughly comprises hardware, along with any associated systems software. It begins with the hardware implementation relationship surveyed in section 3.1 (C/Δ) plus the pure dyadic topic of systems software (C/C) and builds up from there. The band of three layers at the top of the hierarchy then corresponds roughly to applications software. It begins with the implementation relationship surveyed in section 3.2 (Δ/C) and similarly builds up from there. Essentially, each of these two bands starts with a primitive implementation relationship in its lowest layer, which then gets compounded at the middle layer through an indefinite number of interactions (*). These interactions then combine to implement (/) something new in the band's highest layer.

Each row in the table has been augmented with characterizations via ME. In the *isolated* column, the expressions focus on computing abstracted from its context. There are interaction relationships ($\leftrightarrow$) here, along with instances of the generic domain symbol (Δ), but they are only in service of explaining the use of computing in these layers. In contrast, computing is shown in the context of its use in the *contextual* column, including interactions with people and the world. This adds further interaction relationships and generic domain symbols. For the upper two layers, the isolated and contextual representations converge, as the explicit representation of computing (C) disappears here.

Within the hardware band, the lowest layer is where a computing *platform* (i.e., a computational device of some sort) is implemented in some technology.[5] Platforms can vary from the very small, such as an individual chip or a region of a chip, to handheld devices such as phones, to desktop computers, and finally on up to the largest supercomputers. They can involve a single processor or thousands of processors. They can be anywhere from low-performance power sippers to high-performance energy hogs. They can stand on their own or be embedded in sensors, appliances, robots, or living creatures. This is the domain of computer hardware (C/Δ), but it also includes the lowest levels of systems software (C/C) required for these platforms to run. In context, it also includes interaction with other domains (C$\leftrightarrow\Delta$), whether people via human–computer interaction or the world via sensors and effectors (and their combination into robots).

In the middle of the hardware band is the *network* layer, where arbitrary numbers of platforms interact. Networking, as discussed in section 4.4, is a form of pure dyadic/polyadic computing in that it concerns computers interacting with each other: C*. The C here abstracts over hardware and systems software, representing the combination of both. In context, this layer expands to include everything from sensor networks to social networks.

At the top of the hardware band is the *cloud* layer, which focuses on the pooling and sharing of distributed resources, in effect implementing a metacomputer out of a network of existing computers. The cloud layer is defined in terms of an ideal computational conceptualization that masks as much as possible the underlying reality of a heterogeneous collection of networked resources that are physically distributed in arbitrary ways. Each user, instead of being presented with a cacophony of distributed resources, sees a unified view of a virtual computational resource.

In many ways, *cloud* is not an ideal label for this layer. Cloud computing[6] can be viewed as just the latest fad, and label, for achieving some fraction of the idealization that defines this layer. The cloud layer, in fact, was called the *grid* layer in earlier versions of table 5.2. Grid computing grew out of computational sciences, where historically it focused on the pooling and sharing of distributed online resources—supercomputers, data repositories, scarce experimental equipment, and so forth—for large-scale scientific collaborations.[7] Given that one of the inventors of grid computing was at the Information Sciences Institute (ISI), leading one of the larger research groups in this area, and that cloud computing had not yet appeared on the scene, it was the natural name for this layer in earlier days. Grids also include interactions with noncomputational aspects of the world, such as experimental equipment, implying that they actually better capture the contextual sense of this layer. But this ideal is now more widely known as cloud computing, thus this current choice of label.

Labels of course are epiphenomenal and easily changeable. What really matters is the content to which the label refers; in this case the idealization described above. There are numerous technical differences as to how systems labeled *clouds* are implemented versus those labeled *grids*, any of which can be of critical importance for particular applications, but here we are talking about an idealization that spans the space of technical possibilities—including clouds, grids, and other approaches, such as peer-to-peer systems—rather than focusing on any particular approach to implementing the ideal.

Above the cloud layer, the hardware band implements the applications software band. Simpler software systems and research efforts might omit the cloud layer, or even the network layer, to perch directly on top of the network or platform layer, but the full complexity and richness of software systems and research requires all three lower layers. No matter in what manner this is done, however, the first layer implemented in the upper band is the *entity* layer, where computation implements/simulates various aspects of the world. This can include static entities, such as representations of data/information/knowledge, as well as active entities that implement or simulate activity from one or more of the great scientific domains. The entity layer acts as the inverse of the platform layer with respect to how it exploits the dyadic implementation relationship, focusing on computing implementing/simulating anything and everything versus anything and everything implementing computing.

Above the entity layer is the *environment* layer. Its relationship to the entity layer is analogous to that already seen between the network layer and the platform layer. Here, arbitrary numbers of entities interact to yield a virtual environment in the isolated case and a mixed reality environment in the contextual case. This is actually a broader notion than a standard virtual or mixed reality environment, including databases, sets of connected web pages, a social network composed of people and computers, a community modeling environment composed of data and simulation models,[8] or an online virtual world/environment. It is where all of the content about the domains of interest is instantiated and combined.

At the top of the applications software band, and thus of the entire hierarchy, is the *organization* layer. It stands in relationship to the environment layer as the cloud layer stands to the network layer. An organization goes beyond simply comprising a set of interacting things to implementing a new kind of entity from the interacting things. The term *virtual organiza-tion* is sometimes limited to human organizations that are facilitated by computational means. But teams of agents also yield virtual organizations, as do combinations of computational and living entities. The Electric Elves project discussed in section 4.4 used teams of agents to facilitate the work-ings of human organizations, for example, and the robot–agent–person (RAP) teams discussed later in the same section yield virtual organizations composed of robots, agents, and people. Group science based on grid computing also yields virtual organizations.

The systems architecture, in conjunction with the ME language, helps provide an alternative perspective on what Peter Denning has referred to as *windows of computing mechanics*.[9] Denning was concerned with telling the stories defining the great principles of computing and found that he could organize these stories into five categories:

- Computation: What can be computed; limits of computing.
- Communication: Sending messages from one point to another.
- Coordination: Multiple entities cooperating toward a single result.
- Automation: Performing cognitive tasks by computer.
- Recollection: Storing and retrieving information.

But, given that the category boundaries were blurry, he visualized these as five overlapping windows into a complex whole rather than as disjoint subsets.

As defined by Denning, computation combines theoretical computer science—at the core of monadic computing, C—plus physical realizations, C/P (or C/Δ). Traditionally, theoretical computer science provided the grounding for the bottom layers in both bands of the systems architecture—platform and entity—but it also extends to cover at least some aspects of higher layers as well. The physical realization aspect of computation clearly maps onto the isolated variant of the platform layer. Communication maps onto the isolated variant of the network layer: C*. It could also conceivably be extended to the environment layer as well—covering communication among entities—but it does not appear to be so as currently defined. Coor-dination maps onto the contextual variant of the cloud layer, $\Delta\leftrightarrow C/(C\leftrightarrow\Delta)^*$, and the organization layer, Δ/Δ^*, concerned as it is with human–human, human–computer, and computer–computer combinations. Automation maps onto the platform and entity layers, with Δ instantiated by s: C/s and s/C, respectively (or combined to form C/s/C).

Mapping of the final window, recollection, is a bit messier. Aspects of recollection, having to do with data and databases, map onto the entity and environment layers, but those parts concerned with things like the memory hierarchy in computers—registers, cache, main memory, disks, and so forth—do not belong here. They could be thought of as reflecting part of the platform layer that is missing from the computation window, but it may be more useful to think of them as indicating a need for the extension of the architecture to an additional band below the existing hardware band. In this *component* band, we could talk about the individual parts of computers, how they interact via buses and other means, and how they combine to form working computers. The memory hierarchy would compose part of this band.

This comparison reveals potential gaps in the windows concerned with the applications software band, particularly aspects of the entity and environment layers not concerning S or s; and contextual aspects of the hardware band, such as when sensing and effecting are implicated. These might be good areas within which to search for additional stories. The comparison also reveals that the systems architecture may ultimately need to be extended to a third *component* band, below the existing hardware band.

As mentioned earlier, this systems architecture, along with the dyadic map and the systematic generation and decomposition of ME expressions, are used in the remainder of this chapter to analyze four complex aspects of computing sciences. The first analysis, in section 5.1, is of a segment of polyadic computing that mixes real and virtual worlds in such a way as to yield virtual reality, ubiquitous computing, prosthetics, and other complex forms of embedding (often in conjunction with simulation) of computing, people, and the world. Systematic ME expressions are the main tool here.

The second analysis, in section 5.2, focuses on how science is pursued rather than on domains of scientific study themselves. The pursuit of science is traditionally a social activity (S) where people (scientists) exist in particular relationships with their domains of study (S+Δ), but the people are increasingly being augmented or replaced by computing: (S$\leftrightarrow$C)+Δ or C+Δ, respectively. This is where computational science and the various flavors of informatics exist and is unfortunately too often the only perspective many scientists from other domains have of computing. Systematic ME expressions will also be used here to understand better these particular variants of computing and thus to place them in their rightful context within the rest of the broad domain of computing.

The third analysis, in section 5.3, concerns understanding the conceptual and technical bases for two research institutions at the University of Southern California (USC) with which I have had significant associations: the ISI and the Institute for Creative Technologies (ICT). Both are large, diverse organizations engaged in computing research, but the analyses help explicate their unique natures. In the process, they also illustrate how these macrostructure forms can aid in understanding computing organizations as well as computing disciplines. The systems architecture and the dyadic computing table are, respectively, critical to understanding these two organizations.

The fourth analysis, in section 5.4, also emphasizes a big-picture view of organizations, but this time the organizations are academic computing departments, schools, and colleges. All three forms of macrostructure are leveraged to understand the scope and organization of such units. The analysis argues for an acceptance of the full breadth of the computing sciences within academia and discusses how the tools provided here could help bring conceptual coherence to academic computing units.

5.1 Mixed Worlds

Given the ME language, the simplest way to denote the overall world within which we live is as Δ. This is the generic symbol across the scientific domains, implicitly including S along with P, L, and C. We can be more explicit, however, about our relationship to this overall world by representing how we are embedded as part of it: $\Delta/(S\leftrightarrow\Delta)$. By interacting with the world around us, we effectively contribute to implementing a world in which we are an integral part. This section focuses on a space of variations and elaborations on the delta in the denominator; that is, the aspect of the world with which we interact. In particular, we will consider combinations of the world and computing that fundamentally alter the world with which we interact, causing the computer to disappear from sight by shifting the locus of interaction from the computer to this altered world. The generic for this shift in the denominator is $S\leftrightarrow\Delta/C$, to yield $\Delta/(S\leftrightarrow\Delta/C)$ overall, but we will explore several variants of this expression that are based on specializing the right side of the denominator in the directions of computational simulation, δ/C, and embedded computing, $\Delta/(C\leftrightarrow\Delta)$. The engendered space is diverse, highly polyadic, and includes an array of important directions for the future of computing. It ultimately also is integrated via a single ME expression.

Let's start with simulation. A straightforward substitution in the overall expression yields $\Delta/(S\leftrightarrow\delta/C)$, but we could also consider denoting it as $\delta/(S\leftrightarrow\delta/C)$. The former leaves open whether the jointly implemented world is real or simulated, whereas the latter insists the new world is a simulation. We will not go into the subtleties of this question here and instead simply go with the more generic version that uses Δ. Either way, however, it should be clear that this is a representation of *virtual reality*, where the human is embedded in a virtual world. The computer effectively disappears when the human becomes perceptually, cognitively, and emotionally immersed in the simulated world, with the resulting mindset of interacting directly with this new world rather than with the computer underlying it (or the real world). The *Star Trek* Holodeck[10] can serve as an idealization, and ultimate goal, for this paradigm. ICT had as a core part of its founding vision the creation of the Holodeck (along with an initial executive director who had been an executive vice president at Paramount, the home of *Star Trek*).

Virtual worlds incorporate territories, public and private spaces, ownership of property and goods, economies, personal relationships, and crime. Sometimes these activities are totally divorced from the real world, and sometimes they are closely intertwined with it, where crime in the virtual world can lead to criminal charges in the real world, relationships in the virtual world turn into or replace relationships in the virtual world—to the extent where one Korean couple let their own child die of neglect while they raised a virtual child[11]—exchange rates exist between real-world currencies and the currencies in some virtual worlds[12]; and concepts from the virtual world, such as earning points for deeds, are being implemented in the real world, in what are called *alternate reality games*.[13] Increasing the sophistication of virtual worlds remains an important research topic in computing, but so also does the isolation they encourage from the real world.

Mixed reality, in its most general sense, provides a hybrid between virtual reality and the real world, yielding a new world in the denominator that is implemented by interactions between the real and virtual worlds: $\Delta/[S \leftrightarrow \Delta/(\delta/C \leftrightarrow \Delta)]$.[14] *Augmented reality* is a variant of mixed reality that maintains the person as part of the real world but overlays computational presentation on top of it.[15] It can be viewed as presenting to the human a hybrid world that is implemented by the existing world plus the computational world, where what is in the real world helps to determine what is presented via the computational world: $\Delta/[S \leftarrow \Delta/(\delta/C \leftarrow \Delta)]$. Augmented reality apps such as *Layar* are starting to appear on smart phones. They combine live video feeds from the phone's camera with localization data—from its GPS and compass—and information from the Internet to overlay onto the visual scene information and offers relevant to what is currently seen.

Augmented virtuality takes the opposite tack from augmented reality. Rather than overlaying the virtual world on the real world, it creates a new

Figure 5.3
The Gunslinger mixed reality interactive entertainment environment (University of Southern California).
Image courtesy of Steve Cohn / Steven Cohn Photography.

hybrid world by adding real objects to the virtual world: $\Delta/[S\leftrightarrow\delta/(\delta/C\leftrightarrow\Delta)]$. The top delta within the denominator here is lowercase because the world with which the person interacts is still largely a simulated one. Figure 5.3, for example, shows how a physical mockup of an Old West saloon was recently combined at ICT with virtual humans on screens to yield a sophisticated interactive entertainment experience.[16]

Let's shift our focus for now to when the substitution involves embedded computing rather than simulation: $\Delta/[S\leftrightarrow\Delta/(C\leftrightarrow\Delta)]$. Computers have long been embedded in objects with which we interact, from toys to appliances and cars. Current trends, however, enhance this basic notion in one of several ways. If the inner denominator takes on a replicated and networked form, yielding $\Delta/[S\leftrightarrow\Delta/(C\leftrightarrow\Delta)^*]$, we have *ubiquitous computing*.[17,18] This topic was so hot for a while that it ended up receiving multiple names, such as pervasive computing, things that think, and the Internet of things. At its core, it imagines a world in which computing is ubiquitously embedded in physical objects that are then networked together. Here, computing disappears because it is masked by the real world instead of a simulated world.

If the embedded computing expression is instead modified so that computing implements a simulation, $\Delta/[S\leftrightarrow\Delta/(\delta/C\leftrightarrow\Delta)]$, we are back to the expression for mixed reality, but by a different path. The focus here, however, is on *prosthetics* and *smart/augmented things*, where the computing embedded within real objects enhances their functionality by making them more lifelike (via l/C) or more human-like (via s/C) to yield $\Delta/[S\leftrightarrow\Delta/(l/C\leftrightarrow\Delta)]$ or $\Delta/[S\leftrightarrow\Delta/(s/C\leftrightarrow\Delta)]$, respectively; or to yield $\Delta/(S\leftrightarrow\Delta/[(s\leftrightarrow l)/C\leftrightarrow\Delta])$ for their combination. The terminology can be confusing in this context, because the terms *smart* and *think* may be used to refer to anything that is computational—as it was above for things that think—or lifelike, rather than something that is necessarily human-like, but we will work our way through this.

Modern prosthetics—such as replacement arms and legs—are increasingly computational, although they clearly have an important physical side as well. Figure 5.4, for example, shows a recent prosthetic arm developed by the Johns Hopkins Applied Physics Laboratory for the Defense Advanced Research Projects Agency (DARPA).[19] Once attached to a person, this arm is to be controlled by direct neural connections, as discussed under brain–computer interfaces in chapter 4. Such a prosthetic can be denoted via the expression above for lifelike things, but the expression can also be specialized and simplified by recognizing that the physical (P) and computing (C) domains jointly simulate an aspect of life (l): $\Delta/[S\leftrightarrow l/(C\leftrightarrow P)]$. This can also be simplified further by recognizing that it is the human body rather than the mind with which the prosthetic interacts and that the interaction implements just a new bit of life rather than the whole world: $L/[L\leftrightarrow l/(P\leftrightarrow C)]$. Notice that this essentially yields a form of robot, $l/(P\leftrightarrow C)$, embedded within a living system, or what is termed a *cyborg*.[20] It is also possible to consider the prosthetic as not being embedded, but simply attached, yielding an interaction relationship. However, it is still reasonable to consider that what remains of the original biological system plus the attached prosthetic forms a new life form, leaving us with the same ME expression as before. The only difference is whether the top level L that is implemented is considered to represent the original life form or a new one.

The area of *cognitive prosthetics* concerns cognitive aids that bring patients with neurologic damage closer to normal levels of cognitive function.[21] They can be denoted by the expression above for human-like things, but this expression can also be converted into a form analogous to life prosthetics, although even simpler because we can omit the physical component: $S/(S\leftrightarrow s/C)$. The brain implant shown in figure 2.10 provides an

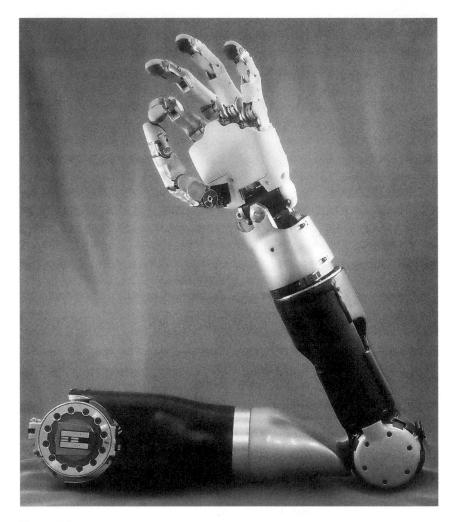

Figure 5.4
Johns Hopkins Applied Physics Laboratory neurally controlled Modular Prosthetic Limb.
Image courtesy of DARPA/JHUAPL/HDT Engineering Services.

example of such a cognitive prostheses, there replacing part of a damaged hippocampus. Prosthetics, both life and social, are nominally intended to regain lost functionality, but there may be no technical limitation keeping them from also being used to go beyond existing human capabilities. We are already seeing such issues concerning life prosthetics, where questions are raised as to whether a prosthetic leg might provide an advantage for its possessor in a race against unmodified humans.[22]

The area of smart/augmented things also leverages simulations of the life (l/C) or social (s/C) domains, but instead of these simulations being embedded within an existing living (L) or social (S) entity, they are embedded into physical objects (P)—such as rooms, buildings, bridges, roads, and waterways—to make them more lifelike and/or human-like. Smart buildings, for example, have sensors, computing, and actuators embedded into their physical structures to monitor and adjust their performance—controlling temperature, materials stress, air quality, security, lighting, music, and so forth—much like an animal's biological systems monitor and adjust its body functions. This converts a situation that was originally $\Delta/(S\leftrightarrow P)$—where the world just comprises people interacting with the physical domain—into a variant of the expression above for lifelike things: $\Delta/[S\leftrightarrow L/(l/C\leftrightarrow P)]$. Similarly, a smart bridge has embedded computing plus sensors that detect whether the strain on any of its structures is close to a dangerous level.[23] They may eventually even possess actuators that will automatically rebalance the stress to keep the bridge safe.

One thing I have wondered about on occasion is whether there is an underlying commonality between the traditionally disjoint topics of virtual reality and ubiquitous computing—based on how they both embed/hide computing within some kind of world interface—and whether there might thus be some eventual combination of them that will be even more revolutionary than either is individually. By seeing how both of these threads come together via a common expression for mixed reality—which can be extended to $\Delta/[S\leftrightarrow \Delta/(\delta/C\leftrightarrow \Delta)^*]$ to include the replicated network aspects—we can see how this might come about.

In summary, in this analysis we have explored how a broad range of state-of-the-art polyadic computing topics can be understood and related by systematically varying ME expressions within a limited scope, finishing up with a single generic expression for these sets of mixed reality topics. This expression neatly characterizes the kinds of mixed worlds, and bodies, we will likely inhabit increasingly in the future. They will have computation so pervasively embedded within them that reality may become unrecognizable. They will also have the real and virtual so closely entangled that it will make little difference in many cases whether something is part of one or the other. The novel issues, both pragmatic and ethical, raised by such a possibility are of course staggering. Do we, for example, enable Big Brother from *1984*[24] or Skynet from *The Terminator*[25] by creating smart environments? Or, what does it mean to be human if we start computationally augmenting human intelligence, and do we end up with something like the Borg from *Star Trek*?[26]

5.2 Pursuing Science

The previous section began with the idea that the world as a whole could be represented as Δ. Here, this usage of Δ is extended to represent the entire subject matter of science, as it spans the study of all four of the great domains. Science is, however, not just an abstract notion that comprises everything either in existence or that can be brought into existence but also a human activity that involves understanding and shaping. This is the pursuit of science that has traditionally been a human (S) activity, but which increasingly involves computing (C) as well as or instead of people. In the extreme this could be automated science, but mostly it involves a combination of people and computers in the form of computational science and informatics.

We can still call individuals who pursue science in the broad sense used in this book *scientists*, although conventionally they may go either by this or one of many other names, whether engineer, doctor, or teacher (all of whom participate in shaping and understanding great scientific domains) or something else. A scientist must minimally *have knowledge about their domain*—in the form of data, laws, models, and so forth—and *interact with the domain* in some way. In the ME language, a scientist's relationship to his or her knowledge can be represented as δ/S; that is, as an implementation (although generally a simulation, model, or representation in this case) by a human of a domain. In simpler and more standard terms, scientists have mental representations of aspects of their domains. Depending on the circumstances, we may choose to represent a scientist as either simply a person (S) or a person who internally models a domain: δ/S. Most often, it will be the latter unless there is a compelling reason for the former.

A scientist's interaction with his or her domain is also easy to denote in the ME language. If we view such interactions as taking the form of either understanding or shaping, then understanding amounts to influence from the domain to the scientist, $\delta/S \leftarrow \Delta$, whereas shaping reverses the direction, so that there is influence flowing from the scientist to the domain, $\delta/S{\rightarrow}\Delta$. In its simplest form, these two expressions characterize what it means to perform science/understanding versus engineering/ shaping, with their duality represented by reversing the direction of the arrow. The unity of science/understanding and engineering/shaping yields a fusion of these two representations, resulting in a single bidirectional arrow for science in the broad sense: $\delta/S{\leftrightarrow}\Delta$.

In addition to representing the duality between science/understanding and engineering/shaping, this expression also embodies and distinguishes the two traditional pillars of science: theory (as grounded in mathematics) and experimentation. The modeling relation (δ/S) represents what goes on inside a scientist's head independent of any direct interaction with the domain. This is the realm of theory. In contrast, the interaction relationship represents the process of experimentation. Mere passive observation of a domain only requires influence in one direction, from the domain to the scientist, but controlled experimentation implies a full bidirectional interaction, reflecting the need for scientists to shape their environment to study it. The simplest way of representing this in ME is just $S{\leftrightarrow}\Delta$. To emphasize explicitly that it is a scientist who is involved in these experimental interactions, we could use $\delta/S{\leftrightarrow}\Delta$, but when we want to emphasize the contrast between theory and experimentation, it makes sense to use the simpler expression for experimentation.

Bottom line, $\delta/S{\leftrightarrow}\Delta$ concisely expresses how science is composed of both understanding and shaping, as well as how it involves both theory and experiment. It can be viewed as an ME representation for the pursuit of science, at least as traditionally engaged in by individual scientists. Still, it misses three increasingly important aspects of modern science: (1) the role of computing in the pursuit of science, (2) science as a community pursuit, and (3) the convergence of the first two aspects in the development of grid-supported virtual organizations. We will examine all three of these aspects in the remainder of this section, with a particular emphasis on the first.

Computing's involvement in the pursuit of science generally falls within computational science or some form of informatics. The former emphasizes simulation and the latter data. The terms *data-intensive computing* and *eScience* are also coming into vogue for informatics that involves massive amounts of data, although the term *eScience* can also take on a broader meaning, including such things as the automated control of experiments and simulations; the collection, storage, management, and communication of data in a distributed environment; and the kinds of virtual organizations that will be discussed later.

Computational science can be thought of as having grown up in support of physicists, if we trace its roots back to work in scientific computing and numerical analysis that existed before the name *computational science* itself came into vogue. Informatics instead initially grew up more in support of biologists (in the forms of bioinformatics and biomedical informatics). However, both have since become broadened to include a wide variety of disciplines across the domains. We now see, for example, computational physics, computational chemistry, computational biology, and computational sociology. We also see cheminformatics, neuroinformatics, geoinformatics, energy informatics, social informatics, and business informatics.

Simulation has become so central to the scientific method that computational science is often referred to as the *third pillar of science*.[27] I exploited such a notion myself at the turn of the millennium in helping to make the case for building a high-performance computing center at USC. Simulations are increasingly replacing experiments in circumstances where experiments are difficult, costly, or dangerous to perform. They become particularly feasible and useful when the basic principles in the domain of interest are well enough understood to enable *good enough* simulations to be built yet the interactions among these principles are too complex and difficult to enable conclusions to be drawn from them by hand (i.e., analytically from the theory embodied by the principles).

Computing has long had a role in managing and processing the data generated by experiments and simulations, whether explicitly labeled as informatics or not. But often, this has been considered as rather mundane, comprising such things as the management of data files and the performance of standard statistical analyses. More recently, this area has come into its own as a significant intellectual endeavor, with a proposal that data-intensive computing amounts to a *fourth paradigm for science*, after theory, experiment, and computational science.[28] This elevation appears largely due to two factors. First, the amount of data available has dramatically increased to petabytes and beyond—Google, for example, recently announced the online availability of 500 billion words from 5 million books for research purposes[29]—increasing both the challenges and the opportunities. Second, the autonomy and sophistication of computational analyses has grown to include, for example, natural language processing to extract results from the literature, information integration to combine data from multiple sources, machine learning to discover regularities in the data, and automated hypothesizing of models.

Unfortunately, although the criticality of computing within science is becoming increasingly acknowledged—as witnessed by these proposals of a third pillar and a fourth paradigm—such disciplines still provide the only prism through which many scientists view computing, making it unsurprising that they mistakenly judge it as merely a tool for the performance of science. There are of course exceptions—such as Richard Dawkins[30] and David Baltimore,[31] who have emphasized the central role of information within biology, and physicists who have been investigating various aspects of digital physics—but the message has yet to become pervasive. As we use the ME language to analyze computational science and informatics, it should become clearer how the traditional uses of computing in science fit within the larger picture of computing that is the basis for this book. It should also become clearer how these new approaches relate to theory and experimentation, enabling an assessment of the proposals for new pillars and paradigms.

Let's start with computational science and its core technology of simulation. Section 3.2.1 was devoted to a fairly extensive, although still far from exhaustive, discussion of simulation. In the ME language, computational simulation is simply expressed as δ/C, denoting that the domain phenomena are produced via an approximate form of computational implementation. However, when simulation is used in the pursuit of science, it requires a bit more than this; in particular, unless the process of science is completely automated, it requires a scientist to set up the simulations and to analyze the data. To draw the sharpest contrast with theory, we will use S for the scientist here, yielding a representation for the use of simulation in science as $S \leftrightarrow \delta/C$.

One way to think about the relationship of simulation to the two preexisting pillars, of theory and experiment, is to view it as falling between them, yielding an implicitly one-dimensional representation of the space of scientific methods. Rohrlich, for example, talks in these terms—describing simulation as *theoretical model experimentation*.[32] However, I have found it preferable instead to go with a two-dimensional interpretation of this space—as in table 5.3—via a move analogous to that taken in the shifting of research and development from one to two dimensions in the identification of Pasteur's quadrant (see chapter 6). The dimensions in table 5.3 characterize two aspects of how domain phenomena are represented to the scientist. The horizontal dimension is *real* versus *synthetic*. A phenomenon is a real representation of itself, whereas anything else is a synthetic representation of it. The vertical dimension is *understandable* versus *executable*. This is similar to a glass box versus black box distinction, with its core being whether the representation can be understood and reasoned about versus simply supporting execution for result generation.

Table 5.3
A two-dimensional categorization of the three pillars of science

	Real	Synthetic
Understandable		Theory: δ/S
Executable	Experiment: S⟷Δ	Simulation: S⟷δ/C

Both dimensions concern the nature of the representations used for the domain, whether real versus synthetic along the horizontal or understandable versus executable along the vertical.

This table, particularly when accompanied by the corresponding ME expressions, reveals the essences of these three approaches to science while also clarifying their inherent similarities and differences. To begin with, it implies that experimentation is real and executable, whereas theory is synthetic and understandable. With experimentation, we run the real world to see what happens: S⟷Δ. With theory, we mentally implement a synthetic representation of the world, δ/S, to derive its properties analytically. Clearly, not all theories are sufficiently understandable or mathematically tractable in practice to enable the kinds of human-driven analysis that are desired, but that is in principle what such theories are about. As earlier, we use S here to represent scientists, so as to enhance the contrast between a theorist, whose primary activity consists of working with an internal representation of his or her domain, and an experimentalist, who in the purest form merely leverages an internal model of his or her domain for designing and interpreting experiments.

If we compare these expressions for theory and experimentation with the one previously derived for simulation, S⟷δ/C, the correspondences and differences should become apparent. Let's start with experimentation. Simulation resembles experimentation in providing an executable version of the domain with which scientists can interact. Simulation thus shares experimentation's strength of enabling science to proceed when it is too difficult analytically to derive results from theories. Some theory is necessary to build the simulation—which could be shown by replacing the S in the expression with δ/S—but the remainder is now done by the computational implementation, δ/C, enabling humans to shift a good deal of their effort from the implementation role they maintain in theory to the interaction role that underlies experimentation. Where simulation differs from experimentation is in its use of computational implementation rather than natural implementation mechanisms, and thus in yielding synthetic rather than real data. Sciences of the artificial, such as computing, where even the real data are synthetic to some extent, tend to blur the distinction between simulation and experimentation.

In the other direction, simulation resembles theory in being based on a synthetic representation of the world—but δ/C rather than δ/S—and thus enabling science to proceed when experiments are costly, dangerous, unethical, illegal, intractable, or simply impossible. Representational formalisms for scientific content that combine both understandability and executability, such as programming languages based on mathematical equations or logical sentences, tend to blur the distinction between theory and simulation.

Based on this picture, simulation can be viewed as situated between theory and experimentation, if we proceed down in the table from theory and then turn left to reach experimentation, hitting simulation as the corner is turned. The other corner, which can also be considered as sitting between theory and experimentation, has been left empty in the table. This could be considered the ideal corner methodologically, as it compromises on neither understandability nor reality, but unfortunately the rules for how the world works cannot simply be read out and understood. This cell could conceivably be filled by *observation* for cases where how the world works is so obvious that it essentially acts as a theory of itself, but we will leave that open for now.

Because simulation shares attributes with both theory and experimentation, it can offer a unique combination of strengths as a means of furthering science. The goal in general is to leverage this combination when the individual weaknesses of theory and experimentation make them less appropriate. Hartmann identifies five overall uses of simulation in science:

1. Technique: Investigate the detailed dynamics of a system.
2. Heuristic tool: Develop hypotheses, models, and theories.
3. Substitute for experiment: Perform numerical experiments.
4. Tool for experimentalists: Support experiments.
5. Pedagogical tool: Gain an understanding of a process.[33]

One way to understand this list is that use (1) derives directly from executability, analogously to how it is traditionally supported by experimentation, whereas use (3) derives directly from its synthetic nature, analogously to how it is traditionally supported by theory. The other three then originate in combinations of these two uses, replacing experiments in helping theorists (use 2), experimentalists (use 4), and students (use 5) understand detailed system dynamics.

Because of what simulation shares with both theory and experiment, it is also subject to some of the inherent weaknesses of both. As with theory, the synthetic nature of simulation implies that the embodied assumptions are critical to the quality of the derived results. As with experimentation, the lack of understandability of simulations implies a constant risk of misinterpretation and overinterpretation of the derived results. Although it is all too possible to run into trouble when using simulations if either of these limitations is ignored, the appropriate use of simulation can be, and has been, a great boon to scientific progress.

From this discussion, a good case can be made for thinking of simulation, and computational science more generally, as providing a distinct (third) pillar of science. However, as a pillar of its own, it must be understood not to be a completely independent one. It is a hybrid of the other two, albeit with an additional computational twist.

Moshe Vardi, editor in chief of the *Communications of the ACM*, recently reached a rather different conclusion: that theory and simulation are the same pillar, or *leg* as he called it, at a suitable level of abstraction.[34] His argument is easily stated in the ME language, but we need to start with a different take on how to represent theory. Instead of δ/S, which emphasizes the scientist's representation of the domain, we can use $S \leftrightarrow \delta/M$, where we will use M as the symbol for mathematics. According to this expression, theory consists of a human interacting with a mathematical representation of a domain, yielding a structure that is parallel with the one we already have for simulation: $S \leftrightarrow \delta/C$. Vardi actually ignores the role of the scientist in these expressions—effectively yielding δ/M and δ/C for theory and simulation, respectively—and then appeals to abstraction over the nature of the simulation to say that these are fundamentally the same.

We could alternatively reach the same conclusion by keeping the full expressions while exploiting the argument to be made in chapter 6 that mathematics is part of computing. We then simply generalize from M to C in the expression for theory to yield the one for simulation. In contrast to Vardi's approach, this actually subsumes theory as a part of simulation, analogously to how we will propose to subsume mathematics as part of computing in chapter 6.

Either of these perspectives on Vardi's position essentially amounts to a collapsing of the two rows in table 5.3 into a single row, abstracting away the difference between understandable and executable. Although this abstraction does yield a useful viewpoint, it isn't complete in and of itself because it ignores that a useful alternative abstraction can also be obtained by collapsing the two columns, thus ignoring the difference between real and synthetic, to map simulation onto experimentation. Whereas to conceive computational science as an independent third pillar overemphasizes the differences between simulation and the preexisting legs, to identify simulation completely with theory (or experiment) obscures one set of differences or the other.

We have spent considerable time on computational science and its core of simulation to do justice to the subtlety and complexity of its relationships with theory and experimentation. Informatics—and data-intensive science in general—is more straightforward, although still far from trivial in its relationships. A few aspects of it, particularly topics such as data representation, properly fit as forms of implementation (δ/C), but the lion's share concerns the computational (C) facilitation of the interaction ($\leftrightarrow$) between scientists (S) and their executable systems, whether these systems are the real world (Δ) or a simulation of it (δ/C). This can be expressed as (S$\leftrightarrow$C)$\leftrightarrow${Δ,δ/C} to reflect that it is a human–computer team that now interacts with the executable system.

As Vardi maps the third pillar onto theory, he maps the fourth paradigm onto experimentation. This makes considerable sense from several perspectives. First, the dominant relationship in the informatics expressions is one of interaction. There is a human–computer team interacting with an executable system. With suitable abstraction, this becomes indistinguishable from the expression for experimentation: S$\leftrightarrow$$\Delta$. Second, the use of computing to handle experimental data is a generalization of the traditional use of mathematics—statistics in particular—for this purpose. Thus, as with theory and simulation, a generalization from mathematics to computing leads to an identification of informatics with experimentation. Although just as in the earlier case, the generalization goes from mathematics to computing here, so informatics should subsume traditional experimentation (and statistics) rather than the other way around.

What informatics additionally brings to the table is the automation of a range of experimental activities, from the planning and setting up of experiments, to operating experimental equipment, to managing the data in large-scale distributed computing environments, to syntactic and semantic integration across different types of data, to analyzing the data via both traditional statistical techniques and newer machine learning algorithms, and even to drawing conclusions and building models from the processed data. We also need to be aware that when we are talking about experimentation here, we must include experiments with simulations as well as with the real world, although this is not itself a differentiator between statistics and informatics.

If we now pull up from the details of defining and discriminating computational science and informatics, we reach a bigger picture of *human–computer science*, where computers do whatever they can to assist scientists. This can be expressed in a variety of manners, but two of the simpler variants are $(\delta/S \leftrightarrow \delta/C) \leftrightarrow \Delta$ and $\delta/(S \leftrightarrow C) \leftrightarrow \Delta$. The first expression denotes that the human scientist (δ/S) interacts with a computer that embodies simulations and/or representations of the domain (δ/C) and that this pair then interacts with the domain itself ($\leftrightarrow \Delta$). Simulation (δ/C) can be viewed as being embedded in this equation as part of the support for experimentation ($\leftrightarrow \Delta$). The second expression represents a human–computer team that jointly does theory/simulation, $\delta/(S \leftrightarrow C)$, and experimentation/informatics, $(S \leftrightarrow C) \leftrightarrow \Delta$. This form most closely parallels Vardi's published perspective, but in both of these forms it should be clear that the computer is either augmenting or substituting for the human in the human's normal pursuit of science. If there were to be complete substitution, we would get automated science: $\delta/C \leftrightarrow \Delta$.

The two expressions above for human–computer science can capture computing's role in both computational science and informatics via a single C plus two distinct relationships with the scientific domain—implementation for computational science and interaction for informatics. However, in the process they downplay the special case where computing provides informatics support for its own simulations rather than for real-world experiments. This can be fixed by adding a new C either to the left or right side of these expressions. Adding it on the left of the first expression, for example, yields $[\delta/S \leftrightarrow (\delta/C \leftrightarrow \delta/C)] \leftrightarrow \Delta$. This variant maintains the distinctness of the real world, on the right of the interaction, from all of the synthetic (man- or computer-made) aspects of the scientific enterprise on the left side while splitting the informatics/representational aspect of computing ($\delta/C \leftrightarrow$) from the computational science (simulation) aspect (δ/C). If the extra C is instead added on the right side, we get either $(\delta/S \leftrightarrow \delta/C) \leftrightarrow \{\Delta, \delta/C\}$ or $\delta/(S \leftrightarrow C) \leftrightarrow \{\Delta, \delta/C\}$. The left sides of these equations correspond to theory and representation, whereas their right sides correspond to execution of both the real world and simulations of it. The interaction relationship represents the informatics aspects. These variants emphasize the parallels both between simulation and experimentation and between the role of humans and computers in theory/representation and informatics.

Computational science and informatics are thus aspects of polyadic computing in which computers (C) join with people (S) to increase our knowledge of some great scientific domain (P, S, L, or C). Together they cut a broad swath across computing, including forms of computational simulation (δ/C), human–computer interaction (S$\leftrightarrow$C), and computational interaction with other domains (C$\leftrightarrow\Delta$). Because of their extreme computational demands, they can—and often do—also drive development of advanced processors (C/Δ) along with networking and parallel/distributed computing (C*). Yet they still remain just one such swath.

Up until now in this discussion, we have focused on an individual scientist operating in isolation. But science increasingly rarely proceeds in this manner. In general, communities pursue it, with significant fragments of computing technology being developed in support of these communities. The World Wide Web, for example, was invented to support scientific data sharing over the Internet. The Grid was invented to enable sharing of large-scale computational resources—massive data sets, scarce instruments, supercomputers, and so forth—by distributed scientific communities. If we consider society as an indefinite number of interacting people, S*, then the process of science as a societal activity can be captured by δ/S*$\leftrightarrow\Delta$.[35] We can, however, also view this process as (δ/S$\leftrightarrow\Delta$)*, emphasizing the interactions among multiple people who are independently pursuing their own theoretical and experimental work, or we can combine these communitarian and individualistic extremes into a representation of groups of scientific communities interacting, (δ/S*$\leftrightarrow\Delta$)*. This probably comes closest to reality, representing groups of one or more scientists working closely together on common experiments and theory while interacting more loosely with other groups of scientists.

When computing is added to this picture—particularly when the computers are also multiplied and connected via networks to form distributed computing systems and grids—it gets richer and more complex. If we start with the last expression from individual science—δ/(S$\leftrightarrow$C)$\leftrightarrow\{\Delta,\delta$/C$\}$—there are even more ways we can potentially add stars, depending on which group interactions are being emphasized. The left side of the equation can, for example, become δ/(S*$\leftrightarrow$C*), δ/(S$\leftrightarrow$C)*, or [δ/(S$\leftrightarrow$C)]*. The first reflects groups of people working with groups of computers; the second represents groups of human–computer pairs working together to represent and theorize; and the third denotes interactions among individual human–computer scientific pairs. We can also combine all of these to yield [δ/(S*$\leftrightarrow$C*)*]*. The right side of the expression can in turn become $\{\Delta,\delta$/C*$\}$, $\{\Delta,(\delta$/C)*$\}$, or $\{\Delta,\delta$/C$\}$*, with the combination of all three yielding $\{\Delta,(\delta$/C*)*$\}$*. The first can be read as either the world itself or a simulation of it implemented by a parallel/distributed computer. The second involves the world plus multiple interacting simulations. The third involves interactions among multiple computational simulations and parts of the real world. The fourth combines all three.

If we combine all of the possible group interactions on both sides of the expression and add the possibility of interactions among multiple instances of the whole expression, we get $([\delta/(S^*\leftrightarrow C^*)^*]^*\leftrightarrow\{\Delta,(\delta/C^*)^*\}^*)^*$. This expression has become quite complex, but we can always abstract it back down to something much simpler, like $\delta/(S\leftrightarrow C)^*\leftrightarrow\{\Delta,\delta/C\}^*$, without too much loss of meaning. Here, teams of people and computers jointly theorize and experiment with some combination of the real world and simulations.

Given this final generic approximation for communities engaged in computational science and informatics, it can now be specialized to represent particular subdisciplines by replacing the domain wildcard, Δ, with any one of the domains. So, for example, the human–computer pursuit of biological science becomes $l/(S\leftrightarrow C)^*\leftrightarrow\{L,l/C\}^*$, with bioinformatics and biomedical informatics one fragment, $l/(S\leftrightarrow C)^*\leftrightarrow L$, and computational and systems biology another, l/C^*. Similarly, the combination of cheminformatics and computational chemistry becomes $p/(S\leftrightarrow C)^*\leftrightarrow\{P,p/C\}^*$, with the corresponding fragments; and the interdisciplinary field of cognitive science becomes $s/(S\leftrightarrow C)^*\leftrightarrow\{S,s/C\}^*$, although we could also add a factor here in the right side to signify that the intermediary of computational models of neurons $(s/l/C)$ may also be used.

In summary, we have used systematic variations in ME expressions in this section to explore several aspects of the pursuit of science: the similarities and differences among theory, experimentation, simulation, and large-scale data analysis; the use of computing in science via computational science and informatics, along with the extent to which they yield new approaches to science; and the community aspect of science, including computing's support of such communities. Some of the expressions grew quite complex in the process, but abstractions were always available to help in understanding them.

5.3   Research Institutes

The previous section focused on the pursuit of science and, in particular, on the use of computing in the pursuit of science. This section continues this concern with the pursuit of science but shifts the focus to analyzing a particular class of organizations that pursue the science of computing—academic research institutes. This will be limited to two research institutes with which I am particularly familiar: USC's ISI and ICT. Historically, it would make sense to start with ISI, given that I spent twenty years there before joining ICT and that the relational approach emerged from attempts at understanding and organizing a decade's worth of interdisciplinary new directions activities at ISI. However, the ICT analysis is simpler, so it helps to start with that.

ICT's mission is to "create compelling immersive systems for effective learning for military, entertainment and educational purposes."[36] Figure 1.3 provided a good example, displaying an image from an environment designed to help soldiers learn multiperson, cross-cultural negotiation skills in stability and support operations.[37] But other environments and games have been developed, for example, to help clinicians learn to deal with soldiers suffering from posttraumatic stress disorder (PTSD)[38] and to guide visitors through an exhibition at the Boston Museum of Science (figure 4.12).[39] In support of such applications, ICT research focuses on (a) the construction of virtual humans, including both their minds and bodies (figures 1.3 and 4.12); (b) photo-realistic graphics (figure 3.17), three-dimensional displays (figure 4.13), and other forms of output for human consumption (such as scent); (c) recognition and understanding of human bodies, behaviors, and thoughts; (d) the development of immersive and mixed reality environments (figure 5.3); and (e) the use of such environments, often along with games defined in them, for learning.

The analysis here is relatively simple because of ICT's focused mission, yielding, in table 5.4, a set of overlays on the dyadic map. The first thing to notice about this chart is that ICT's research concerns the relationship

Table 5.4
Regions of the dyadic table covered to some degree by research at ICT

	C+P	C+L	C+S	C+C
C/Δ				
Δ/C		SmartBody	Cognitive architectures and capabilities	
C←Δ		Body, gesture, and expression tracking; Light Stage		
C↔Δ		Immersive environments and games; dialogue and rapport		
C→Δ		Graphics; three-dimensional displays; Scent Collar		

Regions that are not covered by ICT are blank.

of computing (C) to the social (S) and life (L) domains. It is thus limited to the middle two columns in the table: C+S and C+L. The second thing to notice is that there is no work on the implementation of computing (C/Δ). The institute thus occupies a compact region of the full table—covering implementations/simulations of, and interactions with, the life and social domains—although clearly not covering absolutely everything within this region. Research on virtual humans (a) covers only part of the computational implementation (Δ/C) row; in particular, s/C for minds and l/C for bodies. Research on output modalities for human consumption (b) covers only the corresponding regions of the acting-and-shaping row (C→Δ), affecting as it does both the human mind and body. Research on recognition and understanding of people (c) likewise covers only the corresponding regions of the sensing-and-understanding row (C←Δ), and immersive environments and games for learning (d and e) cover only the corresponding regions in the bidirectional-interaction row (C↔Δ).

Mixed reality (d) is an interesting special case, as it clearly involves interactions with the physical domain as well as with people, but it is actually the people—and their bodies in particular—rather than the computers who participate in this interaction in the systems so far investigated. If we take this into account, along with the fact that the people interact with what is simulated computationally rather than with computing directly, we end up with an expression of Δ/{P,δ/C}↔S/L. The dyadic version of this abstracts away much of this elaboration, however, leaving us with just the interaction between the computer and the human: C↔S.

As opposed to ICT, which has a focused mission and has only been in existence for a bit over a decade, ISI has pursued a much broader mission for four decades. The traditional way to characterize ISI's technical expertise has been via a straightforward, two-level outline, with organizational divisions at the top level and technological foci listed below. Table 5.5 shows such an outline from 2003, during the era when the earliest versions of the relational architecture were developed. ME annotations were not used in these outlines back in 2003 but have been added to the technological foci in the table to help in clarifying the topics and thus the actual overall foci of the divisions. For simplicity, we will stay with this 2003 version of ISI throughout this analysis while acknowledging that ISI has continued to evolve significantly since then, including at least one major reorganization.

From the ME annotations, it can be seen that the first two divisions—Advanced Systems and Computational Sciences—both focused on some form of implementation involving computers (Δ/C, C/Δ), which can be

Table 5.5
Traditional outline of ISI's technological foci, organized by division, as of 2003

Division	Technological Foci		
Advanced Systems	Grid technology: C/C*	System on a chip: C/P	Biomimetic and bioinspired: l/C/P
Computational Sciences	VLSI engineering: C/P	Large-scale simulation: δ/C*	Advanced compilers: C/C
Computer Networks	Security: Δ↔C*	Sensor networks: (Δ→C)*	Network architectures: C*
Distributed Scalable Systems	Advanced resource management: Δ↔Δ/C	N-dimensional information: δ/C	Human-centered systems: S↔C
Dynamic Systems	Embedded real-time systems: P/(C↔P)	Scalable embedded systems: P/(C↔P)	Sensor systems: Δ→C
Integration Sciences	Signal processing algorithms: Δ→C	Mixed-mode signals: Δ→C	Space electronics: P→C/P
Intelligent Systems	Intelligent agents/ robots: C↔(s↔l)/C, Δ↔(s↔l)/(C↔P)	Knowledge: δ/s/C	Natural language: s/C↔S
MOSIS	Device and circuit modeling: C/P	Test structures: C/P	Wafer-level reliability: C/P

combined to form Δ/C/Δ. There does not appear to be a more precise characterization of them at this level, nor an inherent distinction between them based on their foci at this level. The Computer Networks Division not surprisingly concentrated on multiple computers interacting, C*, but also paid some attention to them interacting with other things (sensor networks). The Distributed Scalable Systems Division is harder to characterize, but from the expressions could perhaps be said to emphasize interaction with information systems: ↔Δ/C. In contrast to the first two divisions, which focused on implementation, the Dynamic Systems and Integration Sciences Divisions primarily focused on interactions between computing and the world, Δ↔C, albeit with some instances of implementation occurring in the context of embedding, P/(C↔P). Other than the focus on embedding in the Dynamic Systems Division, these two divisions are also difficult to tell apart at this level. The Intelligent Systems Division, true to its name, concentrated on artificial intelligence; that is, systems in which s/C played a key role. MOSIS—which originally stood for *Metal Oxide Silicon Implementation System*, but which was known simply by its acronym for many years before its name was changed to the Silicon Systems Division—focused on the physical implementation of computing: C/P.[40]

An attempt at mapping these topics to the dyadic table proved uninformative, as both the institute and many of its divisions were scattered across the table. This is consistent with ISI's nature as a research institute with a broad base in computing, but whose specific foci are primarily determined bottom-up by the interests of individual division directors and project leaders. An alternative approach is to view ISI's research areas through the lens of the more applied systems architecture. ISI's work traditionally ranged from basic research to applications, missing just the most extreme positions at the two ends of the spectrum. But no matter where an individual effort fell along this spectrum, it was almost guaranteed to be inherently practical, yielding useful technologies and systems, due to the need for sizable contracts and grants in order to support ISI's full-time researchers. It thus should not be a major surprise that such an approach might prove effective in understanding ISI.

In the context of the systems architecture, three of ISI's divisions in 2003—Dynamic Systems, Integration Sciences, and MOSIS—can be seen to have concentrated on the platform layer within the hardware band, with MOSIS dealing with it in isolation and the other two including the context. The Computational Sciences Division also focused primarily on the platform layer, but now with a strong dose of systems software—compilers and simulation software. The work on simulation software might appear more properly to belong to the entity and environment layers, but the emphasis was on low-level aspects of how to implement such software on parallel computers rather than on how actually to simulate entities from other domains.

The Computer Networks Division focused, appropriately enough, one layer up from platforms, at the network layer. Although this is within the hardware band, much of this division's activity concerned the systems software that enabled networks to operate rather than the physical hardware itself. The Advanced Systems Division also was mostly circumscribed within the hardware band, covering both actual hardware and systems software, with major emphases at both the platform and cloud layers. Biomimetic hardware in some sense brings in an aspect of the entity layer—simulating aspects of a region of the brain—even though this was actually done in hardware rather than software. The other two divisions— Distributed Scalable Systems and Intelligent Systems—spanned the software band, although the latter also included physical (reconfigurable) robots down at the platform layer.

This hierarchical analysis yields a more concise way of characterizing ISI's divisions than would have been possible with the dyadic map. Although the analysis still has rough edges, more probably cannot be expected given the nature of ISI's divisions and the organic manner in which they grew. Still, this section's analyses have shown overall how two forms of macrostructure—the dyadic map and the systems architecture—which are grounded in the relational approach, can be leveraged to understand the nature and structure of a pair of leading-edge computing research institutions. These, however, are far from the only organizations that are analyzable via these macrostructures; in the next section we shall, for example, apply these same two forms of macrostructure, plus systematic explorations with the ME language, to understand academic computing organizations. Nor are the uses of these macrostructures limited to the understanding of organizations. The dyadic map aids in understanding the whole domain of computing, its subdisciplines, how its subdisciplines interact, and how computing interacts with the other scientific domains. The systems architecture can also be applied, for example, to understand complex computing systems.

5.4 Academic Computing

This section resembles the previous in bearing on academic organizations that pursue the science of computing, rather than on the science of computing itself, but the focus here shifts from research institutes to academic departments, schools, and colleges in the United States. A similar discussion may be appropriate for such organizations outside of the United States, but I am insufficiently familiar with them to include them explicitly. This section also breaks from the previous section in going beyond simply being descriptive to include a normative aspect.

At the core of academic computing in most universities are computer science and computer engineering departments, although in some places they may be combined to yield computer science and engineering departments; or electrical engineering may also be added into the mix to form electrical engineering and computer science departments. Some universities also have departments focused on informatics, information sciences, or computational sciences, each of which may stand on its own or be coupled in some fashion with computer science. Multiple departments focused on different aspects of computing may also be aggregated into higher-level units, yielding for example: the School of Computer Science at Carnegie Mellon University; the School of Information and Computer Science at the University of California, Irvine; the School of Informatics and Computing at the University of Indiana; and the College of Computing at the Georgia Institute of Technology.

If computer science and engineering were really about science and engineering, respectively, then we might denote computer science as C→S and computer engineering as S→C, signifying people understanding versus shaping computing. In the first publication on the relational architecture for computing, I actually proposed rationalizing the split between computer science and engineering in this fashion, with computer science focused on the science of computing—as characterized by an early version of the dyadic table—and computer engineering focused on the shaping of computing, as characterized by an early version of the systems architecture.[41] However, this turned out to be a mistake for two reasons. The most critical reason goes back to the early discussion of the difficulty in distinguishing understanding from shaping in computing and of how their intertwining has actually been a key factor in the rapid progress of the field. Thus, rather than being a useful step forward, reifying the split by placing a departmental boundary between understanding and shaping would be a step back toward the more traditional model of science versus engineering and away from the future of increasingly tight intertwining.

The other reason was that in proposing that computer engineering should focus on shaping, it left a number of my computer engineering colleagues at USC with the impression that I was denying that what they did was science. Although I was talking about what computer engineering ought to be, at least if it were really to focus on the shaping of computing, rather than what it actually was—the understanding and shaping of computer hardware—any proposal to strip an academic department of what is perceived as its science component rightfully leads to significant concerns.

So, we will proceed here with the traditional notion of the distinction between computer science and engineering as being between hardware versus software, or how computers can be built versus how they can be used. One high-level approach for representing such a distinction in the ME language is then as Δ/C for computer science versus C/Δ for computer engineering. There is an appeal and a natural symmetry in such an approach to representing computer science and engineering, yet it proves to be inadequate in several respects. Let's focus on computer science, which is what I know the best. First, there are good reasons to question whether Δ/C is the right place to start in characterizing academic computer science. Three broad specializations of this expression are clearly within the normal boundaries of computer science: theory and algorithms, C; systems software, such as compilers and operating systems, C/C; and artificial intelligence, s/C. But two other obvious specializations of the expression—l/C and p/C—are more paradigmatically computational science rather than computer science, and even artificial intelligence may only be accepted as nonperipheral by some because of its long history as a key component of the discipline. Second, distributed computing and networking, C^*, would likely be considered more core than would artificial intelligence or other aspects of computational science.

Together, these objections suggest that C/C^*—that is, the rightmost column in the dyadic table, which covers both forms of pure dyadic computing ($C+C$) plus, implicitly by abstraction, monadic computing—might be a more appropriate place to start when characterizing the core of computer science as a discipline. If computational science, with its focus on simulation, were now represented as δ/C, informatics as $\Delta\leftrightarrow C$, and computer engineering as C/Δ, we could get a single expression for the combination of these disciplines as $\Delta\leftrightarrow\delta/C/C^*/\Delta$. Extending the approximate delta to a full delta to cover generically both implementation and simulation yields $\Delta\leftrightarrow\Delta/C/C^*/\Delta$.

This single expression spans monadic computing plus all of the dyadic relationships in table 5.1 under suitable abstraction. It can also be simplified and enhanced in various useful ways. If C/C^* is simplified to just C, we get $\Delta\leftrightarrow\Delta/C/\Delta$. If computer science is now viewed as just C, this expression can be seen as a different way of talking about all of academic computing or as an expression for the basic forms of multidisciplinary computing. If, instead of simplifying the expression, we enhance it by replacing the implemented Δ by Δ/Δ^*, we essentially get a variant of the in-context systems architecture: $\Delta\leftrightarrow\Delta/\Delta^*/C/C^*/\Delta$. Extending the bottommost Δ in the same manner then yields an expression for what the systems hierarchy might look like if it were to include the component band: $\Delta\leftrightarrow\Delta/\Delta^*/C/C^*/\Delta/\Delta^*$.

To a large extent, this all says that building academic computing out of the existing four mainstream disciplines is a reasonable approach. However, significant issues remain. First, in this picture, none of the four traditional disciplines handle true computational implementation of other domains: Δ/C (sans δ/C). Either a new discipline would be required or one of the existing ones would need to be extended beyond its traditional boundaries. Second, disciplines best described as $C/\delta/C$—such as artificial intelligence and artificial life—run into a different problem. They are effectively split between computational science for δ/C—aside from artificial intelligence, which is usually found within computer rather than computational science—and either computer engineering or computer science, depending on where C/δ rightly belongs. C/δ is currently more likely to be found in computer science, because it is all software, but by its expression may more appropriately belong in computer engineering. Third, mixed interaction disciplines, such as human–computer interaction and robotics, would be part of informatics by this mapping, whereas the former currently tends to be within computer or cognitive science, and the latter tends to either be in computer science or in some other engineering discipline, such as electrical or mechanical. Similarly, information technology would show up as a combination of informatics—for the human–computer interaction aspect—plus one of the other three disciplines for the objects that are being created.

Still, given that the existing set of disciplines was not planned in a top-down manner, they do not do too bad a job of covering the computing sciences. The bigger problems arise when universities either (1) lack departments focused on some of these disciplines, and the ones that do exist do not view their own boundaries as being broad enough to cover the missing pieces; or (2) all of the relevant departments exist, but each defines itself too narrowly. This problem of narrow disciplinary and departmental boundaries is a critical one, and one that will get even more problematic as an ever-larger fraction of the field focuses on mixed dyadic and polyadic computing.

In general, as discussed back in chapter 1, drawing narrow boundaries around disciplines and departments causes many forms of interdisciplinary research to fall between the cracks, a result that can be dysfunctional both for scientific progress in general and for the individuals involved in particular. My personal experience with this involved working across two departments on the combination of psychologically motivated artificial intelligence and computational modeling of human cognition: C/s/C. The fact that in some ways I had managed to situate myself outside of the paradigm boundaries drawn by colleagues in both of my home departments, in conjunction with my later decade working on highly multidisciplinary new directions activities, made me a confirmed advocate for broad field boundaries. Computing does, and should, involve everything in which C plays a central role, whether monadic, pure or mixed dyadic, or polyadic computing. Any such area that involves scientific activity—in the broad sense—should be able to find a home in academic computing.

Let's now focus more specifically on computer science departments and on how they organize and describe themselves before returning to the bigger picture of computing as a whole. Computer science departments have historically organized themselves around rather simplistic decompositions of the field; for example, theory, software systems, hardware systems (when these are not assigned to a separate computer engineering department), and artificial intelligence. Such an organization can be mapped directly onto a combination of monadic and dyadic computing: Theory covers much of monadic computing (C), software systems is mostly pure dyadic computing (C+C), hardware systems cover a single cell in the dyadic table (C/P), and artificial intelligence can be considered as covering two cells (s/C and C/s).

This mapping spans monadic computing and pure dyadic computing, plus a smattering of topics in mixed dyadic computing. The rest of mixed dyadic computing, along with most of polyadic computing, is often then either reduced to fringe status in computer science or simply viewed as outside of the pale, although some specific topics may be shoe-horned into the existing buckets by abstracting away their full richness. For example, ubiquitous computing will generally be lumped in with software and/or hardware systems. But, as just discussed, other important topics may be left without an academic home, particularly when there are only computer science and computer engineering departments. Table 5.1, however, not only makes explicit the full breadth of computing—at least for dyadic computing—but also provides an organization over this richness. In the process, it ultimately reveals how these simplistic departmental decompositions can be arbitrary, inhomogeneous, and incomplete.

Partly in response to an early version of the relational architecture, and partly based on an analysis of where it had particular strengths, USC's Computer Science Department reorganized itself in 2002 around four nonstandard topics: *computation, interaction, autonomy,* and *immersion.* Computation was to cover monadic computing (C) plus much of the implementation relationships between computing and the noncomputing domains (C/Δ and Δ/C, except for C/C); it included such topics as theory, algorithms, high-performance computing (including simulation), and exotic implementation technologies for computers (such as neural, molecular, and quantum). Interaction was to cover interactions among computers (C*)—both networking and distributed/grid computing—including situations, such as in figure 4.5, where the interacting computers were part of sensor networks: (P→C)*. Autonomy was to cover the ability of computer systems to operate independently of human control, in the form of artificial intelligence and intelligent robotics: s/C and P⟷s/C in simplistic form, respectively. Immersion was to cover the embedding of people within computational environments, including human–computer interaction, graphics, virtual reality, simulation, and games. Such embedding would have been represented as C[S] or (Δ/C)[S], given the use at that time of square brackets to denote embedding; but now, depending on whether the embedded person is considered to be part of the computational environment—as in many modern games—or just interacting with the computational environment, immersion would be represented as δ/(C⇔S) or δ/C⇔S, respectively.

Although developed independently, these four topics turn out to map reasonably well onto Denning's windows of computing mechanics discussed in the introduction to this chapter: computation to computation, interaction to a combination of communication and coordination, and autonomy to automation. The fit isn't perfect of course, as our notion of computation included not only theory and physical realization but also simulation, and our notion of interaction mapped to two of his windows. His recollection window was not an explicit part of our model but likely would have fallen within interaction, given our work in various forms of distributed databases and information systems. Our notion of immersion could be mapped to part of his interaction window, given that this window included human–computer interaction.

The department did succeed in reorganizing itself along these lines and attracted some positive notice in the process for the innovativeness of this structure. However, the experiment was ultimately a failure. Many people did not understand the subtleties behind the definitions of the areas, nor did they particularly care to do so. They were confused, for example, as to why networking was part of interaction, given that interaction to most computer scientists refers to human–computer interaction. Nor could they understand why human–computer interaction, the standard interaction discipline, would be part of immersion rather than interaction. This ultimately led to *regularizing* the topics, by mapping them onto more conventional areas: computation onto theory, interaction onto systems, autonomy onto artificial intelligence, and immersion onto graphics. Although the novel labels remained for some time as a means of grouping the faculty and research in the department, they no longer reflected much that was actually different from the norm.

By 2009, the USC Computer Science Department had again been reorganized, this time into seven groups: (1) artificial intelligence, agents, natural language, and vision; (2) databases and information management; (3) graphics, games, and multimedia; (4) robotics, brain theory, and computational neuroscience; (5) software systems and engineering; (6) systems, distributed systems, and communication networks; and (7) theory and computational sciences.[42] This is a variation on a second strategy used by various departments of describing themselves in terms of long, explicit lists of areas of interest to their faculty.

Seven isn't a huge number of areas in this context. The Computer Science Department at the University of Texas as Austin lists twelve areas.[43] The Electrical Engineering and Computer Science Department at the University of California, Berkeley, lists twenty areas,[44] and the equivalent department at the Massachusetts Institute of Technology lists twenty-three,[45] although MIT actually goes even further by stating that it has "many, many more." The Computer Science Department at the University of Illinois at Urbana-Champaign is the champion, however, at least out of those I have looked at, listing thirty-six areas.[46] But the names for each of USC's seven areas are themselves simply lists of between one and four topics each, for a total listing of nineteen topics and a position among the leaders in list size (although structured hierarchically for some organizational gain).

Each of USC's seven areas, along with each of its actual list of nineteen topics, could conceivably be described in ME, but this by itself would lend only marginal coherence to the department's portrayal of itself. In general, such a laundry-list approach is comforting for faculty—it enables them to pursue their academic lives within their self-described affinity groups—and leaves little room for doubt what the department does, but it does a disservice to anyone who wants to understand computing in general or the department's principal research foci. What is needed is either a list with fewer areas or more structure over the areas.

One strategy for reducing the number of areas is to impose more constrained boundaries on computer science so that it inherently encompasses fewer subdisciplines. For example, if it were defined strictly as C/C*, it would admit within the boundary only monadic plus pure dyadic computing, covering all of computing that has no multidisciplinary flavor to it. A more open variation would be to accommodate some multidisciplinary work, but only as long as the across-domain relationships are *in service of computing*. Under such a regime, quantum computing (C/P) would be allowed because it both yields radically new types of computers and drives the development of fundamentally new kinds of algorithms for core computing problems. In contrast, simulation (δ/C) would not be included because it is primarily a use of computing in service of some other field, even though work in such an area may provide a range of fundamental challenges for computing itself. This kind of definition ends up keeping most, if not all, of informatics and computational science outside the pale of computer science.

The most inclusive form of definition for computer science would be to include all of computing science. What I would argue for is either computer science departments that accept this last broad definition, in terms of all of computing science, or the institution of schools or colleges that define themselves in this fashion (with computer science then being just one computing discipline within a broader such organization). Given the identification of computing as a great scientific domain, the latter actually seems the most appropriate choice in most cases. Either way, however, this does not mean that every department, school, or college must pursue every topic within these broad boundaries. Most are simply too small for this and thus need to focus their resources on a smaller set of topics where they can reach critical mass. But the justification for not covering a topic within this boundary should not be that it is outside of the realm of computing or even of academic computing. My hope instead is that the relational approach, and possibly even the dyadic table and the ME language, will enable departments to tell more coherent and interesting stories about what they do while still acknowledging the ever increasing importance of the diversity within the computing sciences provided by mixed dyadic and polyadic computing.

One such possibility would be to start with the top-level structure outlined via heavy borders in table 5.6. This partitions computing into five broad bins that cover all of monadic computing—which is shoe-horned into a new cell in the top left corner—and dyadic computing, plus the more homogeneous aspects of polyadic computing: (1) C, monadic computing; (2) C/C, pure implementation; (3) C*, pure interaction; (4) {P,S,L}/C/{P,S,L}, mixed implementation; and (5) C↔{P,S,L}, mixed interaction.

The mixed implementation and interaction bins require a bit more explanation. The ideal structure for mixed implementation would appear to be a matrix, as indicated internally by the gray borders within this bin. The idea is that there are important commonalities in both the horizontal and vertical dimensions here. Horizontally, there are significant commonalities across the different approaches to implementing computers and across the various forms of computational implementation/simulation. Hopefully, this came across when these two topics were discussed in chapter 3. Vertically, there can be a strong commonality of knowledge and techniques underlying the two implementation directions when the same noncomputing domain is involved, whether cast in terms of P/C/P or C/p/C, L/C/L or C/l/C, or S/C/S or C/s/C. This cuts across both hardware and computational science, also including areas such as artificial intelli-

Table 5.6

Possible top-level structure for academic computing based on a partitioning of monadic, dyadic, and the more homogeneous regions of polyadic computing

C: theory, algorithms	C+P	C+L	C+S	C+C
C/Δ	Mechanical, electromechanical, electronic, optical, quantum, chemical, precomputing, analog	Phylogenetic, ontogenetic, immunologic, neural, collective, biomolecular, evolutionary, autonomic, swarm, biomimetics	Human cognition, mechanical Turks, Wizard of Oz, crowdsourcing, artificial intelligence	Compilers, OS, emulation, reflection, abstractions, procedures, architectures, languages, databases
Δ/C	Computational science, graphics, numerical analysis, virtual environments, digital physics	Artificial life, systems biology, neural networks, virtual humans	Artificial intelligence, cognitive modeling, computational sociology, econometrics	
C←Δ	Sensors, scanners, computer vision, optical character recognition, localization	Eye, gesture, expression and movement tracking, biosensors	IT industry (hardware and software), input devices, learning, authorization, speech understanding	Networking, security, parallel and distributed computing, grids, clouds, multirobot and multiagent systems, automated programming and debugging, self-monitoring
C↔Δ	Robots, informatics	Brain-computer interfaces, assistive robotics, bio/medical informatics	Computer and software engineering, human-computer interaction, full immersion, games, natural language, social robotics	
C→Δ	Locomotion, fabrication, manipulation	Bioeffectors, haptics, sensory immersion	Presentation, screens, printers, graphics, speech generation, cognitive augmentation, computational thinking	

gence, neural networks, and the pair of biomimetics and systems biology. If it were to prove possible to create such a matrix structure in academia, it might enable the necessary interactions in both directions.

Within mixed interaction, the same gray borders can be found across the horizontal dimension of domains, representing the same form of sharing that can occur within each direction of interaction. The wavy borders partitioning the vertical dimension, of directionality, represent a blending across the border; in particular, that each cell of bidirectional interaction is grounded in the unidirectional interaction cells on either side of it. If this variant form of matrix structure could also prove feasible in an academic environment, it would be ideal for this bin.

Any particular department, school, or college may work across some or all of these bins and may particularly specialize in one or more of them. Further details could then be provided by subdivisions within the bins that correspond to more specialized areas—such as artificial intelligence (s/C/s), systems biology (l/C), and computational physics (p/C), which all reside within mixed implementation. Other less homogeneous polyadic topics, such as intelligent robotics [Δ↔(s↔l)/(P↔C)], would still cross the bin boundaries; in this case including both artificial life [l/(C↔P)] and artificial intelligence (s/C) from mixed implementation and robotics (Δ↔C) from mixed interaction. But if broad boundaries were used here for bins, any topic that has a bin as part of its expression would be considered part of the bin. Intelligent robotics would thus be welcome within both mixed implementation and mixed interaction and also within both the artificial life and artificial intelligence parts of mixed implementation.

In summary, in this analysis all three macrostructure forms are leveraged in understanding academic computing, providing multiple perspectives on it. A pitch is also made for defining coverage boundaries broadly and more coherently. Most importantly, we need to be sure that academic computing is structured in a manner that will facilitate rather than impede the doubt-less future of increased polyadic computing. Changes here will not be easy, but inaction would be increasingly damaging.

6 Computing as a Great Scientific Domain

In the preface and chapter 1, the notion of a *great scientific domain* was introduced as comprising the understanding and shaping of a significant domain of content. The computing sciences were assumed to provide one such domain, with the physical, life, and social sciences providing the other three. The equivalence this implies between the computing sciences and the three more traditional domains provides part of the motivation and rationale for the relational approach that is explored in this book, although neither the approach itself nor the results produced by it literally depend on the validity of this assumption. Still, the relational approach is more compelling if computing is in fact the fourth great scientific domain. And, beyond this, the truth of such a claim could have a major impact, independently of the relational approach, on how computing is viewed by people both within and without the field. This could ultimately be of more importance to the field than the relational approach itself, despite the latter underlying much of the novel technical material in this book.

In this chapter, we examine this claim in more depth, both looking further into what it means to be a great scientific domain and evaluating the extent to which computing qualifies. This starts, in section 6.1, with a crisper definition of a great scientific domain that provides criteria for membership in the set of such domains. Although this definition is new, it is in large part intended to correspond to the traditional, albeit informal and implicit, notions that underlie how we think about the physical, life, and social sciences. The material here takes off from the earlier discussion on science and great scientific domains, where the inclusion of both understanding and shaping was proposed and the traditional top-level distinction between natural and artificial was criticized. This gets us fully back into philosophy of science, with all of the caveats about such an activity mentioned then.

This material is also partially derived from my reflections on computing as a scientific domain, introducing considerations that have been central to computing since its inception but that may not typically be part of the thinking about the three traditional domains. As mentioned in the preface, this does introduce some circularity into the overall process of defining great scientific domains and then evaluating whether computing is such a domain according to whether or not it meets the definition. To break this circularity requires a judgment that the definition is appropriate on its own, irrespective of what was considered in developing it. The discussion surrounding this definition is intended to contribute to such a judgment.

After the definition of a great scientific domain, the remaining step is to evaluate whether computing meets it (section 6.2). This material does not by itself remove the circularity just discussed, but it does argue for computing being a great scientific domain under the assumption that the definition is accepted. It also explores the proposal that mathematics, rather than being either a great scientific domain itself or not part of science at all, is properly part of the computing sciences.

Each of these two steps may be controversial in its own way. The definition of a great scientific domain likely includes both more and less than what many might think should qualify, including a nontraditional broadening of what is considered science and the elimination of several major candidates for status as great scientific domains. As part of the evaluation of computing as a great scientific domain, the proposal to subsume mathematics within the computing sciences may raise controversy within the mathematics community. But neither of these discussions is intended as the last word on their respective topics; rather, each is instead intended to raise important issues and to initiate discussions on them. The hope is that even readers who do not agree with the proposals as stated will be motivated to think along new lines and that this will ultimately help move forward our understanding.

This chapter could quite logically end with the second step, of evaluating computing as a great scientific domain in section 6.2. But it seemed useful to include a bit of a final diversion at this point—a relational analysis of *Time* magazine's "Best Inventions of the Year" for 2007–2009—before wrapping everything up in chapter 7. Inventions are more about shaping than understanding, but shaping is fully part of a great scientific domain according to the definition provided here; and, even without this, the ability to shape is a major indication of the level of understanding. The ability to yield useful inventions also says much about the significance of a domain. Thus, in examining these inventions, we will attend to the percentage that involves computing as one indicator of both our level of understanding of the domain and of the domain's importance. *Time's* selections are by no means limited to computing, intending to cover the best inventions across the board. For example, in 2007 they covered everything from a Spandex space suit[1] to a new steam engine for cars.[2] However, computing does often play a key role.

We will also use this analysis as a form of final exam for the relational approach, exploring the degree to which these annual lists of inventions, as developed by *Time* magazine rather than by me, are representable within the metascience expression (ME) language and the extent to which these expressions reflect the hypothesized present-and-future importance of polyadic computing. These lists are also provided simply because they are fun and provide a bit of a wow factor. They thus serve to pull us back up from the hard slogging through philosophy of science embodied in the rest of this penultimate chapter and refocus us back on the exciting present and future of the computing sciences.

6.1 Great Scientific Domains

In its essence, a great scientific domain concerns the *understanding and shaping of the interactions among a coherent, distinctive, and extensive body of structures and processes*. This definition maintains the combination of understanding and shaping that we saw earlier but goes beyond the vague notion of a significant domain of content to interactions among a body of structures and processes, where the structures and processes must be sufficiently coherent, distinctive, and extensive. The most critical extension is the focus on interactions among structures and processes. Both structures and processes were discussed briefly in chapter 1 and used in characterizing the form taken by the subject matter of scientific domains. Interaction between them was glossed over there, but here it becomes central; although such interactions are not required for science itself to be occurring, they are at the core of the richness inherent to a great scientific domain. We will expand on this further in this section as we go through the definition piece by piece and apply it to the existing three domains. This implies that there will be some repetition of earlier material in order to be complete here, but it will be kept to as little as possible.

To start, the critical role of *understanding* in a great scientific domain goes without saying. Without it, there cannot be the least pretension toward being a science. The key nonstandard aspect here is that, as mentioned in chapter 1, I have come to accept the notion that any enterprise that *tends to increase our understanding of the world over time* should be considered as essentially scientific, and thus part of science. This is not intended to be a precise philosophical statement but a pragmatically useful notion that focuses on whether or not an activity—as opposed to a theory—is scientific. Still, if we do contrast it with standard ideas in philosophy of science, we can see that it is more akin to Lakatos's concept of a *progressive research program*[3] than to Popper's focus on *falsifiability*.[4] It is, however, not focused specifically on Lakatos's conception of the role of correct predictions in establishing progressiveness. The ability to make novel correct predictions provides one means of assessing whether the world is better understood over time, but it need not be the only way. This approach is actually closest in spirit to the newer Bayesian approaches to the philosophy of science, where the concern isn't directly with either hypothesis confirmation or falsifiability but with changes in the subjective probability of hypotheses being valid.[5] Changes in such probabilities reflect an increase in understanding.

In general, it is expected that good science in a domain should apply one from among the best methods available for furthering our understanding of the domain. This suggests a form of *methodological pluralism* in which multiple methods may be necessary to increase our understanding of individual domains, and those methods that are best in one domain may not necessarily be best in other domains. However, this need not go anywhere near as far as Feyerabend's *epistemological anarchy*, with its denial of preeminence for any particular methods and its notion that conventional science is just one among many ideologies.[6] It is, for example, possible to rank many methods by the degree of veracity they can guarantee. All else being equal, the stronger such method should be used when applicable.

Domains can be ranked by the strength of the methods they are able effectively to use, with the physical sciences traditionally able to use stronger methods than the life sciences and the life sciences stronger methods than the social sciences. But this should not be confused with a claim that this hierarchy correlates with the quality of the science pursued within the domain. We have the need to understand all of these domains, and good science is equally possible within each based on the best methods available for them. Of course, even good science can be relatively unproductive if the best methods available in a domain are insufficient to increase our understanding of it to any significant extent.

Using poor methods when better ones are available is one of the hallmarks of bad science, as is misuse of even the best methods. At some point, bad science crosses over into the realm of non-science, although the line of demarcation may not be clear as the amount of understanding asymptotically approaches zero (and the amount of misunderstanding swamps the amount of understanding). However, what is clear is that there should be no place for either bad science or non-science in science research and education.

My bottom line is that the term *science* is appropriate for all human intellectual endeavors that tend to increase our understanding over time, whether pursued by a restricted set of methods that are geared toward answers with high certainties—such as mathematical proofs and quantitative experiments with accompanying measures of statistical significance—or weaker methods that yield more uncertain progress, yet do yield increases in understanding all the same. This is not intended to advocate for the use of weaker methods when stronger ones are applicable but merely to acknowledge that although the best method for a particular area may be far from perfect, using such a method may still be better than shunning the area as unsuitable for scientific study merely because more rigorous methods do not apply. The critical and analytical approaches common in the humanities, along with the reasoned argument approach favored in much of philosophy, are prime examples of weak but still potentially useful methods in their respective contexts. Such activities do come under the heading of understanding and as such are candidates for participation in great scientific domains.

To some extent, this can be viewed as a return to the original notion of philosophy, or *love of wisdom*, from which modern science descended through the splintering off of natural philosophy. A friend of my son who has recently started a PhD program in philosophy once strove to convince me that philosophy should still be thought of as the generic name, encompassing not only what is currently studied in philosophy but also all of science as well. But philosophy, except for work in areas such as logic, has been associated for so long with primarily very weak methods, focused essentially on argumentation, that it seems too late to put that Humpty Dumpty back together again. Still, whether the generic is called philosophy, or science, or even *Wissenschaft*—a German word for science that includes not only those academic disciplines typically labeled as science in English but also other areas of academic study, such as the humanities[7]—the key point is to consider how our understanding is increased across the full range of subjects of interest, along with the methods best able to increase this understanding.

The concept of *shaping* leads to still more novel territory with respect to a conventional notion of science. The task of shaping the world is generally considered the realm of engineering. However, use of the term *engineering* is conventionally limited to quantitative, mathematical approaches to shaping, leading to a traditional focus in engineering on shaping the physical aspects of the world. Yet, beyond the physical world, humans shape the living world through a range of activities that create, alter, and destroy both plant and animal life. The creation of life is affected by human activities such as agriculture and ranching. Alteration of life occurs, for example, through medical and veterinary interventions in people and animals and through everyday activities—at least for farmers—such as irrigating and fertilizing crops. Destruction of life occurs through hunting, fishing, harvesting, murder, and war. Creation, alteration, and destruction of life are studied in, for example, schools of human and veterinary medicine, where we learn how to alter living bodies through medical interventions; schools of agriculture and departments of horticulture, where people learn to shape the world of plants and animals through selective breeding and other techniques; and military academies and schools, where people learn to disable and kill other people (among other subjects).

None of these activities traditionally go by the name of engineering, and they mostly use methodologies that differ radically from the highly quantitative approaches typical in traditional (physical) engineering, but they all can be thought of as part of a very large and broad domain of *life engineering* that is shaping lives in ever more novel ways. So, too, can work in newer areas, such as synthetic biology,[8] which concerns synthesizing new biological functions and systems, and genetic engineering,[9] in which selective breeding is taken to a high art through direct genetic manipulation. There do exist departments of biomedical engineering and a much smaller assortment of departments of biological engineering, but they by themselves fail to achieve the breadth within the life sciences that traditional schools of engineering achieve within the physical sciences.

Within the social domain, there is a notion of social engineering in political science that has a particular focus on shaping large-scale human attitudes and behavior.[10] The term is also used separately in computing for approaches that scammers use online to mislead people into divulging confidential information, such as in *phishing*, where forged e-mail pretending to be from a legitimate organization or individual solicits confidential information.[11] However, as with the domain of life, the shaping of the social domain has a much richer history under a variety of other names. All human education and training, rearing of children, lawmaking, propaganda and psychological operations, advertising, counseling, and much of

Table 6.1
Quadrant model of scientific research

		Considerations for Use?	
		No	Yes
Quest for Fundamental Understanding?	Yes	Pure basic research (Bohr)	Use-inspired basic research (Pasteur)
	No		Pure applied research (Edison)

speech, discussion, and argumentation may in reality also be considered aspects of a much more broadly defined domain of social engineering. These are all activities that can shape the thoughts and behavior of human individuals and groups. The synthetic, performance aspects of the humanities—which study, for example, how to write books and paint portraits—as well as the study of how the resulting artifacts can affect individuals and society, can also be considered part of social engineering.

The distinction between science and engineering can be thought about in a number of different ways. Sometimes it is considered as a difference between *basic* (or *pure*) and *applied* work. Denying the fundamental nature of this distinction for the research enterprise was the basis of *Pasteur's quadrant*, which refactored the research spectrum into two orthogonal dimensions, as reproduced in table 6.1.[12] The traditional basic versus applied distinction corresponds to the main diagonal of this table, but the book advocates more of a focus on the top right quadrant, where the French scientist Louis Pasteur stands as an example of *use-inspired basic research*. Essentially, Stokes is arguing for the necessity of a particular form of combination of understanding and shaping.

One of the ironies of use-inspired research—whether basic or applied, or considered as engineering science—being deprecated as in some manner less respectable than pure science, is that the former needs to be held up to stronger guarantees of veracity—and thus must limit itself more assiduously to stronger methods—than the latter. The more understanding is to be used in service of shaping, and the more critical is the shaping, the more confidence is required in the results. Pure basic research can muddle along tolerably well for quite some time with relatively weak methods, but when the results are to be applied, confidence is no longer an armchair game. This is true when the shaping is to occur within the same domain, such as when the understanding of physics is to be leveraged in designing a bridge.

But it is just as true, and sometimes even more crucial, when understanding from one domain is to support shaping in another; such as when knowledge from the physical, life, or computing domain is to be used in formulating laws, regulations, and policies within the social domain. Thus, use-inspired research (or engineering science) has more of an intrinsic driver toward strong methods than does pure research (or basic science). In basic science, the preference for strong methods is culturally driven, whereas in engineering science it is driven by the inherent logic of use.

A different way of viewing the distinction between science and engineering is as *knowing what* versus *knowing how*; or, equivalently, of understanding facts versus procedures. This perspective casts both as forms of understanding—just of different forms of knowledge—and thus can be used to make the case that engineering should really be thought of as one aspect of a broader understanding-based notion of science. Although this is an important point to acknowledge, such a notion still leaves much of shaping outside of science.

The distinction in this book between understanding and shaping concerns the nature of the relationship between people—whether called scientists or engineers—and the domain of interest.[13] As discussed in chapter 5, the people who devote their lives to working with scientific domains are part of the social domain and thus not part of their domain of study itself—unless of course they are either social scientists or life scientists studying human bodies—however, they do interact with their chosen domain, yielding a flow of influence from the domain to the person, from the person to the domain, or in both directions. Understanding is a flow of influence from a domain to a person: $\Delta \rightarrow S$. This notion captures the essence of what science is about (i.e., learning about the world from the world) while glossing over any a priori distinctions concerning which domains may be considered sciences, which methods may be considered scientific, or which people are doing the understanding. Shaping is a reverse flow of influence, from a person to a domain: $S \rightarrow \Delta$. It captures the essence of engineering—how people alter both themselves and the world around them—but bears the same relationship to it as does understanding to science. Bringing understanding and shaping together enables bidirectional, interactive flow between people and the world: $S \leftrightarrow \Delta$. Understanding and shaping can be mapped onto the two dimensions in Pasteur's quadrant if shaping is mapped onto use, but use really concerns one's goals rather than one's actions. In truth, both understanding and shaping may be use-inspired or not.

This approach yields a different way of cutting up the scientific pie that makes particular sense when examining computing, but which need not be limited to just that domain. It should be clear that the physical, life, and social domains each comprises a broad swath of understanding and shaping activities. Rather than labeling a subset of these activities as science and using a miscellany of labels for shaping, the idea is to include both activities within each great scientific domain. This takes a cue from the computing sciences, where these activities are inherently intertwined. It also leverages the additional notions from chapter 1 that such intertwining has actually accelerated progress in computing and that the other domains are heading inevitably in this direction.

But what exactly can each domain be said to understand and shape? Are there any constraints on what may be the subject matter of a great domain? This is where the key additional feature of the definition, concerning the *interactions* among *structures* and *processes*, comes to the fore. This clause is not intended to imply that interactions are the only phenomena of relevance within a great scientific domain. Instead, it signifies that a domain cannot be a great scientific domain unless it includes significant interactions among structures and processes. Structures are the things of interest in a scientific domain, comprising such things as subatomic particles, atoms, molecules, rocks, rivers, planets, and stars in the physical sciences; organic molecules, cells, organs, organisms, and (non-human) social groups in the life sciences; and people, their minds, and the articles that they produce and use in the social sciences. Structures need not be physically embodied, potentially including pure abstractions, such as the concept of beauty or a theorem in mathematics, but can be difficult to understand and shape unless they are embodied in some form that enables them to be shared and preserved. Processes actively alter structures over time. This includes elementary forces, chemical reactions, the creation and erosion of landmasses, and the birth and evolution of the cosmos in the physical sciences; the creation, evolution, maintenance, and death of organisms and their components in the life sciences; and varying genres of cognition and behavior in the social sciences.

There is a richness and vitality in each of the great scientific domains that arises from the interactions among its structures and processes. It is difficult to imagine processes without structures on which they can operate. There are, however, important intellectual domains that possess significant structure with little to no process. The humanities are a prime example. According to one definition, the humanities are "Those branches of knowledge, such as philosophy, literature, and art, that are concerned with human thought and culture; the liberal arts."[14] They clearly fall within the broad realm of understanding—and of shaping as well, as they involve the creation of artifacts and the molding of minds—although they are not conventionally considered a science and certainly not a part of engineering.

The humanities are full of structures—books, paintings, statues, and so forth—and analyses of such structures, but there is little process to interact with these structures. When there is process, it is principally the human activity involved in the creation and analysis of the structures. The study of human activity, however, is properly within the domain of the social sciences as broadly construed. Without processes, the humanities yield a *static domain* that falls short of the scientific fertility produced by *dynamic domains* in which processes are also central components. Without processes, there is little or no need for experiments. Analysis and theory have roles in a static science—as they do in the humanities—in dissecting and explaining the domain's structures, but experiments exist to illuminate the inner workings of complex processes and their interactions with structures. Essentially, experiments enable understanding of the consequences of interactions by running the world to see what happens.

The ability to run controlled experiments is often taken as a defining characteristic of science, and the relative inability of some scientific fields— such as those concerned with the past—to do so has been used as a criticism of them. A focus on dynamics explains why experiments are so important in science, but it also implies that the ability to perform experiments is a second-order criterion. Dynamics are central to a great scientific domain, and it can be hard—although not necessarily impossible—to make significant progress in a dynamic domain without the ability to perform experiments. Like historical domains, static domains also have little room for experiments, but for them it is because experiments generally are not useful rather than because they cannot be performed.

Although a static domain such as the humanities can be of undoubted intellectual and pragmatic importance, it does not possess the additional richness yielded by active processes and thus, according to the definition here, cannot on its own amount to a great scientific domain. Such a domain still can, however, comprise a scientific enterprise that tends to increase our understanding over time and even form an important component of a more comprehensive domain that does fully embrace interactions among structures and processes. Given the focus of the humanities on human thought and culture, it seems to make the most sense to include them as part of the social domain. Within the social sciences, the humanities would then focus on structures that are not necessarily of great functional utility but that help to reveal the essential human condition. The analytical and critical methods of the humanities are attuned to dealing with such structures, where the stronger methods used in other parts of the social sciences may be unavailable.

What about mathematics? It clearly possesses the rigor of the most stringent sciences and plays a central role as a tool in all of the sciences. People do refer to the mathematical sciences, or to the formal sciences, which "are the branches of knowledge that are concerned with formal systems, such as logic, mathematics, theoretical computer science, information theory, systems theory, decision theory, statistics, and some aspects of linguistics."[15] I even received my BS in mathematical sciences—although, in contrast to a pure mathematics major, mathematical sciences at Stanford also included computer science, which had not yet been separated into its own undergraduate major, plus statistics and operations research. Yet mathematics never fit as a discipline within the physical, life, or social sciences. Nor has it seemed to many quite like a scientific domain all on its own. There has in fact been a long-standing ambivalence over whether mathematics should be considered a science. One possible explanation for this awkward status is that mathematics is largely a *static science of the artificial*.

As with the humanities, mathematics concentrates on structure. Mathematics can be defined as "the systematic treatment of magnitude, relationships between figures and forms, and relations between quantities expressed symbolically."[16] There is a process in mathematics, *proof*, which generates new structures (proved theorems) from existing structures (axioms); however, proof is a process engaged in by mathematicians—or occasionally by computers—rather than being a process in the domain of study itself. Mathematics may also be used to model the dynamics of processes via sets of equations, but again the processes being modeled are not themselves part of mathematics. The descriptions of processes (models) and products of processes (proofs) can be part of the domain of mathematics, but these are static descriptions—structures—rather than processes. Thus, according to our definition, mathematics is not a great scientific domain. It is more like the humanities in being a static domain that is essentially all about structures. In consequence, it is also like the humanities in lacking a significant experimental component.

Mathematics is artificial because its structures—expressions, equations, theorems, proofs, and so forth—are human made. Some have argued that mathematical expressions are reflections of abstract but unobservable truths of the universe, so that what mathematicians study is no more human made than is the subject matter of the physical, life, and social sciences. Such an argument, based essentially on the reality (but unobservability) of Platonic ideals, can in fact be made for anything traditionally considered artificial and conceivably could thus be marshaled as another general argument against the distinction between natural and artificial. However, the important point—that there is doubt about mathematics as a science because its structures are not generally observable in the world without human shaping, and that this is thus akin to the concerns some people have about computing as a science—is independent of whether the subject matter is considered artificial versus natural but unobservable.

Despite being both static and artificial, mathematics obviously fits the model of science used in this book—it has clearly increased our understanding in many ways. The next section contains a proposal for resolving the long-standing conundrum of the relationship of mathematics to science by including it as a static component of the computing sciences.

Beyond requiring the dynamics of interactions among structures and processes, the definition of a great scientific domain also demands that the body of structures and processes be coherent, distinctive, and extensive. *Coherence* is straightforward. The domain should encompass a related body of material rather than consist of a disparate amalgam of topics. For the three traditional domains, their coherence is succinctly reflected in their single-word names: physical, life, and social. Although single-word names can in theory cloak complexly disjunctive concepts, they do not appear to do so here. *Distinctiveness* requires that the domain possess a core body of structures and processes that are different from those studied by the other great domains. This is not to say that the great scientific domains must be completely disjoint—in fact, the significance of overlaps among domains is central to the relational approach—but that their core questions and methods should be sufficiently distinct from each other to enable a significant distance to be maintained among them. Without this, two domains would best be thought of in combination as a single great scientific domain rather than as distinct great domains. *Extensiveness* requires that the domain's core body of distinct material be sufficiently large to justify the appellation of *great*. Without it, the domain would be relatively insignificant scientifically.

All three of the traditional great scientific domains meet these additional requirements. Given that only two life science disciplines are itemized in figure 1.1, you might be led to question whether it is sufficiently extensive to be a great scientific domain. In fact, the life sciences are some-times bundled with the physical sciences into the single larger domain of the *natural sciences*. However, biology is quite distinct in subject matter and methodology from the physical sciences and is furthermore at least as rich in subject matter as the physical sciences are en masse. The fact that there are few top-level disciplines listed within the domain seems to be more of a historical accident, in terms of how the domain developed and how pieces of it were labeled, than an indication that it should be subjugated within a single broader domain.

One intriguing discipline that does not fully meet the three additional requirements is philosophy. Although philosophy may be considered as part of the humanities, it is important enough in the history of science, and different enough from the mainstream of humanities, to deserve its own discussion. To begin, philosophy is definitely extensive, being—or at one time having been—concerned with a wide variety of important topics, from ethics to meaning, mind, existence, and origins. Its subject matter is also largely distinct from that of the other domains, with many of its topics being ones that no other domain is willing or able to approach. Although there are across-domain overlaps, such as in a concern with the human mind, this is no different in kind from the overlaps that can occur among the other domains.

A key problem from the perspective of the additional requirements is that, as currently constituted, philosophy is incoherent in the set of topics it covers; it covers bits and pieces from all over the map. It seems likely that this stems from philosophy having been reduced over the centuries from comprising a scientific domain—or perhaps all scientific domains—to a weak scientific methodology that is based largely on analysis and argu-mentation, at least for the form of analytic philosophy that dominates in English-speaking countries.[17] The philosopher Alex Rosenberg captured this nicely in saying that philosophy's "major components are easy to list, and the subjects of some of them are even relatively easy to understand. The trouble is trying to figure out what they have to do with one another, why combined they constitute one discipline—philosophy, [sic] instead of being parts of other subjects, or their own independent areas of inquiry."[18]

As an outsider looking in on the history of philosophy, I do see signifi-cant contributions to our understanding in formulating certain classes of important questions and in suggesting, exploring, and criticizing potential answers to them. But its methods—other than logic, which more properly seems to belong with mathematics—are not generally strong enough to yield definitive answers to questions. As stronger methods have been developed in various domains, these domains separated from philosophy—as natural philosophy became natural science—leaving the discipline of philosophy with a patchwork of topics not amenable to stronger methods. Philosophy thus appears to have become a *Swiss cheese discipline*, full of holes where it used to own the content. Rosenberg actually provides a definition of philosophy that matches this notion almost exactly. He claims that philosophy deals with two sets of questions: "First, the questions that science—physical, biological, social, behavioral—cannot answer now and perhaps may never be able to answer. Second, the questions about why the sciences cannot answer the first lot of questions."[19]

Under such circumstances, when overlaps exist with disciplines that use stronger methods, the conflict can be problematic for philosophy. Instead of being a coherent scientific domain at this point, philosophy is instead a weak methodology applied to a set of topics brought together only by being amenable to no stronger methods. Although such an activity can still be important and useful, this conclusion does imply that not only is philosophy not—at least any longer—a great scientific domain itself, but also that it does not fit within any one of the extant domains. Instead it is a combination of a methodology that is potentially usable in any domain plus a disparate set of domain fragments.

Philosophy is thus part of science but limited to topics that (1) fall within the four great scientific domains while remaining outside the applicability of the accepted methods within these domains or (2) fall outside of the four domains. Given that philosophy is part of science, it should be clear how philosophy of science can be considered as part of a broader discipline of *metascience*—which concerns the understanding and shaping of science itself via a range of methods that include but are not limited to those of philosophy—and thus how the ME language received its name.

Philosophy's status provides an interesting contrast with the humanities. The humanities were defined earlier in terms of their subject matter, but they also embody a characteristic analytical method that has been developed for investigating this subject matter. It is possible to view the humanities as focused on this method, rather than on its traditional subject matter, with the method then being exploitable wherever it might be applicable. The development of critical code studies, where the analytical method is applied to the understanding of computer programming, can be viewed as such a stretch, although it can alternatively be considered as a within-domain extension if we reconceive of computer programs as cultural artifacts.

Generally, given what has happened to philosophy by becoming ori-ented around a method rather than a subject, it could be dangerous for the humanities to go down the same path. Philosophy seems to have become a prime example of a discipline with what can only be called a *perverse definition*. By, at least implicitly, defining the field in terms of a weak scientific method, any time one of its domains of study becomes amenable to stronger methods, it is no longer part of philosophy. Thus, progress in science, or in this case scientific methodology, can weaken the field. Limiting the set of scientific methods acceptable within a domain is always risky, but it in particular becomes perverse in cases where stronger methods are, or could become, available.

It is important to note, however, that a perverse field definition, such as the one discussed here for philosophy, says nothing in and of itself about the quality of scientific work produced by the field; it merely concerns the nature of the boundaries drawn around the field. There may also be other definitions of the same field that are immune from such a problem. For example, defining philosophy in terms of "the study of general and fun-damental problems, such as those connected with existence, knowledge, values, reason, mind, and language"[20] attempts to lay out the subject matter of modern philosophy directly, in this case focusing mostly on issues within the social domain. The intended source of coherence here is the limitation to *general and fundamental problems*. Unfortunately, however, this is a rather vague notion that could include many other topics—such as the origins of life—that are not now listed, presumably because they are now being approached via stronger methods. Even worse, the same source goes on to say that "Philosophy is distinguished from other ways of addressing such problems by its critical, generally systematic approach and its reliance on rational argument," bringing the perverse aspect fully back into the definition.

If, in general, we take a discipline to be perversely defined whenever scientific progress can weaken it, we also reach an important lesson for artificial intelligence (AI), a part of computing for which perverse defini-tions have been rife. One classical definition of AI is "The study of how to make computers do things at which, at the moment, people are better."[21] This definition was intended to provide a pragmatic way of delimiting what the field covered without getting lost in philosophical intricacies, but if taken seriously it means that whenever the field succeeds in getting a computer to do something as well as a human it is no longer part of AI. This definition thus restricts AI to the margins of understanding, largely denying it the ability to become a cumulative discipline embodying within-discipline successes upon which it can build.

Although this definition is perverse, its source of perversity is not the same as that for philosophy, as it does not embody a methodological limitation. However, a second perverse way of defining AI does impose methodological limitations, in terms of the kinds of technologies that are acceptable within AI. Most typically, this has limited AI to symbolic approaches to intelligence, focused on representations, or even more narrowly to logical approaches. Both of these restrictions eliminate, for example, approaches based on statistical or neural models, risking the field's becoming irrelevant as success with such methods grows.

When these two forms of perversity are combined, we can end up with the notion that any technology well enough understood so as to be algorithmic is no longer AI. Or, in other words, a computational system is only intelligent if we cannot understand it. Such a notion has been used, for example, to try to deny that the Deep Blue chess program[22] was an instance of AI. This denial was not because Deep Blue could now play chess as well as people—succumbing to the first perverse definition above—but because the search algorithms and other techniques that it used were by then well understood. Fortunately, most of these perverse forms of definition were never accepted by more than a fraction of the field of AI, or were limited to people outside of the field, or were eventually dropped as the field matured. They therefore did not end up as permanent traps.

What about theology, the study of God? Notably, it actually—and perhaps surprisingly—seems to fulfill the definition provided at the beginning of this section and thus could be a candidate for a great scientific domain. It has, however, shared the perversity of philosophy at times, such as when its focus has been on supernatural explanations of perceptible phenomena. Once stronger methods became available for studying these phenomena, theology became irrelevant to them, and the scope of theological applicability shrank. But even when limited to areas in which stronger methods have not been applicable, such as the nature of God, there is a more fundamental question of whether theology is scientific in the sense of tending to increase our understanding over time. If God does not exist, then it is either the study of nothing, and cannot fulfill this criterion, or it is the study of human imaginings of God, which properly belongs within the social domain. If God does exist, there would still be a real question as to whether theology actually is helping us understand him/her/it better over time and how we would know whether or not it is actually doing so. Without some form of demonstrably increasing understanding, it isn't a science. Still, it is worth noting that even theology can be discussed in these same terms.

In defining great scientific domains, the greatness of a domain has been concentrated in the combination of understanding and shaping, the prevalence of dynamics (i.e., interactions among structures and processes) and the extensiveness of the subject matter. The depth[23] and importance of the questions at the heart of the domain have not been considered explicitly as criteria, nor has the surprisingness of the answers provided to these questions. These issues have been taken for granted mostly because of an assumption on my part that any domain meeting the other criteria will answer questions of sufficient depth and yield results of sufficient importance that occasionally surprise us that these need not be stated explicitly as part of the definition. If this assumption ultimately proves not to hold, modifications of the definition would be needed.

In summary, the definition provided here stretches the normal boundaries of how we view scientific domains in (1) how broadly it construes the process of understanding that is at the heart of science; (2) the inclusion of shaping as well as understanding within great scientific domains; and (3) a focus on significant interactions among structures and processes as the key to greatness. It maps well onto the three traditional great domains while making specific recommendations about the positioning of other subject areas that might have been considered a priori for inclusion as great scientific domains but that do not meet the criteria specified by the definition. This definition is likely to be controversial in a number of ways and may need to continue to evolve over time, but it at least gives us a basis on which to ask about the status of computing in the next section. It also, more generally, provides a coherent top-level organization over much of human intellectual activity—whether normally considered science, engineering, humanities, or one of the professions—upon which the relational approach then builds further organization and insights.

6.2 Computing

Does computing form the basis for a great scientific domain? As with the three traditional domains, this question is best answered in pieces, starting with the combination of understanding and shaping and then proceeding through interactions, coherence, distinctiveness, and extensiveness. We will also return in this section to the question of how mathematics fits into the sciences.

The drive to understand is at the heart of the theoretical and experimental segments of the computing sciences, whether the goal is to understand if **P=NP**, a core problem in theoretical computer science mentioned in chapter 2, or whether it is to understand the principles for designing better computer architectures.[24] The first goal is a highly abstract one, whose answer will almost certainly take the form of a mathematical proof. The second goal involves principles, but for real working objects. Achieving such a goal generally involves detailed experimentation with existing artifacts—computers in this case—plus possibly the design and construction of new artifacts, whether real or simulated, that enable further experimentation, including focused hypothesis testing. This is the kind of activity that leads to thinking about computing as a science of the artificial, or as engineering science, as it is focused on understanding man-made artifacts and how to improve them. The term *ergalics* has recently been coined to refer specifically to the process of understanding computational tools and artifacts, with the goal of developing predictive models for them.[25] However, this term is not generally accepted at this point, and understanding in computing can also take the form of puzzling out the nature of computing that occurs in the natural world, whether in biological systems or the universe as a whole. All of this is understanding and a core part of the science of computing.

Much of the understanding in computing is in service of shaping, as with the computer architecture example above. Other parts are more directly driven by an abstract need to understand. Determining whether **P=NP** may have a huge practical impact if it turns out that **P** actually equals **NP**—many important problems that are infeasible to solve at present could become tractable—but the more likely answer, that **P≠NP**, may end up being of purely theoretical interest. In the reverse direction, some shaping within computing is in service of understanding. Much of the systems side of academic computing is focused on the construction of research prototypes in support of analysis and experimentation and ultimately of understanding. But this is dwarfed by the shaping that goes on in industry in creating hardware and software products for the market. Because shaping is thus such a significant and obvious segment of computing, little more needs to be said about it here.

One question I have been asked in the context of this work, and which was mentioned in passing back in chapter 1, is whether computing is just a form of engineering rather than a great scientific domain. The notion is that, sure, there is some science that gets done as part of the engineering, but it is *just* engineering science—of secondary importance and in a subordinate position—rather than being either a full partner with engineering or of major significance overall in the world of science. Were this true, computing would mostly amount to shaping, with a bit of subsidiary understanding, and may not qualify as a great scientific domain.

A good analogy for this view of computing would be premodern medicine. It engaged in significant shaping of human life with a very primitive understanding of the underlying biology, yet even then it was not inherently just a form of engineering, in the sense of *life engineering* discussed earlier. It was instead part of an incipient great scientific domain, concerned with understanding and shaping a distinct body of material, but with an as-yet-underdeveloped base of understanding. Social science has similar issues; although for them there is a significant body of understanding, it just does not always relate as well as could be desired to the kinds of shaping attempted in areas such as education and economics. Yet, the social sciences still form one of the three traditional great scientific domains.

I could point out the breadth of work that exists in theoretical computer science and throw in all of mathematics, as it will shortly be claimed as part of the domain of computing. There is also much quantitative understanding about various aspects of computing that has come out of experimental computer science. The formulation of ergalics is attempting to take this even a step further, as is Peter Denning's push to articulate the great principles of computing.[26] I will not attempt to survey all of this work to try to make the case more specifically, as what really matters is that the domain of computing concerns a subject matter that has the potential for a full combination of understanding and shaping. Whether or not computing is premodern or modern, à la medicine, it has this potential.

Furthermore, my sense is that this kind of question often comes up because of computing being largely a science of the artificial. There is a tendency on the part of many automatically to label any such domain as engineering because the shaping comes before, and is necessary for, the understanding. The arguments against the fundamental nature of the distinction between natural and artificial (chapter 1), in combination with the identification of a variety of forms of natural computing (section 3.1) and the questions being raised about whether the physical, life, and social domains are fundamentally computational (section 3.2.2), should eventually correct such misunderstandings.

To evaluate the second aspect of the definition of a great scientific domain—concerning interactions among structures and processes—with respect to computing, we must hark back to the definition of computing in chapter 1 as the *transformation of information*. The mapping between structures and processes on the one hand and information transformation on the other is straightforward: Information provides the structures in computing whereas transformation provides the processes. The dynamics implied by their interaction is at the heart of what makes computing what it is—software defines, and hardware executes, complex processes on wide varieties of informational structures. There are subdisciplines of computing that focus almost completely on structures. For example, the field of knowledge representation within artificial intelligence focuses on how formally to represent knowledge about the world. But even there, the intent is ultimately to support reasoning processes that can transform an initial body of knowledge into new information that is more directly useful.

The domain of computing is also *coherent*, as evidenced by the simple non-disjunctive definition provided for it in chapter 1. With respect to *distinctiveness*, the structures and processes embodied by computing can be used to model the structures and processes from the other domains—for example, it is possible to create a computational model of Earth's climate and how it changes—but they are not themselves part of these other domains. Information and its transformation are simply not part of what is studied in the physical, life, or social sciences, except perhaps indirectly, through human information processing, within the social domain.

This is where mathematics comes back into the picture. We have already concluded that mathematics is not a great scientific domain because of its lack of the kinds of complex dynamics that could only arise from having a significant process component to interact with its structures. But the structures at the heart of mathematics are informational, just as are those in computing. Information theory is a branch of mathematics (and engineering) that is focused on the quantification of information. And beyond this, if we review the definition of mathematics provided earlier in this chapter—"the systematic treatment of magnitude, relationships between figures and forms, and relations between quantities expressed symbolically"—a case can be made that all of mathematics is about information. According to the theory of *formalism*, "statements of mathematics and logic can be thought of as statements about the consequences of certain string manipulation rules."[27] In fact, according to such an approach, the content of mathematics and computing are essentially indistinguishable. Some formalists have recently gone so far as to propose that "all of our formal mathematical knowledge should be systematically encoded in computer-readable formats, so as to facilitate automated proof checking of mathematical proofs and the use of interactive theorem proving in the development of mathematical theories and computer software."[28]

The inherently mathematical processes that do exist, such as calculation and proof, are computational, as noticed early on by the British mathematician Alan Turing, one of the most significant figures in the early development of computer science. These processes would traditionally only be performed by people, making experimentation with them difficult and likely keeping the focus on the static structures. Whether or not for this reason, mathematics remained mainly analytical rather than experimental and focused little of its attention on the nature of these processes.

With both mathematics and computing focused on information and its transformation, there appears to be little to distinguish between them except that mathematics has principally limited itself to a region of this overall scientific domain that is concerned with the creation and analysis of (static) informational structures. With the advent of computers, the study of information transformation became more feasible, including the extensive use of experimental methods. Computing has thus been able to expand to cover the full range of interactions between informational structures and processes.

This suggests that computing and mathematics should ultimately be merged into a single domain. In many universities, computing actually grew out of mathematics but then likely had to separate itself from its erstwhile host in order to work more freely outside of the narrowing constraints of mainstream mathematics. If mathematics had instead been more welcoming toward the full extent of information transformation—including the complete range of understanding and shaping activities implicated—along with the methods appropriate for its study, computing may have remained a part of mathematics. In such a case, this domain might have been called the mathematical sciences, in concert with my undergraduate major. However, within the joint focus on information, mathematics has remained focused on its more limited niche of structure creation and analysis, whereas computing took on the more general question of interactions among such structures and processes. For this de facto reason and for the related but more principled reason that great scientific domains are, at their essence, about the dynamics of interaction among structures and processes rather than just about structures, computing appears to be a more appropriate label for this domain.

Subsuming mathematics within the computing sciences in this fashion should enable a rationalization of the study of information transformation while also finally laying to rest the long-standing ambivalence concerning whether mathematics is a science. According to the arguments here, it isn't a great scientific domain on its own, but it is a key analytical component of a domain that is: computing. Its static nature is removed as an issue by its becoming a theoretical facet of a fully active domain, and its artificiality is handled by the earlier arguments about artificiality in computing. Potential worries about computing being again constrained by the more limited methodology in mathematics would need to be dealt with, but with the mass of experimental computing that has been built up since the days when computing was part of mathematics in various universities, this would likely be less of a problem than it was back then.

A less controversial approach might be to consider the fourth domain to be about information rather than computing, with the traditional forms of computing and mathematics then both being part of the domain of information sciences. Computing is, after all, defined in terms of the transformation of information, and the impetus for this work began at the Information Sciences Institute. Still, I am partial to the label computing. I cannot rule out that part of this preference may stem from having grown up in computer science. But there is a deeper reason. The term *information* emphasizes structure and thus connotes a static discipline. Yet a great scientific domain must, by definition, be dynamic. Computing, with its inherently dynamic nature, thus seems more appropriate as the name for a great domain, even if it may be more controversial in application. But, either way, it is the concept that a fourth great scientific domain does exist along the lines described here that is the key idea to take away, with the actual label for it being of secondary importance at best.

The one component of the definition of a great scientific domain not yet discussed is *extensiveness*. The focus here is not on how much science has been done with respect to computing—that question was discussed earlier in the material concerning how central understanding is in computing—but on the breadth of the subject matter covered by the domain. If computing were a meager domain, lacking in sufficient subject matter, it would not be on a par with the other great domains. Fortunately, computing passes this test with flying colors. First, it is worth noting in passing that with the addition of mathematics, computing immediately inherits the existing extensiveness of mathematics. But the two more significant arguments are based on (1) the breadth of computing phenomena that have been produced through the joint efforts of academia and industry (as well as natural forms to a lesser extent) and (2) the breadth of possibilities implied by results from theoretical computer science on universal computing devices.

Consider all that computers currently do and all that we can anticipate them doing in the future. Some of this was mentioned in chapter 1, much more was covered in chapters 3 and 4, and some additional bits found their way into chapter 5. Further discussions of such possibilities can also be found elsewhere, such as in the collection of essays about the future of computing in *The Invisible Future*.[29] Or you can just think about the many roles computers play in your everyday life—from games, to communications, to the control of appliances and cars—to begin to get the picture. The flexibility inherent to universal Turing machines (section 2.1) is critical here. It enables, for example, computers to simulate just about any phenomena present in any of the three other domains (section 3.2.1), including everything from subatomic to astronomical processes within the physical domain; cells, organs, and organisms within the life domain; and human thought processes and behavior within the social domain. It is even conceivable that much of this will eventually go beyond simulation to actual implementations of new bits of reality (section 3.2.2).

At the end of the previous section, it was mentioned that the depth of the questions asked and the importance and surprisingness of the answers generated were currently implicit rather than explicit parts of the definition of a great scientific domain. Just in passing, we can note the depth of questions such as whether there are functions that are uncomputable, whether **P=NP**, and whether the universe is fundamentally computational. An answer has been provided for the first of these questions but not yet for the second or third. We can also note that the importance overall of answers to questions about computing must go without saying at this point in the penetration of computing into so much of our lives and that a range of surprising answers have been returned in areas such as uncomputability, intractability, thrashing, choice uncertainty, file compression, perfect codes, error correcting codes for deep-space operations, and processing freezes in interrupt codes.[30]

Thus, computing looks like it should meet even these additional criteria, should it ultimately prove appropriate to make them explicit parts of the definition of a great scientific domain. But regardless, the conclusion we are driven to is that computing is a great scientific domain according to our definition. It is the fourth such domain because there are three already well recognized, and the other candidates have been dismissed as great scientific domains on their own. Each reader of this material will have to decide for his or herself whether the circularity of this definition-and-evaluation process has been sufficiently broken so as to make this a meaningful claim. However, if the consensus judgment ultimately is against either the specific definition or claim made here, it will hopefully be replaced with an improved version rather than being dropped completely. But, if some essential form of the claim does hold up, the implications are stunning. Computing could no longer be viewed as just the trade of programming, or as just the information technology industry, or as just a handmaiden to the other sciences. It instead will have been revealed as a scientific domain of great importance and vitality that would deserve to be, and would demand to be, acknowledged as an equal partner with the other great scientific domains.

6.3   Best Inventions of the Year

While I was in the early stages of writing this book, *Time* magazine came out with its list of "The Best Inventions of the Year for 2008."[31] I was immediately struck by how many of the inventions involved computing and how many of these illustrated the inherently multidisciplinary—either dyadic or polyadic—nature of much of the present and future of computing. So I went back and examined the previous list, for 2007,[32] which had the same properties, and later added in the list from 2009.[33] Of the 47 inventions listed in 2007, 18 (38 percent) had computing as a major component; of the 50 in 2008, 17 (34 percent) featured computing; and of the 50 in 2009, 16 (32 percent) had a similar emphasis. In total, 51 of the 147 (35 percent) best inventions across these three years involved a significant component of computing, reflecting the broad impact of computing science in shaping our world. And even beyond the one third of the lists that obviously involved computing were other inventions that almost certainly also used computers in some manner, such as electric cars and retail DNA tests. But the lists already reveal such a rich body of interdisciplinary inventions without the need to dig for additional submerged applications of computing that we can follow their lead and also gloss over these more subtle combinations.

From the perspective of the centrality of multidisciplinarity in the present and future of computing, it is interesting to note that all 51 of the obvious uses of computing were dyadic or polyadic, with all but one of them being mixed. The lone pure example, from 2008, was the discovery of the *46th Mersenne Prime*.[34] A Mersenne prime is a prime number—an integer divisible only by itself and 1—that is one less than a power of two; that is, it is of the form $2^n - 1$ for some value of n. The 46th Mersenne prime is $2^{43,112,609} - 1$, a number with more than 10 million digits. It was discovered by the Great Internet Mersenne Prime Search (GIMPS),[35] an effort in large-scale computational mathematics that can be viewed as implementing the process of mathematics via a network of computers: M/C*. But, with mathematics considered as part of computing, this becomes C/C*.

A few of the other inventions could conceivably be considered examples of monadic computing at some level of abstraction, but I'm going to go ahead and claim them for multidisciplinary (i.e., mixed dyadic or polyadic) computing because each has at least one noncomputational aspect that is critical for understanding both the full richness of the invention and why it was chosen to be part of the list. A typical example is the *Orbital Internet*, number 9 on the 2008 list.[36] At some level of abstraction, it can be considered as an instance of monadic (C) or pure dyadic (C*) computing, but what made this invention stand out was its existence in outer space, implying that its interaction with the surrounding physical domain (C*↔P) is central to its selection.

The eighteen computing-related inventions from 2007 are shown in table 6.2, grouped according to the categories provided by *Time*. Six are listed under the heading of computers and two more under robots. If we add in the iPhone, this amounts to half (nine) of the computing-related inventions. The other half is spread across entertainment, living, architecture, fashion, and health. The additional invention categories that are provided by *Time*, but that are missing from this list, are cars & buses, aircraft, space, law & order, and environment. Computing is almost certainly hidden in some of these, but as previously mentioned we will not worry about it for these instances.

In the table, brief English explanations have been added for each invention, with each also being modeled as an ME expression covering the essential domains and relationships that make it what it is. We will not go into detail on all of these inventions here, but a few are worth explicit mention in passing, beginning with the invention of the year in 2007: the iPhone.[37] It is a small device but rich in functionality and relationships. It thus has a relatively complex description in the ME language. The iPhone is a computing device implemented via the physical domain (C/P)—that is, by standard electronic circuits—that supports a variety of applications (Δ/C). It interacts with a user's body (hands, fingers, eyes, and ears) and mind (indirectly, but critically, through the body that implements the mind), S/L↔, while also interacting with the physical world (sensing the iPhone's orientation and location, sending and receiving electromagnetic signals, etc.), the web (via its wireless data connection), and one other person at a time (via its voice connection), ↔{P,C*,S}. Apple itself is only

Table 6.2

Examples of dyadic and polyadic computing from *Time* magazine's list of best inventions of 2007

Category	Invention	Description	ME Expression
Invention of the Year	iPhone	Smart phone	S/L↔Δ/C/P↔ {P,C*,S}
Robots	Weed 'Em and Reap	Robot weeder	P↔(s↔l)/(C↔P)
	A Robot You Can Relate To	Social robot	{P,S/L}↔ (s↔l)/(C↔P)
Entertainment	Sound Tracker	Track radio/ television listening	(S↔P)→C
	Reading Glasses	Subtitle display	C/P→S
Living	The $1,000 Football Helmet	Monitor impacts	(L↔P)→C
	An ATM for Books	Print books on demand	C/P→P→S
Architecture	Water Works	Waterfall display	C/P→S
Fashion	Can You Feel Me	Emotion sense/ display	S/L→C/P→S
	Hot or Not?	Social retailing	(P↔S/L)↔(C↔S)*
Computers	Bending Reality	Flexible display	C/P→S
	Size Matters	45-nanometer processors	C/P
	Discard the Cord	Wireless charging	C/P (or P→C)
	Flexible Fiber	Bendable cables	C/P
	The $150 Laptop	One laptop per child	Δ/C/P↔S
	Take a Walk	Street-level map images	p/C↔S
Health	Joint Venture	Foot-ankle prosthesis	L↔l/(C↔P)
	Healing Hand	Glove for CPR	L→C→S

directly responsible for the device (C/P), some of its software (Δ/C), and its interaction abilities (↔), but the other components of the expression jointly elucidate the richness of the interactions this small device enables.

At the other extreme are three dyadic inventions involving new physical implementations of computers (C/P): *Size Matters* further shrinks the dimensions of the circuits that implement computers[38]; *Discard the Cord* replaces cords with a wireless charging system (which can alternatively be thought of as P→C if the power system is considered as outside of the computer)[39]; and *Flexible Fiber* provides fiber-optic cables that can bend without losing functionality, for use in communication and computation.[40] *The $150 Laptop* conceivably could also have been modeled as dyadic computing (C/P) because of its emphasis on developing hardware for particularly cheap computers, but its innovativeness derives at least as much from its driving focus on usability by children anywhere in the world.[41] Dropping interaction (↔) with the social domain of children (S) and the software that enables this (Δ/C) from the expression would therefore hide much of what makes it innovative.

One interesting trend that shows up in the ME expressions for 2007 is the large number of inventions that provide output for human consumption. Three of these are new display technologies (C/P→S): *Reading Glasses* provides a mini-display that attaches to eyeglasses and presents subtitles to the hearing impaired[42]; *Water Works* displays information via a waterfall[43]; and *Bending Reality* provides flexible displays.[44] *Can You Feel Me* combines a new form of display—a form of computational fabric that is based on controlling the pattern and color of clothing—with sensing of the wearer's emotional state (S/L→C) to present this state to observers (figure 4.14). Although *Healing Hand* does not develop a new form of display, it similarly combines sensing—in this case of chest compression intensity and frequency during cardiopulmonary resuscitation (L→C)—with feedback to the person performing resuscitation (C→S).[45] *An ATM for Books* also does not create a new form of display but does develop cost-effective printing on demand, a form of asynchronous display technology that is mediated through purely physical objects (books).[46]

In 2008, *Time* ordered the list of inventions by importance, from 1 to 50, rather than by category. So the selected items are presented in table 6.3 as per this order, rather than grouped by category. As with 2007, there are instances of new computer hardware in the 2008 list, such as the *World's Fastest Computer*, which uses more than 100,000 processors—some conventional and others the Cell processor,[47] which is likely most well known for its presence in Sony's Playstation 3—to exceed one quadrillion

Table 6.3

Examples of dyadic and polyadic computing from *Time* magazine's list of best inventions of 2008

Rank	Invention	Description	ME Expression
4	Hulu.com	Online television distribution	$\delta/C{\rightarrow}C^*{\rightarrow}S°$
9	The Orbital Internet		$C^*{\leftrightarrow}P$
10	The World's Fastest Computer	Petaflop cluster	$(C/P)^*$
13	The Memristor	Circuit with memory	C/P
14	The Bionic Hand	Hand prosthesis	$L{\leftrightarrow}l/(C{\leftrightarrow}P)$
15	The Direct-to-Web Supervillain Musical		$\delta/C{\rightarrow}C^*{\rightarrow}S°$
17	The Mobile, Dexterous, Social Robot		$\{S,P\}{\leftrightarrow}(s{\leftrightarrow}l)/(C{\leftrightarrow}P)$
18	The New Mars Rover		$\{S,P\}{\leftrightarrow}(s{\leftrightarrow}l)/(C{\leftrightarrow}P)$
20	The Everything Game	Evolution of life	$S{\leftrightarrow}[(s/l)^*{\leftrightarrow}p]/C$
24	Bionic Contacts	Lens display	$C/P{\rightarrow}S/L$
27	Bubble Photography	Virtual backgrounds	$P^*{\rightarrow}C{\rightarrow}S$
29	The 46th Mersenne Prime		C/C^*
30	The Internet of Things	Everything sensing and connected	$(P{\rightarrow}C)^*$
32	Facebook for Spies		$(C{\leftrightarrow}S{\leftrightarrow}\Delta)^*$
42	Disemvoweling	Blog moderation	$S°{\leftrightarrow}(\delta/C)^*{\leftrightarrow}S°$
47	Google's Floating Data Center		$C^*{\leftrightarrow}P$
50	A Camera for the Blind		$P{\rightarrow}C{\rightarrow}S/L$

operations per second (a petaflop)[48]; and the *Memristor*, which provides "a new kind of circuit that remembers its history when turned off."[49] There are also a few new output devices, such as *Bionic Contacts*, which provides a computer display on a contact lens,[50] and devices that go all of the way from sensing to output for humans, such as *A Camera for the Blind*, which converts images from a camera intro Braille-like patterns that can be felt on the forehead (figure 6.1).[51]

Beyond these two classes of inventions that are repeats from 2007, there are also a couple of new, albeit small, clusters of inventions. There is a pair of intelligent robots: $(s{\leftrightarrow}l)/(C{\leftrightarrow}P)$. *The Mobile, Dexterous, Social Robot* com-

Figure 6.1
The Touch Sight *Camera for the Blind* enables text viewed by a camera to be felt on
the forehead.
Image courtesy of Liqing Zhou, http://www.liqingzhou.com/.

bines the abilities to move around, perceive its environment through
cameras, dexterously grasp objects with its hands and arms, and interact
with people via speech and an emotionally expressive face (figure 6.2).[52]
The *New Mars Rover*—more formally known as the Mars Science Laboratory—
interacts with both the physical environment and human controllers.[53]
There are also two instances of multiple interacting computers in new
relationships with the physical world: *The Orbital Internet*, as already mentioned, creates a computer network in outer space, and *Google's Floating
Data Center* locates computer servers out at sea, where wind and waves
provide power and seawater provides cooling.[54]

One of the most complicated inventions, at least according to the length
of its encoding in ME, is *The Everything Game*, in which gamers toy with
species creation and evolution in a complex implementation/simulation
of a physical, living, and social world (figure 6.3).[55] It provides a particularly rich and diverse example of the kinds of computational implementation discussed in section 3.2.

In 2009, *Time* once again ordered the inventions by importance, with
half of the top ten including computing (table 6.4). Robots, cyborgs, and
bionics (biomimetic prosthetics) of various sorts are once again a popular
topic in the list. *The Robo-Penguin*, a robot that "flies" underwater like a

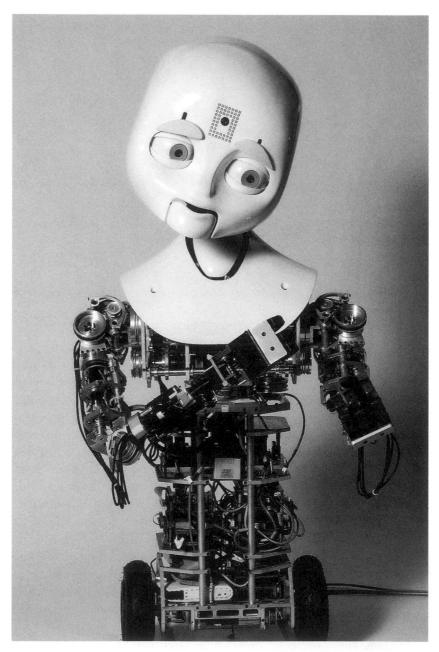

Figure 6.2
The Nexi *Mobile, Dexterous, Social Robot* can move, sense, grasp, and interact via speech and facial expressions (Massachusetts Institute of Technology).
Image courtesy of Mikey Siegel, Personal Robots group, MIT Media Lab.

Figure 6.3
The Everything Game (*Spore*) combines multispecies evolution and interaction in a galaxy-wide environment.
Spore image used with permission of Electronic Arts Inc.

Table 6.4
Examples of dyadic and polyadic computing from *Time* magazine's list of best inventions of 2009

Rank	Invention	Description	ME Expression
4	The Smart Thermostat	Manage energy usage	P↔C↔S
5	Controller-Free Gaming	Body and voice tracking	S/L↔Δ/C
6	Teleportation	Teleporting data	(C→C)/P
9	Tweeting by Thinking	Brain–computer interface	S/L↔C→C°
10	The Electric Eye	Visual prosthesis	Δ→C→S/L
14	The Handheld Ultrasound	Body scanning	L→C→S
17	The Planetary Skin	Ecological sensing	(P↔L)→C*→S*
23	Cyborg Beetle	Remote-controlled insect	S→C→L
26	The Robo-Penguin	Robotic swimmer	l/(P↔C)↔P
27	The Universal Unicycle	Robotic unicycle	S/L↔ P/(P↔C)↔P
32	The School of One	Individualized learning	S↔Δ/C
37	Packing, Improved	Disk packing	p/C
30	The Eyeborg	Camera eye	(P→C)↔L
46	The Smart Bullet	Microchips in bullets	Δ←P/(P↔C)
47	The Fashion Robot	Humanoid model	P↔s/l/(C↔P)
48	The 3D Camera		Δ→P/(P↔C)

Figure 6.4
Model of *The Electric Eye*, a neurally connected optical prosthetic (Massachusetts Institute of Technology).
Image courtesy of Shawn K. Kelly, Boston Retinal Implant Project.

penguin (figure 3.11), and *The Fashion Robot*, a humanoid robot modeling a wedding dress,[56] are autonomous robots. On the cyborg side, *The Electric Eye*, where an eyeglass-mounted camera communicates wirelessly to a chip that is physically attached to a human's eyeball and interfaced to his or her brain (figure 6.4),[57] augments human perceptual abilities, and *Tweeting by Thinking*—where short messages are composed mentally and distributed over the Internet via a brain–computer interface and Twitter[58]—augments human action abilities. *The Cyborg Beetle*—where electrodes are embedded in the optic lobes and flight muscles of a beetle, enabling a human wirelessly to control the insect's takeoff, hovering, and flight behavior (figure 4.8)[59]—can be viewed as augmenting the beetle's perceptual abilities, linking incoming radio signals directly to its brain, or as a complete bypass of the beetle's brain to enable external control of its actions. *The Eyeborg*, where a wireless video camera is worn in a human eye socket,[60] is also a cyborg-oriented item, but in this case, at least as far as I can tell, the only connections between the camera and the human is that the person is wearing it in place of his or her own eye and that he or she can examine the resulting video. There is no direct brain–computer interaction in this case.

Beyond the "sexy" topics of robots and cyborgs, there are automated devices, sensory systems—including *The Planetary Skin*, which uses a sensor network distributed over land, sea, air, and space to provide integrated worldwide monitoring of the environment[61]—plus a form of computer-based individualized education, and even a piece of theoretical computer science, concerned with a bin packing problem for disks of varying sizes. There is also an entry for the quantum teleportation of information.[62]

In summary, across these three years of *Time*'s best inventions, there is a strong showing for mixed polyadic computational shaping. Computing, and multidisciplinary computing in particular, clearly forms a compelling part of the cusp between the present and future that is represented by these inventions. All of the inventions could be characterized by expressions in the ME language, enabling it to pass a representational test that was composed from externally selected topics. It also proved possible to leverage the resulting ME expressions to extract a few interesting patterns from the lists, yielding a supplemental benefit from the analysis. Hopefully, the wow factor in these lists has been self-evident.

7 Conclusion

In some significant sense, this book can be viewed as a general rallying cry for computing. By casting the field in terms of the *computing sciences* and analyzing it via the *relational approach*, the goal has been to further a vision of its broad scope and essential multidisciplinarity; its intellectual stature as a scientific domain that is on a par with the physical, life, and social sciences; and both its vital present and exciting future. But it has also been intended as a vehicle for substantive contributions on many of these particular aspects of the overall vision. In this chapter, we conclude both of these aspects of this book with a review of these main points.

Computing is about the *transformation of information*, with the computing sciences forming a *great scientific domain* that concerns the *understanding and shaping of information transformation*. Information provides the structures that are at the heart of what is studied. Transformation comprises processes that modify this information. It is the interactions among these structures and processes, whether natural or human made, that yield the dynamic richness of computing. As has been argued, such interactions, along with the dynamics that they imply, are central to affording a suitable basis for a great scientific domain.

The idea that science consists of the *understanding* of some segment of the world is fundamental and noncontroversial. In defining great scientific domains, however, arguments have been presented for expanding on this basic notion in multiple ways. The acceptable approaches to understanding have been pushed beyond the standard use of quantitative, high certainty, methods—as exemplified, for example, by the traditional scientific method—to anything that tends to increase our understanding over time. The complementary activity of *shaping*—the influencing of a domain's subject matter—has also been added as a full partner with understanding in such domains. The resulting intertwining of understanding and shaping, which has characterized computing since its beginning and which seems likely to play an ever increasing role in the other domains, has been proposed as a strength within a scientific domain rather than as a sign that its status as a true science should be doubted. Part of this comes down to questioning the fundamental status of the long-standing dichotomy between what is natural versus what is artificial. But part also comes down to the pragmatic utility and increasing inevitability of such intertwining across the sciences.

The idea that science studies both structures and processes is likely also noncontroversial. More unusual is the notion that the existence of substantial interactions among structures and processes is central to supporting a great scientific domain. Major intellectual disciplines such as mathematics and the humanities have been ruled out as great scientific domains on their own because of their largely static focus on structures. Yet, at the same time it has been argued that they should be seen as full participants in the scientific enterprise, where they serve as important, albeit static, components of two great scientific domains—the computing and social sciences, respectively—that study comparable structures, but which also have a substantial focus on the complex interactions that occur between these structures and the processes that accompany them. Such interactions appear to be the key aspect of computing that has enabled it to go beyond mathematics in how it studies information, as well as being the key reason experimentation plays such an important role in computing versus mathematics.

It has also been proposed that the interactions among structures and processes within a great scientific domain should be *coherent, distinctive, and extensive*. Altogether, a definition of a great scientific domain is yielded that amounts to the *understanding and shaping of the interactions among a coherent, distinctive, and extensive body of structures and processes*. With this definition in hand, we were able to say something about the status of both philosophy and theology with respect to science, concluding that the former fits as part of science, but only as a weak methodology that may occasionally still be the best available across some aspects of the four domains and beyond; and the latter, although it maintains the form of a great scientific domain, remains questionable in terms of whether it actually tends to increase our understanding over time. More importantly, we were also able to ask whether computing met the definition. Although potential issues of circularity remain, because of computing being considered during the development of the definition, the particular argument provided that it meets the definition is not anticipated to be controversial.

With a hopefully growing consensus that computing does actually form the fourth great scientific domain, it reaches a plane of equality with the physical, life, and social sciences. This means that computing is not just a respectable scientific discipline, rather than merely being a part of engineering or the maker of useful tools, but in fact an entire domain of science. If true computational implementation of the other domains ultimately pans out, computing may even prove to be the most fundamental and important of the four domains, replacing the physical sciences as the base to which all else is reduced.

The parity between the computing sciences and the other three domains is part of the motivation for the relational approach, which looks broadly across computing at the domains involved in its various topic areas and the *implementation* and *interaction* relationships that are implicated among these domains. The *relational architecture* and its accompanying *metascience expression (ME) language* facilitate breaking down various aspects of computing into their constituent parts and understanding how these parts work together. They also help understand the commonalities and differences across these aspects, yielding a novel relational taxonomy over the domain that has been leveraged to survey some of the past, and much of what is exciting for the present and future, of computing.

The relational approach makes clear the essential multidisciplinarity of computing. There is monadic computing, within which progress was absolutely essential in the early days of the field and where continued progress continues to be critical and anticipated. There is also pure dyadic computing, where computing relates to itself. But the relational architecture reveals how much of conventional computing is already multidisciplinary, as well as how much of computing's exciting future is mixed dyadic or polyadic.

Going beyond the relational taxonomy, three forms of relational macrostructure have been introduced—(1) a two-dimensional map of dyadic computing, (2) the systematic synthesis, decomposition, and comparison of ME expressions, and (3) a hierarchical systems architecture—and used to analyze mixed worlds, the pursuit of science, university-based computing research institutions, and academic computing departments and schools. These analyses have provided insight into these topics themselves while also providing feedback on the utility of the relational approach. The last analysis has also included a particular appeal for the use of broad disciplinary boundaries within academic computing. Some universities come close to embracing the full scope of the computing sciences within single units, with schools of computing or departments of information and computer science, whereas others continue with narrowly construed departments that remain chary of the impurity implied by both the intertwining of understanding and shaping and multidisciplinarity. However, embracing both is critical for enabling the exciting future of computing.

With computing raised to the status of a great scientific domain and the resulting embrace of both intertwining and multidisciplinarity, the full scope of the computing sciences can finally be appreciated. Thinking of it as only hardware, software, mathematics, tools, engineering, or whatever could not be further off the mark. It spans all of the fields that contribute to the understanding and shaping of information transformation, including computer science and engineering, information science and technology, informatics and computational science, and mathematics. The inclusion of mathematics within the computing sciences may be one of the more surprising and controversial implications, but in addition to simply seeming to make sense, it finally tells a coherent story about the role of mathematics in science.

Computing is a scientific domain that is far from having already seen its best days. It remains a grand adventure, with much still to be understood and tremendous ongoing potential for practical impact. Hopefully, much of this has come across as one has read this book. But I also hope that this book has provided food for thought in general about the nature, structure, and stature of computing, even if important areas have been omitted or mischaracterized in the attempt to cover so much ground; and especially even if aspects of the overall argument ultimately prove to be off the mark. If the material here serves to fertilize a broader discussion within the community that eventually leads to a better understanding of computing, I will be satisfied. This book is intended to be just one step, albeit a significant one, toward a better understanding of computing and its role in the world and toward the development of the relational approach and its application to understanding (and shaping) the sciences.

Notes

Preface

1. Although *computing science* is an uncommon term in the United States, the term is used in some universities in Canada and the United Kingdom in place of *computer science*.

2. Although I cannot locate *unidisciplinary* in any dictionary, it seems like a much more appropriate antonym for *multidisciplinary* than *non-multidisciplinary*.

3. The prefix *meta-* can mean transcendent or beyond, as in metaphysics. But its standard epistemological meaning, and how it is most often used in computing, is to denote X *about* X; for example, metadata is data about data. The usage here is focused on this latter sense, with the language intended to support *science about science*. Much of this activity would traditionally be considered as belonging within philosophy of science, rather than being science about science, but as we proceed we will also be arguing for stretching the traditional boundaries of what is considered to be science, yielding a bit of the other meaning of metascience and explaining why this activity may itself be viewed as science.

4. Peter J. Denning, "The great principles of computing," *American Scientist* 98 (Sep–Oct 2010): 369–372.

5. Jeannette M. Wing, "Computational thinking," *Communications of the ACM* 49, no. 3 (March 2006): 33–35.

6. In earlier work, and through much of the development of this book, dyadic computing was called *binary computing* rather than dyadic computing. The term *binary* is a much more familiar way of talking about something composed of two parts and certainly trips off the tongue more easily for computer scientists, but the phrase *binary computing* is so entrenched in referring to computers based on bits rather than decimal numbers that it was ultimately given up as potentially too confusing, particularly for readers on first perusal.

7. A thorough review of existing viewpoints concerning computing as a science can be found in Matti Tedre, "Computing as a science: A survey of competing viewpoints," *Minds and Machines* 21 (2011): 361–387.

8. Definition 6 of *science*. Dictionary.com Unabridged (v 1.1). Random House, Inc. Available at http://dictionary.reference.com/browse/science (accessed September 21, 2009).

9. Wikipedia entry on *Science*. Available at http://en.wikipedia.org/wiki/Science (accessed September 21, 2009).

10. Milind Tambe, W. Lewis Johnson, Randy M. Jones, Frank Koss, John E. Laird, Paul S. Rosenbloom, and Karl B. Schwamb, "Intelligent agents for interactive simulation environments," *AI Magazine* 16 (Spring 1995): 15–39.

11. Allen Newell, "Desires and Diversions," Lecture at Carnegie Mellon University, December 4, 1991.

12. Paul S. Rosenbloom, John E. Laird, and Allen Newell, *The Soar Papers: Research on Integrated Intelligence* (Cambridge, MA: MIT Press, 1993).

13. John E. Laird, Paul S. Rosenbloom, and Allen Newell, *Universal Subgoaling and Chunking: The Automatic Generation and Learning of Goal Hierarchies* (Hingham, MA: Kluwer Academic Publishers, 1986).

14. Paul S. Rosenbloom, "A new framework for Computer Science and Engineering," *IEEE Computer* 37, no. 11 (November 2004): 23–28.

15. Graduate seminar (CS 599) offered at USC during fall 2007 on "New Perspective/ Directions for Computing."

16. Peter J. Denning and Paul S. Rosenbloom, "Computing: The fourth great domain of science," *Communications of the ACM* 52, no. 9 (September 2009): 27–29.

17. Paul S. Rosenbloom, "Ubiquity symposium 'What is computation?': Computing and computation," *Ubiquity* (November 2010).

18. Paul S. Rosenbloom, "The great scientific domains and society: A metascience perspective from the domain of computing," *The International Journal of Science and Society* 1, no. 1 (2009): 133–144.

19. Paul S. Rosenbloom, "Towards a conceptual framework for the digital humanities," *Digital Humanities Quarterly*, 2012. Forthcoming.

20. Paul S. Rosenbloom, "Rethinking cognitive architecture via graphical models," *Cognitive Systems Research* 12, no. 2 (2011): 198–209.

21. Paul S. Rosenbloom, "Combining procedural and declarative knowledge in a graphical architecture," in *Proceedings of the 10th International Conference on Cognitive Modeling*, eds. Dario D. Salvucci and Glenn Gunzelmann (Philadelphia, PA: Drexel University, 2010), 205–210.

22. Wikipedia can be found at http://www.wikipedia.org/.

23. Dictionary.com can be found at http://dictionary.reference.com/.

24. Engadget can be found at http://www.engadget.com/.

25. Slashdot can be found at http://slashdot.org/.

Chapter 1

1. Wikipedia entry on *Artificial life*. Available at http://en.wikipedia.org/wiki/ Artificial_life (accessed December 27, 2010).

2. Wikipedia entry on *DNA nanotechnology*. Available at http://en.wikipedia.org/ wiki/DNA_nanotechnology (accessed December 27, 2010).

3. Wikipedia entry on *Cognitive neuroscience*. Available at http://en.wikipedia.org/ wiki/Cognitive_neuroscience (accessed December 27, 2010).

4. Wikipedia entry on *Cognitive neuropsychology*. Available at http://en.wikipedia .org/wiki/Cognitive_neuropsychology (accessed December 27, 2010).

5. Peter L. Berger and Thomas Luckmann, *The Social Construction of Reality: A Treatise in the Sociology of Knowledge* (Garden City, NY: Anchor Books, 1966).

6. Edwin O. Wilson, *Consilience: The Unity of Knowledge* (New York, NY: Knopf, 1998).

7. Michael Schirber, "Monkey thinks robotic arm into action: Brain impulses translated into 3-D manipulation," MSNBC.com, 2005. Available at http://www.msnbc .msn.com/id/6989239/ (accessed January 7, 2011).

8. N. David Mermin, *Quantum Computer Science* (Cambridge, UK: Cambridge University Press, 2007).

9. Vernor Vinge, "The coming technological singularity: How to survive in the post-human era," *Vision-21 Symposium* (NASA Conference Publication CP-10129) (March 1993).

10. David Traum, Stacy C. Marsella, Jonathan Gratch, Jina Lee, and Arno Hartholt, "Multi-party, multi-issue, multi-strategy negotiation for multi-modal virtual agents," in *Proceedings of the 8th International Conference on Intelligent Virtual Agents* (IVA '08), eds. Helmut Prendinger, James Lester, and Mitsuru Ishizuka (Berlin: Springer-Verlag, 2008), 117–130.

11. Behrokh Khoshnevis, "Automated construction by Contour Crafting—Related robotics and information technologies," *Journal of Automation in Construction* 13, no. 1 (2004): 5–19.

12. Seth Lloyd, *Programming the Universe: A Quantum Computer Scientist Takes On the Cosmos* (New York, NY: Knopf, 2006).

13. Rob St. Amant, *Computing for Ordinary Mortals* (Oxford, UK: Oxford University Press, 2012, Forthcoming).

14. W. Daniel Hillis, *The Pattern on the Stone: The Simple Ideas That Make Computers Work* (New York, NY: Basic Books, 1998).

15. Alan W. Biermann, *Great Ideas in Computer Science: A Gentle Approach,* 2nd edition (Cambridge, MA: MIT Press, 1997).

16. Peter J. Denning, "The great principles of computing," *American Scientist* 98 (Sep–Oct 2010): 369–372.

17. Ibid.

18. Peter J. Denning and Peter A. Freeman, "Computing's paradigm," *Communications of the ACM* 52, no. 12 (December 2009): 28–30.

19. Allen Newell, Alan J. Perlis, and Herbert A. Simon, "Computer science," *Science* 157, no. 3795 (September 1967): 1373–1374.

20. Ibid.

21. Donald Knuth, "Computer science and its relation to mathematics," *American Mathematical Monthly* 81, no. 4 (April 1974): 323–343.

22. Definition of *computer science*. PCMag.com Encyclopedia. Available at http://www.pcmag.com/encyclopedia_term/0,2542,t=computer+science&i=40168,00.asp (accessed September 23, 2009).

23. Wikipedia entry on *Computer science*. Available at http://en.wikipedia.org/wiki/Computer_science (accessed September 23, 2009).

24. *Curriculum Guidelines for Undergraduate Degree Programs in Computer Engineering* (Washington, DC: IEEE Computer Society, 2004).

25. Definition of *information science*. Dictionary.com. The American Heritage® Science Dictionary. Houghton Mifflin Company. Available at http://dictionary.reference.com/browse/information science (accessed August 26, 2011).

26. Definition of *information technology*. Dictionary.com Unabridged. Random House, Inc. Available at http://dictionary.reference.com/browse/information technology (accessed August 26, 2011).

27. Dennis J. Frailey, "Ubiquity symposium 'What is computation?': Computation is process," *Ubiquity* (November 2010).

28. John S. Conery, "Ubiquity symposium 'What is computation?': Computation is symbol manipulation," *Ubiquity* (November 2010).

29. Peter J. Denning, "Ubiquity symposium 'What is computation?': Opening statement," *Ubiquity* (November 2010).

30. Ruzena Bajcsy, "Ubiquity symposium 'What is computation?': Computation and information," *Ubiquity* (November 2010).

31. Paul S. Rosenbloom, "Ubiquity symposium 'What is computation?': Computing and computation," *Ubiquity* (November 2010).

32. Ibid.

33. James Gleick, The Information: A History, a Theory, a Flood (Pantheon Books, 2011).

34. Herbert Simon, *The Sciences of the Artificial* (Cambridge, MA: MIT Press, 1969).

35. Peter J. Denning, "Computing is natural science," *Communications of the ACM* 50, no. 7 (July 2007): 13–18.

36. Jane Austen, *Persuasion* (London: John Murray, 1818).

37. Hetal Vyas, "Astrology is a science: Bombay HC," *Times of India* (February 3, 2011). Available at http://articles.timesofindia.indiatimes.com/2011-02-03/india/28356472_1_astrology-advocate-for-maharashtra-government-dattaram-kumkar (accessed March 29, 2011).

38. Jim Enderby, "Lumpers and splitters: Darwin, Hooker, and the search for order," *Science* 326, no. 5959 (December 2009): 1496–1499.

39. These two ideas, of expanding shaping beyond the physical domain and of intertwining understanding and shaping, echo a similar call in W. Brian Arthur, *The Nature of Technology: What It Is and How It Evolves* (New York, NY: Free Press, 2009), although Arthur uses the terms *phenomena* and *technology* rather than *understanding* and *shaping*. He also introduces a notion of domains encountering each other, which can be loosely mapped onto the central idea of across-domain relationships in this work.

40. Peter Galison, *Image and Logic: A Material Culture of Microphysics* (Chicago, IL: University of Chicago Press, 1997).

41. In a letter to Robert Hooke of February 5, 1676, Isaac Newton stated, "If I have seen further it is by standing on the shoulders of Giants" (as transcribed in Jean-Pierre Maury, *Newton: Understanding the Cosmos, New Horizons*, London: Thames and Hudson, 1992).

42. On Richard Feynman's blackboard when he died in 1988. Available at http://archives.caltech.edu/search_catalog.cfm?search_field=Richard%20Feynman&firstRecToShow=194&totalRecordsFound=269&recsPerPage=1&entry_type=Photo&photo_id=&cat_series= (accessed December 27, 2010).

Chapter 2

1. Home page of the Cognitive Science Society. Available at http://cognitivescience society.org/index.html (accessed December 28, 2010).

2. John L. Hennessy and David A. Patterson, *Computer Architecture: A Quantitative Approach*, 4th edition (San Francisco, CA: Morgan Kaufmann, 2007).

3. C. Gordon Bell and Allen Newell, *Computer Structures: Readings and Examples* (New York, NY: McGraw-Hill, 1971).

4. Allen Newell, *Unified Theories of Cognition* (Cambridge, MA: Harvard University Press, 1990).

5. Paul S. Rosenbloom, John E. Laird, and Allen Newell, *The Soar Papers: Research on Integrated Intelligence* (Cambridge, MA: MIT Press, 1993).

6. Lance Fortnow, "The status of the P versus NP problem," *Communications of the ACM* 52, no. 9 (September 2009): 78–86.

7. Wikipedia entry on *Church–Turing thesis*. Available at http://en.wikipedia.org/wiki/Church-Turing_thesis (accessed October 14, 2009).

8. Alan M. Turing, "On computable numbers, with an application to the entscheidungsproblem," *Proceedings of the London Mathematical Society*, series 2, 42 (November 1936): 230–265.

9. Although the unlimited ability of a universal Turing machine to emulate arbitrary Turing machines is the basis for modern stored-program computers, today's computers are in reality strictly less powerful computationally than Turing machines because of the inability to implement the equivalent of a Turing machine's infinite tape. Still, computers can be considered to be as powerful as Turing machines as long as the problems they solve do not exceed their memory capacity. Within this restricted scope, computers effectively function as universal Turing machines.

10. This dual usage of Δ to represent all of science and to stand in for any particular individual science is semantically inconsistent if you examine it in detail, but using this one abstract symbol for both of these meanings is simple and convenient and has not caused any discernible problems when used in this manner here.

11. Earlier articles on this subject used * as the domain wildcard rather than Δ. But, as will be seen later, * is now reserved for a separate role in the ME language: representing multiple instances of the same domain interacting, as in C*.

12. N. David Mermin, *Quantum Computer Science* (Cambridge, UK: Cambridge University Press, 2007).

13. Peter W. Shor, "Polynomial-time algorithms for prime factorization and discrete logarithms on a quantum computer," *SIAM Journal on Computing* 26, no. 5 (1997): 1484–1509.

14. Home page of the Association for the Advancement of Artificial Intelligence. Available at http://www.aaai.org/home.html (accessed December 28, 2010).

15. Wikipedia entry on *Deep Blue (chess computer)*. Available at http://en.wikipedia.org/wiki/Deep_Blue_(chess_computer) (accessed November 18, 2011).

16. Wikipedia entry on *Watson (computer)*. Available at http://en.wikipedia.org/wiki/Watson_(computer) (accessed August 30, 2011).

17. Jose M. Carmena, Mikhail A. Lebedev, Roy E. Crist, Joseph E. O'Doherty, David M. Santucci, Dragan F. Dimitrov, Parag G. Patil, Craig S. Henriquez, and Miguel A. L. Nicolelis, "Learning to control a brain-machine interface for reaching and grasping by primates," *PLoS Biology* 1, no. 2 (2003): 193–208.

18. William S. Bainbridge and Mihail C. Roco, "Progressive convergence," in *Managing Nano-Bio-Info-Cogno Innovations*, eds. William S. Bainbridge and Mihail C. Roco (Dordrecht, The Netherlands: Springer, 2006), 1–7.

19. John R. Searle, *Mind, Language and Society: Philosophy in the Real World* (New York, NY: Basic Books, 1999), 47.

20. Wikipedia entry on *Artificial life*. Available at http://en.wikipedia/wiki/Artificial_life (accessed December 27, 2010).

21. Wikipedia entry on *Digital physics*. Available at http://en.wikipedia.org/wiki/Digital_physics (accessed October 29, 2010).

22. Charlie Finch, "First-rate art in 'Second Life'," *artnet Magazine* (2007). Available at http://www.artnet.com/magazineus/news/artnetnews/artnetnews1-23-07.asp (accessed December 28, 2010).

23. Definition of *interaction*. Dictionary.com Unabridged. Random House, Inc. Available at http://dictionary.reference.com/browse/interaction (accessed November 3, 2010).

24. Paul S. Rosenbloom, "A new framework for computer science and engineering," *IEEE Computer* 37, no. 11 (November 2004): 23–28.

25. Theodore W. Berger and Dennis L. Glanzman (eds.), *Toward Replacement Parts for the Brain: Implantable Biomimetic Electronics as Neural Prostheses* (Cambridge, MA: MIT Press, 2005).

26. Amazon Mechanical Turk, Beta web page. Available at http://aws.amazon.com/mturk/ (accessed October 30, 2009).

27. Wikipedia entry on *The Turk*. Available at http://en.wikipedia.org/wiki/The_Turk (accessed December 28, 2010).

28. Web Services Architecture: W3C Working Group Note 11 (February 2004). Available at http://www.w3.org/TR/2004/NOTE-ws-arch-20040211/ (accessed October 30, 2009).

29. Wikipedia entry on *Interpreter (computing)*. Available at http://en.wikipedia.org/wiki/Interpreter_(computing) (accessed December 28, 2010).

30. Alfred V. Aho, Monica S. Lam, Ravi Sethi, and Jeffrey D. Ullman, *Compilers: Principles, Techniques, and Tools*, 2nd edition (Upper Saddle River, NJ: Prentice Hall, 2006).

31. Abraham Silberschatz, Peter B. Galvin, and Greg Gagne, *Operating System Concepts* (Hoboken, NJ: Wiley, 2008).

32. Larry L. Peterson and Bruce S. Davie, *Computer Networks: A Systems Approach*, 4th edition (San Francisco, CA: Morgan Kaufmann, 2007).

33. Vijay K. Garg, *Elements of Distributed Computing* (Hoboken, NJ: Wiley, 2002).

34. Embedding was originally visualized as *inside of*.

35. Wikipedia entry on *Reductionism*. Available at http://en.wikipedia.org/wiki/Reductionism (accessed February 18, 2012).

36. Roger Penrose, *The Emperor's New Mind: Concerning Computers, Minds, and The Laws of Physics* (Oxford, UK: Oxford University Press, 1989).

37. Ted G. Lewis, *Network Science: Theory and Applications* (Hoboken, NJ: John Wiley & Sons, 2009).

38. Wikipedia entry on *Massively multiplayer online role-playing game*. Available at http://en.wikipedia.org/wiki/Massively_multiplayer_online_role-playing_game (accessed December 28, 2010).

39. Mark Weiser, "The computer for the twenty-first century," *Scientific American* 265, no. 3 (September 1991): 66–75.

40. To a computer scientist, a language is something used for programming, so the modifier *natural* is added for human languages.

41. Earlier articles on this subject used the exponent n rather than * to denote an arbitrary number of interacting domains.

42. Earlier articles on this subject used parentheses around comma-separated lists of domains rather than curly brackets, but the latter's familiar use in denoting sets makes it ultimately more appropriate.

Chapter 3

1. Jim Motavalli, "The dozens of computers that make modern cars go (and stop)," *New York Times* (February 4, 2010). Available at http://www.nytimes.com/2010/02/05/technology/05electronics.html (accessed March 10, 2012).

2. Wikipedia article on *Microcode*. Available at http://en.wikipedia.org/wiki/Microcode (accessed September 17, 2010).

3. Ian Foster, Carl Kesselman, and Steven Tuecke, "The anatomy of the grid: Enabling scalable virtual organizations," *International Journal of Supercomputer Applications* 15, no. 3 (2001): 200–222.

4. Wikipedia entry on *Cloud computing*. Available at http://en.wikipedia.org/wiki/Cloud_computing (accessed December 8, 2009).

5. Brian C. Smith, "Reflection and semantics in LISP," in *Proceedings of the 11th ACM SIGACT-SIGPLAN Symposium on Principles of Programming Languages* (New York, NY: ACM, 1984): 23–35.

6. Paul S. Rosenbloom, "A world-championship-level Othello program," *Artificial Intelligence* 19, no. 3 (November 1982): 279–320.

7. John F. Reiser (ed.), SAIL. Stanford Artificial Intelligence Lab Memo AIM-289 (August 1976).

8. Wikipedia entry on *Boolean logic*. Available at http://en.wikipedia.org/wiki/Boolean_logic (accessed January 8, 2011).

9. Wikipedia entry on *Analog computer*. Available at http://en.wikipedia.org/wiki/Analog_computer (accessed January 18, 2010).

10. Wikipedia entry on *Antikythera mechanism*. Available at http://en.wikipedia.org/wiki/Antikythera_mechanism (accessed February 12, 2010).

11. Vlad Savov, "Apple engineer uses Lego to rebuild ancient Greek mechanism, will surely try to patent it," *Engadget* (December 10, 2010). Available at http://www.engadget.com/2010/12/10/apple-engineer-uses-lego-to-rebuild-ancient-greek-mechanism-wil/ (accessed December 29, 2010).

12. Michael A. Arbib, *The Handbook of Brain Theory and Neural Networks* (Cambridge, MA: MIT Press, 2003).

13. Frank Rosenblatt, "The perceptron: A probabilistic model for information storage and organization in the brain," *Psychological Review* 65, no. 6 (1958): 386–408.

14. N. David Mermin, *Quantum Computer Science* (Cambridge, UK: Cambridge University Press, 2007).

15. Peter W. Shor, "Polynomial-time algorithms for prime factorization and discrete logarithms on a quantum computer," *SIAM Journal on Scientific and Statistical Computing* 41, no. 2 (1999): 303–332.

16. Dave Bacon and Wim van Dam, "Recent progress in quantum algorithms," *Communications of the ACM* 52, no.2 (2010): 84–93.

17. David Deutsch, "Quantum theory, the Church-Turing principle and the universal quantum computer," *Proceedings of the Royal Society of London A* 400 (1985): 97–117.

18. Wikipedia entry on *Quantum teleportation*. Available at http://en.wikipedia.org/wiki/Quantum_teleportation (accessed January 27, 2010).

19. Wikipedia entry on *Natural computing*. Available at http://en.wikipedia.org/wiki/Natural_computing (accessed January 8, 2011).

20. Wikipedia entry on *Difference engine*. Available at http://en.wikipedia.org/wiki/Difference_engine (accessed January 18, 2010).

21. Wikipedia entry on *Analytical engine*. Available at http://en.wikipedia.org/wiki/Analytical_engine (accessed January 18, 2010).

22. "Babbage Analytical Engine to be digitised," BBC Mobile News Technology (September 21, 2011). Available at http://www.bbc.co.uk/news/technology-15001514 (accessed September 24, 2011).

23. Edward Fredkin and Tommaso Toffoli, "Conservative logic," *International Journal of Theoretical Physics* 21 (1982): 219–253.

24. Wikipedia entry on *Reversible computing*. Available at http://en.wikipedia.org/wiki/Reversible_computing (accessed January 18, 2010).

25. Rolf Landauer, "Irreversibility and heat generation in the computing process," *IBM Journal of Research and Development* 5 (1961): 183–191.

26. R. A. Bissell, E. Cordova, A. E. Kaifer, and J. F. Stoddart, "A chemically and electrochemically switchable molecular shuttle," *Nature* 369 (1994): 133–137.

27. Wikipedia entry on *Relay*. Available at http://en.wikipedia.org/wiki/Relay (accessed January 8, 2011).

28. Wikipedia entry on *Z3 (computer)*. Available at http://en.wikipedia.org/wiki/Z3_(computer) (accessed January 18, 2010).

29. News release entitled "Northrop Grumman Sets New World Record for Fastest Transistor" (March 30, 2009). Available at http://www.irconnect.com/noc/press/pages/news_releases.html?d=162102 (accessed February 5, 2010).

30. Robert F. Service, "Nitrides race beyond the light," *Science* 327, no. 5973 (2010): 1598–1599.

31. Prabhakar R. Bandaru, Chiara Daraio, Sungho Jin, and Apparao M. Rao, "Novel electrical switching behaviour and logic in carbon nanotube Y-junctions," *Nature Materials* 4, no. 9 (2005): 663–666.

32. Y.-M. Lin, C. Dimitrakopoulos, K. A. Jenkins, D. B. Farmer, H.-Y. Chiu, A. Grill, and Ph. Avouris, "100-ghz transistors from wafer-scale epitaxial graphene," *Science* 327, no. 5966 (2010): 662.

33. Wikipedia entry on *Molecular electronics*. Available at http://en.wikipedia.org/wiki/Molecular_electronics (accessed January 18, 2010).

34. Wikipedia entry on *Photonic computing*. Available at http://en.wikipedia.org/wiki/Photonic_computing (accessed January 18, 2010).

35. Wikipedia entry on *Optical fiber*. Available at http://en.wikipedia.org/wiki/Fiberoptic (accessed January 18, 2010).

36. Wikipedia entry on *Optical disc drive*. Available at http://en.wikipedia.org/wiki/Optical_disc_drive (accessed January 18, 2010).

37. Meng Fai Tung, *An Introduction to MEMS Optical Switches*. Available at http://www.docin.com/p-85381809.html (accessed March 17, 2012).

38. Wikipedia entry on *Photonic computing*. Available at http://en.wikipedia.org/wiki/Photonic_computing (accessed January 18, 2010).

39. Wikipedia entry on *Holographic data storage*. Available at http://en.wikipedia.org/wiki/Holographic_data_storage (accessed January 18, 2010).

40. Wikipedia entry on *Chemical computer*. Available at http://en.wikipedia.org/wiki/Chemical_computer (accessed January 18, 2010).

41. Wikipedia entry on *Object-oriented programming*. Available at http://en.wikipedia.org/wiki/Object-oriented_programming (accessed September 14, 2010).

42. Wikipedia entry on *Annealing*. Available at http://en.wikipedia.org/wiki/Annealing_(metallurgy) (accessed September 14, 2010).

43. Wikipedia entry on *Simulated annealing*. Available at http://en.wikipedia.org/wiki/Simulated_annealing (accessed September 14, 2010).

44. David H. Ackley, Geoffrey E. Hinton, and Terrence J. Sejnowski, "A learning algorithm for Boltzmann machines," *Cognitive Science* 9 (1985): 147–169.

45. Richard Dawkins, *The Greatest Show on Earth: The Evidence for Evolution* (New York, NY: Free Press, 2009), 404–405.

46. Wikipedia entry on *Antibody*. Available at http://en.wikipedia.org/wiki/Antibody (accessed February 5, 2010).

47. Wikipedia entry on *List of animals by number of neurons*. Available at http://en.wikipedia.org/wiki/List_of_animals_by_number_of_neurons (accessed February 5, 2010).

48. Wikipedia entry on *Swarm intelligence*. Available at http://en.wikipedia.org/wiki/Swarm_intelligence (accessed February 12, 2010).

49. Leonard M. Adleman, "Computing with DNA," *Scientific American* 279, no. 2 (August 1998): 54–61.

50. Donald Beaver, "A universal molecular computer," Technical Report CSE-95-001, Penn State University (1995).

51. Joanne Macdonald, Yang Li, Marko Sutovic, Harvey Lederman, Kiran Pendri, Wanhong Lu, Benjamin L. Andrews, Darko Stefanovic, and Milan N. Stojanovic, "Medium scale integration of molecular logic gates in an automaton," *Nano Letters* 6, no. 11 (2006): 2598–2603.

52. Ehud Shapiro and Binyamin Gil, "RNA computing in a living cell," *Science* 322 (2008): 387–388.

53. Jonas K. Hannestad, Peter Sandin, and Bo Albinsson, "Self-assembled DNA photonic wire for long-range energy transfer," *Journal of the American Chemical Society* 130, no. 47 (2008): 15889–15895.

54. Thomas B. DeMarse and Karl P. Dockendorf, "Adaptive flight control with living neuronal networks on microelectrode arrays," in *Proceedings of the IEEE International Joint Conference on Neural Networks* 3 (Piscataway, NJ: IEEE, 2005), 1548–1551.

55. Larisa B. Goncharova, Yannick Jacques, Carlos Martin-Vide, Alexander O. Tarakanov, and Jonathan I. Timmis, "Biomolecular immune-computer: theoretical basis and experimental simulator," in *4th International Conference on Artificial Immune Systems,* Lecture Notes in Computer Science 3627, eds. Christian Jacob, Marcin L. Pilat, Peter J. Bentley, and Jonathan Timmis (Berlin: Springer-Verlag, 2005), 72–85.

56. Wikipedia entry on *Biologically inspired computing.* Available at http://en .wikipedia.org/wiki/Biologically_inspired_computing (accessed February 12, 2010).

57. Kenneth A. De Jong, *Evolutionary Computation: A Unified Approach* (Cambridge, MA: MIT Press, 2006).

58. Wikipedia entry on *Cellular automaton.* Available at http://en.wikipedia.org/ wiki/Cellular_automaton (accessed February 15, 2010).

59. Martin Gardner, "The fantastic combinations of John Conway's new solitaire game *life,*" *Scientific American* 223 (1970): 120–123.

60. Stephen Wolfram, *A New Kind of Science* (Champaign, IL: Wolfram Media, 2002).

61. Wikipedia entry on *Developmental robotics.* Available at http://en.wikipedia.org/ wiki/Developmental_robotics (accessed February 12, 2010).

62. Wikipedia entry on *Artificial immune systems.* Available at http://en.wikipedia .org/wiki/Artificial_immune_system (accessed February 12, 2010).

63. Jeffrey O. Kephart and David M. Chess, "The vision of autonomic computing," *IEEE Computer* 36, no. 1 (January 2003): 41–50.

64. The 50 Best Inventions of 2009: The Robo-Penguin. *Time* magazine. Available at http://www.time.com/time/specials/packages/article/0,28804,1934027_1934003 _1933971,00.html (accessed November 24, 2009).

65. Loizos Michael, "Ant-based computing," *Artificial Life* 15, no. 3 (2009): 337–349.

66. Alvin Tamsir, Jeffrey J. Tabor, and Christopher A. Voight, "Robust multicellular computing using genetically encoded NOR gates and chemical 'wires'," *Nature* (December 8, 2010). Available at http://www.nature.com/nature/journal/v469/n7329/full/nature09565.html (accessed March 17, 2012).

67. Grzegorz Rozenberg and Arto Salomaa, *The Mathematical Theory of L Systems* (New York, NY: Academic Press, 1980).

68. David A. Grier, *When Computers Were Human* (Princeton, NJ: Princeton University Press, 2005).

69. Victor Fleming, Mervyn LeRoy, Noel Langley, Florence Ryerson, and Edgar Allan Woolf, *The Wizard of Oz* (Los Angeles, CA: Metro-Goldwyn Mayer, 1939).

70. Wikipedia entry on *Crowdsourcing*. Available at http://en.wikipedia.org/wiki/Crowdsourcing (accessed February 15, 2010).

71. Amazon Mechanical Turk welcome page. Available at https://www.mturk.com/mturk/welcome (accessed February 15, 2010).

72. Tom Simonite, "Building crowds of humans into software," *Technology Review* (August 29, 2011). Available at http://www.technologyreview.com/communications/38447/?a=f (accessed August 30, 2011).

73. Allen Newell and Herbert A. Simon, "Computer science as empirical inquiry: symbols and search," *Communications of the ACM* 19, no. 3 (1976): 113–126.

74. Wikipedia entry on *Information Processing Language*. Available at http://en.wikipedia.org/wiki/Information_Processing_Language (accessed September 19, 2010).

75. Wikipedia entry on *Lisp*. Available at http://en.wikipedia.org/wiki/Lisp (accessed September 19, 2010).

76. Wikipedia entry on *Prolog*. Available at http://en.wikipedia.org/wiki/Prolog (accessed September 22, 2010).

77. Wikipedia entry on *Rule-based system*. Available at http://en.wikipedia.org/wiki/Rule-based_system (accessed September 28, 2010).

78. Wikipedia entry on *Case-based reasoning*. Available at http://en.wikipedia.org/wiki/Case-based_reasoning (accessed September 28, 2010).

79. Wikipedia entry on *Constraint satisfaction*. Available at http://en.wikipedia.org/wiki/Constraint_satisfaction (accessed September 28, 2010).

80. Wikipedia entry on *Multi-agent system*. Available at http://en.wikipedia.org/wiki/Multi-agent_system (accessed September 28, 2010).

81. Judea Pearl, *Probabilistic Reasoning in Intelligent Systems: Networks of Plausible Inference* (San Mateo, CA: Morgan Kaufmann, 1988).

82. Thomas Bayes, "An essay towards solving a problem in the doctrine of chances," *Philosophical Transactions of the Royal Society of London* 53 (1763): 370–418.

83. Pedro Domingos and Daniel Lowd, *Markov Logic: An Interface Layer for Artificial Intelligence* (San Rafael, CA: Morgan and Claypool, 2009).

84. Brian Milch, Bhaskara Marthi, Stuart Russell, David Sontag, Daniel L. Ong, and Andrey Kolobov, "BLOG: Probabilistic models with unknown objects," in *Statistical Relational Learning*, eds. Lise Getoor and Ben Taskar (Cambridge, MA: MIT Press, 2007), 373–398.

85. Sara Reese Hedberg, "DART: Revolutionizing logistics planning," *IEEE Intelligent Systems* 17, no. 3 (2002): 81–83.

86. Usama M. Fayyad, Gregory Piatetsky-Shapiro, and Padhraic Smyth, "From data mining to knowledge discovery in databases," *AI Magazine* 17, no. 3 (1996): 37–54.

87. Feng-Hsiung Hsu, *Behind Deep Blue: Building the Computer that Defeated the World Chess Champion* (Princeton, NJ: Princeton University Press, 2004).

88. Paul S. Rosenbloom, "A world-championship-level Othello program," *Artificial Intelligence* 19, no. 3 (November 1982): 279–320.

89. Wikipedia entry on *Intelligent agent*. Available at http://en.wikipedia.org/wiki/Intelligent_agent (accessed January 8, 2011).

90. Wikipedia entry on *Multi-agent system*. Available at http://en.wikipedia.org/wiki/Multi-agent_system (accessed January 8, 2011).

91. Paul S. Rosenbloom, John E. Laird, and Allen Newell, *The Soar Papers: Research on Integrated Intelligence* (Cambridge, MA: MIT Press, 1993).

92. John R. Anderson, *How Can the Human Mind Occur in the Physical Universe* (Oxford, UK: Oxford University Press, 2007).

93. John E. Laird, *The Soar Cognitive Architecture* (Cambridge, MA: MIT Press, 2012).

94. Daphne Koller and Nir Friedman, *Probabilistic Graphical Models: Principles and Techniques* (Cambridge, MA: MIT Press, 2009).

95. Frank R. Kschischang, Brendan J. Frey, and Hans-Andrea Loeliger, "Factor graphs and the sum-product algorithm," *IEEE Transactions on Information Theory* 47 (2001): 498–519.

96. Paul S. Rosenbloom, "Rethinking cognitive architecture via graphical models," *Cognitive Systems Research* 12, no. 2 (2011): 198–209.

97. Michael I. Jordan and Terence J. Sejnowski, *Graphical Models: Foundations of Neural Computation* (Cambridge, MA: MIT Press, 2001).

98. Wikipedia entry on *ENIAC*. Available at http://en.wikipedia.org/wiki/ENIAC (accessed February 26, 2010).

99. Wikipedia entry on *Computer simulation*. Available at http://en.wikipedia.org/ wiki/Computer_simulation (accessed January 15, 2011).

100. Wikipedia entry on *Tessellation*. Available at http://en.wikipedia.org/wiki/ Tessellation (accessed January 15, 2011).

101. Wikipedia entry on *Differential equation*. Available at http://en.wikipedia.org/ wiki/Differential_equation (accessed February 26, 2010).

102. Wikipedia entry on *Numerical analysis*. Available at http://en.wikipedia.org/ wiki/Numerical_analysis (accessed January 15, 2011).

103. Gene Wagenbreth, Ke-Thia Yao, Dan M. Davis, Robert F. Lucas, and Thomas D. Gottschalk, "Enabling 1,000,000-entity simulations on distributed Linux clusters," in *Proceedings of the 37th Winter Simulation Conference*, eds. Michael E. Kuhl, Natalie M. Steiger, F. Brad Armstrong, and Jeffrey A. Joines (New York, NY: ACM, 2005), 1170–1181.

104. Wikipedia entry on *World of Warcraft*. Available at http://en.wikipedia.org/ wiki/World_of_Warcraft (accessed January 15, 2011).

105. "How many atoms are there in the human body?" *Jefferson Lab Questions and Answers*. Available at http://education.jlab.org/qa/mathatom_04.html (accessed January 15, 2011).

106. Wikipedia entry on *Density functional theory*. Available at http://en.wikipedia .org/wiki/Density_functional_theory (accessed March 16, 2010).

107. Timothy C. Germann and Kai Kadau, "Trillion-atom molecular dynamics becomes a reality," *International Journal of Modern Physics C* 19, no. 9 (2008): 1315–1319.

108. Wikipedia entry on *Molecular dynamics*. Available at http://en.wikipedia.org/ wiki/Molecular_dynamics (accessed March 16, 2010).

109. Masaru Tomita, "Whole cell simulation: A grand challenge of the 21st century," *Trends in Biotechnology* 19, no. 6 (2001): 205–210.

110. Leslie M. Loew and James C. Schaff, "The virtual cell: A software environment for computational cell biology," *Trends in Biotechnology* 19, no. 10 (2001): 401–406.

111. Michael A. Arbib, *The Handbook of Brain Theory and Neural Network* (Cambridge, MA: MIT Press, 2003).

112. E. M. Cherry and F. H. Fenton, "Visualization of spiral and scroll waves in simulated and experimental cardiac tissue," *New Journal of Physics* 10 (2008): 125016.

113. *IUPS Physiome Roadmap.* Available at http://www.physiome.org.nz/roadmap/ roadmap-mar05/attachment_download/file (accessed March 16, 2010).

114. STEP Consortium, *Seeding the EuroPhysiome: A Roadmap to the Virtual Physiological Human* (2007). Available at http://www.europhysiome.org/roadmap (accessed March 16, 2010).

115. Oleg Alexander, Mike Rogers, William Lambeth, Matt Chiang, and Paul Debevec, "Creating a photoreal digital actor: The Digital Emily project," in *Proceedings of the IEEE European Conference on Visual Media Production* (Los Alamitos, CA: IEEE Computer Society, 2009), 176–187.

116. Wikipedia entry on *Motion capture.* Available at http://en.wikipedia.org/wiki/ Motion_capture (accessed January 26, 2011).

117. Jessica K. Hodgins, Wayne L. Wooten, David C. Brogan, and James F. O'Brien, "Animating human athletics," in *Proceedings of SIGGRAPH 95, ACM Computer Graphics* (New York, NY: ACM, 1995): 71–78.

118. Wikipedia entry on *Artificial life.* Available at http://en.wikipedia.org/wiki/ Artificial_life (accessed March 16, 2010).

119. Wikipedia entry on *Finite state machines.* Available at http://en.wikipedia.org/ wiki/Finite-state_machine (accessed January 16, 2011).

120. Mike Oaksford and Nick Chater, *Bayesian Rationality: The Probabilistic Approach to Human Reasoning* (Oxford, UK: Oxford University Press, 2007).

121. Allen Newell, *Unified Theories of Cognition* (Cambridge, MA: Harvard University Press, 1990).

122. Peter J. Denning and Robert L. Brown, "Operating systems," *Scientific American* 251 (September 1984): 94–106.

123. Allen Newell, *Unified Theories of Cognition* (Cambridge, MA: Harvard University Press, 1990).

124. John R. Anderson, *The Architecture of Cognition* (Cambridge, MA: Harvard University Press, 1983).

125. Allen Newell, Paul S. Rosenbloom, and John E. Laird, "Symbolic architectures for cognition," in *Foundations of Cognitive Science*, ed. Michael I. Posner (Cambridge, MA: Bradford Books/MIT Press, 1989), 93–131.

126. Fischer Black and Myron Scholes, "The pricing of options and corporate liabilities," *Journal of Political Economy* 81, no. 3 (1973): 637–654.

127. Wikipedia entry on *Lanchester's laws.* Available at http://en.wikipedia.org/wiki/ Lanchester%27s_laws (accessed January 15, 2011).

128. Jeremy Q. Broughton, Noam Bernstein, Efthimios Kaxiras, and Farid F. Abraham, "Concurrent coupling of length scales: methodology and application," *Physical Review B* 60, no. 4 (July 1999): 2391–2403.

129. Wikipedia entry on *High level architecture (simulation)*. Available at http://en.wikipedia.org/wiki/High_Level_Architecture_(simulation) (accessed January 15, 2011).

130. Gareth Morgan, "Earth project aims to 'simulate everything'," *BBC News* (December 27, 2010). Available at http://www.bbc.co.uk/news/technology-12012082 (accessed December 29, 2010).

131. Yigal Arens and Paul S. Rosenbloom, "Responding to the unexpected," *Communications of the ACM* 46, no. 9 (September 2003): 33–35.

132. James Cameron and Jon Landau, *Avatar* (Los Angeles, CA: 20th Century Fox, 2009).

133. William Swartout, "Lessons learned from virtual humans," *AI Magazine* 31, no. 1 (Spring 2010): 9–20.

134. John R. Searle, *Mind, Language and Society: Philosophy in the Real World* (New York, NY: Basic Books, 1999), 47.

135. John Searle, "The Chinese Room," in *The MIT Encyclopedia of the Cognitive Sciences*, eds. Robert A. Wilson and Frank Keil (Cambridge, MA: MIT Press, 1999), 115–116.

136. Wikipedia entry on *Chinese room*. Available at http://en.wikipedia.org/wiki/Chinese_room (accessed October 22, 2010).

137. Roger Penrose, *The Emperor's New Mind: Concerning Computers, Minds, and the Laws of Physics* (Oxford, UK: Oxford University Press, 1989).

138. A wide variety of definitions of intelligence can be found in Shane Legg and Marcus Hutter, "A collection of definitions of intelligence" (2006). Available at http://www.vetta.org/documents/A-Collection-of-Definitions-of-Intelligence.pdf (accessed March 21, 2010).

139. Edwin G. Boring, "Intelligence as the tests test it," *New Republic* 35 (1923): 35–37.

140. Alan Turing, "Computing machinery and intelligence," *Mind* 59, no. 236 (1950): 433–460.

141. Joseph Weizenbaum, "ELIZA—A computer program for the study of natural language communication between man and machine," *Communications of the ACM* 9, no. 1 (1966): 36–45.

142. Joseph Weizenbaum, *Computer Power and Human Reason: From Judgment to Calculation* (San Francisco: W. H. Freeman, 1976).

143. *The American Heritage Dictionary of the English Language,* 4th edition (Boston, MA: Houghton Mifflin, 2000).

144. Walter V. Bingham, *Aptitudes and Aptitude Testing* (New York, NY: Harper & Brothers, 1937).

145. L. L. Thurstone, *The Nature of Intelligence* (London: Routledge, 1924).

146. Raymond Kurzweil, *The Age of Spiritual Machines: When Computers Exceed Human Intelligence* (New York, NY: Penguin, 2000).

147. *The Columbia Encyclopedia,* 6th edition (Farmington Hills, MI: Gale Group, 2006).

148. Linda S. Gottfredson, "Mainstream science on intelligence: An editorial with 52 signatories, history, and bibliography," *Intelligence* 24, no. (1997): 13–23.

149. Allen Newell, "Physical symbol systems," *Cognitive Science* 4 (1980):135–183.

150. John R. Anderson and Christian L. Lebiere, "The Newell test for a theory of cognition," *Behavioral & Brain Science* 26 (2003): 587–637.

151. Stuart J. Russell and Eric H. Wefald, *Do the Right Thing: Studies in Limited Rationality* (Cambridge, MA: MIT Press, 1991).

152. Paul S. Rosenbloom, John E. Laird, and Allen Newell, *The Soar Papers: Research on Integrated Intelligence* (Cambridge, MA: MIT Press, 1993).

153. Hubert L. Dreyfus, *What Computers Still Can't Do: A Critique of Artificial Reason* (Cambridge, MA: MIT Press, 1992).

154. Nick Bostrom, "Are you living in a computer simulation?" *Philosophical Quarterly* 53, no. 211 (2003): 243–255.

155. Marcus Hutter, *Universal Artificial Intelligence: Sequential Decisions Based on Algorithmic Probability* (Berlin: Springer, 2004).

156. Definition 1 of *life*. Dictionary.com. Available at http://dictionary.reference .com/browse/life (accessed April 02, 2010).

157. Thomas S. Ray, *Evolution, Ecology and Optimization of Digital Organisms*, Santa Fe Institute Working Paper 92–08–042 (1992).

158. Grey Walter, "An imitation of life," *Scientific American* 182, no. 5 (1950): 42–45.

159. Paul S. Rosenbloom, John E. Laird, and Allen Newell, "Meta-levels in Soar," in *Meta-Level Architectures and Reflection*, eds. Pattie Maes and Daniele Nardi (Amsterdam: North Holland, 1988), 227–240.

160. Douglas E. Bernard, Gregory A. Dorais, Chuck Fry, Edward B. Gamble Jr., Bob Kanefsky, James Kurien, William Millar, Nicola Muscettola, P. Pandurang Nayak, Barney Pell, Kanna Rajan, Nicolas Rouquette, Benjamin Smith, and Brian C. Williams, "Design of the Remote Agent experiment for spacecraft autonomy," in *Proceedings of the 1998 IEEE Aerospace Conference* (Piscataway, NJ: IEEE, 1998), 259–281.

161. Lee K. Graham, Franz Oppacher, and Steffen Christensen, "Irreducible complexity in a genetic algorithm," in *Proceedings of the IEEE Congress on Evolutionary Computation*, 3692–3697.

162. Dictionary.com definition 3 of *physical*. Available at http://dictionary .reference.com/browse/physical (accessed April 02, 2010).

163. Wikipedia entry on *Digital physics*. Available at http://en.wikipedia.org/wiki/ Digital_physics (accessed on October 29, 2010).

164. Wikipedia entry on *Physical information*. Available at http://en.wikipedia.org/ wiki/Physical_information (accessed January 17, 2011).

165. Konrad Zuse, "Rechnender Raum," *Elektronische Datenverarbeitung* 8 (1967): 336–344.

166. John Archibald Wheeler, "Information, physics, quantum: The search for links," in *Complexity, Entropy and the Physics of Information*, ed. Wojciech H. Zurek (Boulder, CO: Westview Press, 1990), 5.

167. Stephen Wolfram, *A New Kind of Science* (Champaign, IL: Wolfram Media, 2002).

168. Edward Fredkin, "A computing architecture for physics," in *Proceedings of the 2nd Conference on Computing Frontiers*, eds. Nader Bagherzadeh, Mateo Valero and Alex Ramírez (New York, NY: ACM, 2005), 273–279.

169. Seth Lloyd, *Programming the Universe: A Quantum Computer Scientist Takes On the Cosmos* (New York, NY: Knopf, 2006).

170. Nick Bostrom, "Are you living in a computer simulation?" *Philosophical Quarterly* 53, no. 211 (2003): 243–255.

171. Andy Wachowski, Larry Wachowski, Joel Silver, and Grant Hill, *The Matrix* (Burbank, CA: Warner Bros. Pictures, 1999).

Chapter 4

1. Wikipedia entry on *Photosynthesis*. Available at http://en.wikipedia.org/wiki/ Photosynthesis (accessed January 18, 2011).

2. Wikipedia entry on *Integrated development environment*. Available at http://en .wikipedia.org/wiki/Integrated_development_environment (accessed November 1, 2010).

3. Wikipedia entry on *Automatic programming*. Available at http://en.wikipedia.org/wiki/Automatic_programming (accessed November 1, 2010).

4. Peter J. Denning and Robert Dunham, *The Innovator's Way: Essential Practices for Successful Innovation* (Cambridge, MA: MIT Press, 2010).

5. Jeannette M. Wing, "Computational thinking," *Communications of the ACM* 49, no. 3 (March 2006): 33–35.

6. Jeannette M. Wing, "Computational thinking—What and why?" *The Link* (Spring 2011): 20–23.

7. Mark Marino, "Critical Code Studies" (2006). Available at http://www.electronicbookreview.com/thread/electropoetics/codology/ (accessed November 1, 2010).

8. Wikipedia entry on *Theory of mind*. Available at http://en.wikipedia.org/wiki/Theory_of_mind (accessed January 20, 2011).

9. Wikipedia entry on *Sensor fusion*. Available at http://en.wikipedia.org/wiki/Sensor_fusion (accessed January 20, 2011).

10. This list most likely was adapted from Wikipedia, but it was first used in the class taught on the material in this book, and the exact citation has been lost.

11. Wikipedia entry on *Functional magnetic resonance imaging*. Available at http://en.wikipedia.org/wiki/Functional_magnetic_resonance_imaging (accessed November 3, 2010).

12. Wikipedia entry on *Biometrics*. Available at http://en.wikipedia.org/wiki/Biometrics (accessed November 18, 2010).

13. Wikipedia entry on *User modeling*. Available at http://en.wikipedia.org/wiki/User_modeling (accessed January 26, 2011).

14. Thomas M. Mitchell, Svetlana V. Shinkareva, Andrew Carlson, Kai-Min Chang, Vicente L. Malave, Robert A. Mason, and Marcel A. Just, "Predicting human brain activity associated with the meanings of nouns," *Science* 320 (May 2008): 1191–1195.

15. Wikipedia entry on *Kinect*. Available at http://en.wikipedia.org/wiki/Kinect (accessed November 18, 2010).

16. Michael S. Horn, Erin T. Solovey, and Robert J. K. Jacob, "Tangible programming for informal science learning: Making TUIs work for museums," in *Proceedings of the 7th International Conference on Interaction Design & Children* (New York, NY: ACM, 2008), 194–201.

17. Wikipedia entry on *Computer vision*. Available at http://en.wikipedia.org/wiki/Computer_vision (accessed November 3, 2010).

18. Wikipedia entry on *Speech recognition*. Available at http://en.wikipedia.org/wiki/ Speech_recognition (accessed November 3, 2010).

19. Stan Z. Li, *Markov Random Field Modeling in Image Analysis*, 3rd edition (London: Springer, 2009).

20. Wikipedia entry on *Hidden Markov model*. Available at http://en.wikipedia.org/ wiki/Hidden_Markov_model (accessed November 3, 2010).

21. Geoffrey E. Hinton, Simon Osindero, and Yee-Whye Teh, "A fast learning algorithm for deep belief nets," *Neural Computation* 18 (2006): 1527–1554.

22. Dan C. Ciresan, Ueli Meier, Luca M. Gambardella, and Juergen Schmidhuber, "Deep big simple neural nets for handwritten digit recognition," *Neural Computation* 22, no. 12 (2010): 3207–3220.

23. Patrick Langley, "Bacon: A production system that discovers empirical laws," in *Proceedings of the Fifth International Joint Conference on Artificial Intelligence* (Los Altos, CA: Morgan Kaufmann, 1977): 344.

24. Wikipedia entry on *Wii remote*. Available at http://en.wikipedia.org/wiki/Wii _remote (accessed November 19, 2010).

25. Wikipedia entry on *Remote sensing*. Available at http://en.wikipedia.org/wiki/ Remote_sensing (accessed January 20, 2011).

26. Wikipedia entry on *Wireless sensor network*. Available at http://en.wikipedia.org/ wiki/Wireless_sensor_network (January 20, 2011).

27. The National Ecological Observatory Network (NEON) website. Available at http://www.neoninc.org/ (accessed May 7, 2010).

28. Wikipedia entry on *Body area network*. Available at http://en.wikipedia.org/wiki/ Body_Area_Network (accessed May 7, 2010).

29. Gordon Bell and Jim Gemmell, *Total Recall: How the E-Memory Revolution Will Change Everything* (New York, NY: Dutton, 2009).

30. Wikipedia entry on *Information Awareness Office*. Available at http://en .wikipedia.org/wiki/Information_Awareness_Office (accessed January 20, 2011).

31. George Orwell, *1984* (London: Secker and Warburg, 1949).

32. Jon-Louis Heimerl, "A day in the life of privacy," *Security Week* (October 14, 2011). Available at http://www.securityweek.com/day-life-privacy (accessed March 11, 2012).

33. Behnam Salemi, Mark Moll, and Wei-Min Shen, "SUPERBOT: A deployable, multi-functional, and modular self-reconfigurable robotic system," in *Proceedings of the IEEE/RSJ International Conference on Intelligent Robots and Systems* (Piscataway, NJ: IEEE, 2006).

34. Wikipedia entry on *Programmable matter*. Available at http://en.wikipedia.org/wiki/Programmable_matter (accessed November 24, 2010).

35. Jonathan D. Hiller and Hod Lipson, "Evolving amorphous robots," in *Artificial Life XII: Proceedings of the Twelfth International Conference on the Synthesis and Simulation of Living Systems*, eds. Harold Fellermann, Mark Dörr, Martin M. Hanczyc, Lone Ladegaard Laursen, Sarah Maurer, Daniel Merkle, Pierre-Alain Monnard, Kasper Stoy, and Steen Rasumussen (Cambridge, MA: MIT Press, 2010), 717–724.

36. James Cameron, William Wisher Jr., Stephanie Austin, B. J. Rack, Gale Anne Hurd, and Mario Kassar, *Terminator 2: Judgment Day* (Culver City, CA: TriStar Pictures, 1991).

37. Wikipedia entry on *Robotic surgery*. Available at http://en.wikipedia.org/wiki/Robotic_surgery (accessed November 24, 2010).

38. Wikipedia entry on *Numerical control*. Available at http://en.wikipedia.org/wiki/Numerical_control (accessed November 24, 2010).

39. Wikipedia entry on *Nanorobotics*. Available at http://en.wikipedia.org/wiki/Nanorobotics (accessed November 24, 2010).

40. Wikipedia entry on *Microelectromechanical systems*. Available at http://en.wikipedia.org/wiki/Microelectromechanical_systems (accessed November 24, 2010).

41. Wikipedia entry on *Rapid prototyping*. Available at http://en.wikipedia.org/wiki/Rapid_prototyping (accessed November 24, 2010).

42. Vladimir Mironov, Glenn Prestwich, and Gabor Forgacs, "Bioprinting living structures," *Journal of Materials Chemistry* 17 (2007): 2054–2060.

43. Web page on "Solid freeform fabrication: DIY, on the cheap, and made of pure sugar." Available at http://www.evilmadscientist.com/article.php/candyfab (accessed November 24, 2010).

44. Behrokh Khoshnevis, "Automated construction by Contour Crafting – Related robotics and information technologies," *Journal of Automation in Construction* 13, no. 1 (2004): 5–19.

45. Edward R. Tufte, *Envisioning Information* (Cheshire CT: Graphics Press, 1990).

46. William Swartout, David Traum, Ron Artstein, Dan Noren, Paul Debevec, Kerry Bronnenkant, Josh Williams, Anton Leuski, Shrikanth Narayanan, Diane Piepo, Chad Lane, Jacquelyn Morie, Priti Aggarwal, Matt Liewer, Jen-Yuan Chiang, Jillian Gerten, Selina Chu, and Kyle White, "Ada and Grace: Toward realistic and engaging virtual museum guides," in *Proceedings of the 10th International Conference on Intelligent Virtual Agents*, eds. Jan M. Allbeck, Norman I. Badler, Timothy W. Bickmore, Catherine Pelachaud and Alla Safonova (Berlin: Springer, 2010), 286–300.

47. Wikipedia entry on *Experience design*. Available at http://en.wikipedia.org/wiki/ Experience_design (accessed January 20, 2011).

48. Sunil Bharitkar and Chris Kyriakakis, *Immersive Audio Signal Processing* (Springer, 2006).

49. Andrew Jones, Ian McDowall, Hideshi Yamada, Mark Bolas, and Paul Debevec, "Rendering for an interactive 360° light field display," *ACM Transactions on Graphics* 26, no. 3 (July 2007): 40/1–40/10.

50. D. R. Allee, S. M. Venugopal, R. Shringarpure, K. Kaftanoglu, S. G. Uppili, L. T. Clark, B. Vogt, and E. J. Bawolek, "Threshold voltage instability in a-Si:H TFTs and the implications for flexible displays and circuits," in *Proceedings of the 8th International Meeting on Information Displays* (2008).

51. Bob Metcalf, "Do computational fabrics hold the future of the Internet's web?" *InfoWorld* (July 24, 2000): 88.

52. Wikipedia entry on *Virtual retinal display*. Available at http://en.wikipedia.org/ wiki/Virtual_retinal_display (accessed November 30, 2010).

53. Wikipedia entry on *Haptic technology*. Available at http://en.wikipedia.org/wiki/ Haptic_technology (accessed November 30, 2010).

54. Donald A. Washburn and Lauriann M. Jones, "Could olfactory displays improve data visualization?" *Computing in Science & Engineering* 6, no. 6 (November 2004): 80–83.

55. Wikipedia entry on *Cave automatic virtual environment*. Available at http://en .wikipedia.org/wiki/Cave_Automatic_Virtual_Environment (accessed November 30, 2010).

56. Wikipedia entry on *Informatics (academic field)*. Available at http://en.wikipedia .org/wiki/Informatics_(academic_field) (accessed January 23, 2011).

57. Web archive of the DARPA 2005 Grand Challenge. Available at http://archive .darpa.mil/grandchallenge05/ (accessed March 11, 2012).

58. Web archive of the DARPA Urban Challenge. Available at http://archive.darpa .mil/grandchallenge/ (accessed March 11, 2012).

59. RoboCup website. Available at http://www.robocup.org/ (accessed November 30, 2010).

60. Wikipedia entry on *Future combat systems*. Available at http://en.wikipedia.org/ wiki/Future_Combat_Systems (accessed May 4, 2010).

61. Wikipedia entry on *Software agent*. Available at http://en.wikipedia.org/wiki/ Software_agent (accessed November 30, 2010).

62. Wikipedia entry on *Intelligent agent*. Available at http://en.wikipedia.org/wiki/Intelligent_agent (accessed November 30, 2010).

63. Wikipedia entry on *Multi-agent system*. Available at http://en.wikipedia.org/wiki/Multi-agent_system (accessed November 30, 2010).

64. Hans Chalupsky, Yolanda Gil, Craig A. Knoblock, Kristina Lerman, Jean Oh, David V. Pynadath, Thomas A. Russ, and Milind Tambe, "Electric elves: Applying agent technology to support human organizations," in *Proceedings of Innovative Applications of Artificial Intelligence Conference* eds. Haym Hirsh and Steve A. Chien (Menlo Park, CA: AAAI Press, 2001), 51–58.

65. Wikipedia entry on *Serviced-oriented architecture*. Available at http://en.wikipedia.org/wiki/Service-oriented_architecture (accessed December 2, 2010).

66. David Feil-Seifer and Maja J. Matarić, "Defining socially assistive robotics," in *Proceedings of the IEEE International Conference on Rehabilitation Robotics* (Piscataway, NJ: IEEE, 2005), 465–468.

67. Wikipedia entry on *Social robot*. Available at http://en.wikipedia.org/wiki/Social_robot (accessed December 2, 2010).

68. Wikipedia entry on *Human-robot interaction*. Available at http://en.wikipedia.org/wiki/Human-robot_interaction (accessed December 2, 2010).

69. Michael Lewis, "Designing for human-agent interaction," *AI Magazine* 19, no. 2 (Summer 1998): 67–78.

70. Dylan D. Schmorrow, *Foundations of Augmented Cognition* (Hillsdale, NJ: Lawrence Erlbaum Associates, 2005).

71. Ronald Shusett, Dan O'Bannon, Gary Goldman, Jon Povill, Philip K. Dick, Paul Verhoeven, Mario Kassar, and Andrew G. Vajna, *Total Recall* (Culver City, CA: TriStar Pictures, 1990).

72. Wikipedia entry on *Social network service*. Available at http://en.wikipedia.org/wiki/Social_network_service (accessed December 2, 2010).

73. Wikipedia entry on *Telepresence*. Available at http://en.wikipedia.org/wiki/Telepresence (accessed December 2, 2010).

74. Definition of *telemediation*. Urbandictionary.com. Available at http://www.urbandictionary.com/define.php?term=Telemediation (accessed December 29, 2010).

75. Wikipedia entry on *Distributed systems*. Available at http://en.wikipedia.org/wiki/Distributed_computing (accessed December 2, 2010).

76. *Network Science* (Washington, DC: The National Academies Press, 2005).

77. Wikipedia entry on *Parallel computing*. Available at http://en.wikipedia.org/wiki/Parallel_computing (accessed December 2, 2010).

78. Wikipedia entry on *Computer network*. Available at http://en.wikipedia.org/wiki/ Computer_network (accessed December 2, 2010).

79. Wikipedia entry on *Transistor count*. Available at http://en.wikipedia.org/wiki/ Transistor_count (accessed December 2, 2010).

80. Wikipedia entry on *Cluster (computing)*. Available at http://en.wikipedia.org/ wiki/Cluster_(computing) (accessed May 7, 2010).

81. "China grabs supercomputing leadership spot in latest ranking of world's top 500 supercomputers," Top 500 Supercomputer Sites. Available at http://www.top500 .org/lists/2010/11/press-release (accessed December 2, 2010).

82. Wikipedia entry on *Graphics processing unit*. Available at http://en.wikipedia.org/ wiki/Graphics_processing_unit (accessed December 2, 2010).

83. Wikipedia entry on *Tianhe-1*. Available at http://en.wikipedia.org/wiki/Tianhe-I (accessed December 2, 2010).

84. Wikipedia entry on *Cloud computing*. Available at http://en.wikipedia.org/wiki/ Cloud_computing (accessed December 8, 2009).

85. Ian Foster and Carl Kesselman (eds.), *The Grid 2: Blueprint for a New Computing Infrastructure* (San Francisco, CA: Morgan Kaufmann, 2004).

86. "CERN cranks up its LHC network," *Boffin Watch* (May 12, 2010). Available at http://www.theinquirer.net/inquirer/boffin-watch-blog/1635983/cern-cranks-lhc -network (accessed March 17, 2012).

87. Website for SETI@home. Available at http://setiathome.berkeley.edu/ (accessed May 7, 2010).

88. Wikipedia entry on *Semantic Web*. Available at http://en.wikipedia.org/wiki/ Semantic_Web (accessed December 2, 2010).

89. Paul Scerri, David V. Pynadath, W. Lewis Johnson, Paul S. Rosenbloom, Nathan Schurr, and Milind Tambe, "A prototype infrastructure for distributed robot-agent-person teams," In *Proceedings of the Second International Joint Conference on Autonomous Agents and Multiagent Systems* (New York, NY: ACM, 2003), 433–440.

Chapter 5

1. The two earlier published versions of this table appeared in Paul S. Rosenbloom, "A new framework for Computer Science and Engineering," *IEEE Computer* 37, no. 11 (November 2004): 23–28; and in Peter J. Denning and Paul S. Rosenbloom, "Computing: The fourth great domain of science," *Communications of the ACM* 52, no. 9 (September 2009): 27–29.

2. Larry L. Smarr, Andrew A. Chien, Tom DeFanti, Jason Leigh, and Philip M. Papa-dopoulos, "The OptIPuter," *Communications of the ACM* 46, no. 11 (November 2003): 58–67.

3. David Garlan, Dan Siewiorek, Asim Smailagic, and Peter Steenkiste, "Project Aura: Toward distraction-free pervasive computing," *IEEE Pervasive Computing* 1, no. 2 (April 2002): 22–31.

4. Paul S. Rosenbloom, "A new framework for Computer Science and Computer Engineering," *IEEE Computer* 37, no. 11 (November 2004): 23–28.

5. Some past versions of this architecture have included a microelectronics layer below the platform layer, and it is possible to imagine even more layers below this, but with our primary focus on computing, these can all be omitted here.

6. Wikipedia entry on *Cloud computing*. Available at http://en.wikipedia.org/wiki/Cloud_computing (accessed December 8, 2009).

7. Ian Foster and Carl Kesselman (eds.), *The Grid 2: Blueprint for a New Computing Infrastructure* (San Francisco, CA: Morgan Kaufmann, 2004).

8. Thomas H. Jordan, Philip J. Maechling, and the SCEC/CME Collaboration, "The SCEC community modeling environment: An information infrastructure for system-level earthquake science," *Seismological Research Letters* 74, no. 3 (2003): 44–46.

9. Peter J. Denning, "Great principles of computing," *Communications of the ACM* 46, no. 11 (November 2003): 15–20.

10. Wikipedia entry on *Holodeck*. Available at http://en.wikipedia.org/wiki/Holodeck (accessed January 24, 2011).

11. Mark Tran, "Girl starved to death while parents raised virtual child in online game," *The Guardian* (March 5, 2010). Available at http://www.guardian.co.uk/world/2010/mar/05/korean-girl-starved-online-game (accessed December 2, 2010).

12. Wikipedia entry on *Entropia Universe*. Available at http://en.wikipedia.org/wiki/Entropia_Universe (accessed December 2, 2010).

13. Wikipedia entry on *Alternate reality game*. Available at http://en.wikipedia.org/wiki/Alternate_reality_game (accessed December 2, 2010).

14. Paul Milgram and Fumio Kishino, "Taxonomy of mixed reality visual displays," *IEICE Transactions on Information and Systems*, E77-D, no. 12 (1994): 1321–1329.

15. Wikipedia entry on *Augmented reality*. Available at http://en.wikipedia.org/wiki/Augmented_reality (November 30, 2010).

16. USC ICT Web page on Gunslinger. Available at http://ict.usc.edu/projects/gunslinger/ (accessed January 24, 2011).

17. Mark Weiser, "The computer for the twenty-first century," *Scientific American* 265, no. 3 (September 1991): 66–75.

18. Wikipedia entry on *Ubiquitous computing*. Available at http://en.wikipedia.org/wiki/Ubiquitous_computing (accessed January 24, 2011).

19. Sean Hollister, "DARPA-funded prosthetic arm reaches phase three, would-be cyborgs celebrate," *Engadget* (July 18, 2010). Available at http://www.engadget.com/2010/07/18/darpa-funded-prosthetic-arm-reaches-phase-three-would-be-cyborg/ (accessed October 21, 2010).

20. Manfred E. Clynes and Nathan S. Kline, "Cyborgs and space," *Astronautics* (September 1960): 26–27, 74–75.

21. Elliot Cole, "Cognitive prosthetics: An overview to a method of treatment," *NeuroRehabilitation* 2 (1999): 39–51.

22. Hannah Devlin, "Prosthetics use in Olympics should be forbidden, says sports engineer," *Sunday Times* (June 10, 2010).

23. Saswato R. Das, "'Smart bridges' harness technology to stay safe," *Scientific American* Slide Show (June 17, 2009). Available at http://www.scientificamerican.com/article.cfm?id=smart-bridges-harness-tech (accessed January 24, 2011).

24. George Orwell, *1984* (London: Secker and Warburg, 1949).

25. James Cameron, Gale Anne Hurd, and William Wisher, Jr., *The Terminator* (Los Angeles, CA: Orion Pictures, 1984).

26. Brannon Braga and Ronald D. Moore, *Star Trek: First Contact* (Los Angeles, CA: Paramount Pictures, 1996).

27. Daniel A. Reed, Ruzena Bajcsy, Manuel A. Fernandez, Jose-Marie Griffiths, Randall D. Mott, Jack Dongarra, Chris R. Johnson, Alan S. Inouye, William Miner, Martha K. Matzke, and Terry L. Ponick, *Computational Science: Ensuring America's Competitiveness* (Arlington, VA: President's Information Technology Advisory Committee, 2005).

28. Tony Hey, Stewart Tansley, and Kristin Tolle (eds.), *The Fourth Paradigm: Data-Intensive Scientific Discovery* (Redmond, WA: Microsoft, 2009).

29. Patricia Cohen, "In 500 billion words, new window on culture," *New York Times* (December 16, 2010). Available at http://www.nytimes.com/2010/12/17/books/17words.html?hpw (accessed December 17, 2010).

30. Richard Dawkins, *The Greatest Show on Earth: The Evidence for Evolution* (New York, NY: Free Press, 2009).

31. David Baltimore, "How biology became an information science," in *The Invisible Future: The Seamless Integration of Technology Into Everyday Life*, ed. Peter J. Denning (New York, NY: McGraw-Hill, 2001), 43–56.

32. Fritz Rohrlich, "Computer simulation in the physical sciences," in *PSA 1990: Proceedings of the Biennial Meeting of the Philosophy of Science Association* (Chicago, IL: University of Chicago Press, 1991), 507–518.

33. Stephan Hartmann, "The world as a process: Simulations in the natural and social sciences," in *Modeling and Simulation in the Social Sciences: From the Philosophy of Science Point of View*, eds. Rainer Hegselmann, Ulrich Mueller, and Klaus. G. Troitzsch (Dordrecht, The Netherlands: Kluwer Academic Publishers, 1996), 77–100.

34. Moshe Y. Vardi, "Science has only two legs," *Communications of the ACM* 53, no. 9 (September 2010): 5.

35. This discussion owes a debt to the earlier work published in Paul S. Rosenbloom, "The great scientific domains and society: A metascience perspective from the domain of computing," *The International Journal of Science and Society* 1, no. 1 (2009): 133–144. However, it has been updated here, and the notation used in the ME language has been changed.

36. ICT Internship Web page. Available at http://ict.usc.edu/internships (accessed December 15, 2010).

37. David Traum, Jonathan Gratch, Stacy Marsella, Jina Lee, and Arno Hartholt, "Multi-party, multi-issue, multi-strategy negotiation for multi-modal virtual agents," in *Proceedings of the 8th International Conference on Intelligent Virtual Agents*, eds. Helmut Prendinger, James Lester, and Mitsuru Ishizuka (Berlin: Springer-Verlag, 2008), 117–130.

38. Patrick Kenny, Thomas Parsons, Jonathan Gratch, and Albert Rizzo, "Evaluation of Justina: A virtual patient with PTSD," in *Proceedings of the 8th International Conference on Intelligent Virtual Agents*, eds. Helmut Prendinger, James Lester, and Mitsuru Ishizuka (Berlin: Springer-Verlag, 2008), 394–408.

39. Boston Museum of Science web page on InterFaces: Virtual Humans, Real Friends. Available at http://www.mos.org/interfaces/index.php (accessed December 15, 2010).

40. MOSIS has for many years run a very large scale integration (VLSI) brokering service, letting designers quickly and cheaply get small batches of chips fabricated at foundries.

41. Paul S. Rosenbloom, "A new framework for computer science and engineering," *IEEE Computer* 37, no. 11 (November 2004): 23–28.

42. USC Computer Science Department Research Areas and Labs. Available at http://www.cs.usc.edu/research/labs.html (accessed November 11, 2009).

43. University of Texas at Austin Computer Science Department Research Areas. Available at http://www.cs.utexas.edu/research/areas (accessed March 9, 2012).

44. University of California, Berkeley, Electrical Engineering and Computer Science Research Areas. Available at http://www.eecs.berkeley.edu/Research/Areas/ (accessed January 22, 2011).

45. Massachusetts Institute of Technology Electrical Engineering and Computer Science Mission. Available at http://www.eecs.mit.edu/mission.html (accessed January 22, 2011).

46. University of Illinois at Champaign-Urbana Computer Science Department Research Topics. Available at http://cs.illinois.edu/research (accessed January 22, 2011).

Chapter 6

1. The Best Inventions of the Year: Spandex Space Suit. Available at http://www .time.com/time/specials/2007/article/0,28804,1677329_1678408_1678409,00.html (accessed November 11, 2009).

2. The Best Inventions of the Year: The Return of Steam. Available at http://www .time.com/time/specials/2007/article/0,28804,1677329_1677971_1677973,00.html (accessed November 11, 2009).

3. Imre Lakatos, "Science and pseudoscience," in *The Methodology of Scientific Research Programmes: Philosophical Papers Volume 1*, eds. John Worral and Gregory Currie (Cambridge, UK: Cambridge University Press, 1978), 1–7.

4. Karl Popper, *The Logic of Scientific Discovery* (London: Routledge, 1959).

5. Michael Strevens, "Bayesian approach to philosophy of science," in *Encyclopedia of Philosophy*, 2nd edition, ed. Donald M. Borchert (Detroit, MI: Macmillan Reference, 2006), 495–502.

6. Paul Feyerabend, *Against Method: Outline of an Anarchistic Theory of Knowledge* (London: New Left Books, 1975).

7. Sven O. Hansson, "Science and pseudo-science," in *The Stanford Encyclopedia of Philosophy*, Fall 2008 edition, ed. Edward N. Zalta. Available at http://plato.stanford .edu/archives/fall2008/entries/pseudo-science/ (accessed October 5, 2009).

8. Wikipedia entry on *Synthetic biology*. Available at http://en.wikipedia.org/wiki/ Synthetic_biology (accessed December 27, 2010).

9. Wikipedia entry on *Genetic engineering*. Available at http://en.wikipedia.org/wiki/ Genetic_engineering (accessed December 27, 2010).

10. Wikipedia entry on *Social engineering (political science)*. Available at http://en .wikipedia.org/wiki/Social_engineering_(political_science) (accessed December 27, 2010).

11. Wikipedia entry on *Social engineering (security)*. Available at http://en.wikipedia.org/wiki/Social_engineering_(security) (accessed December 27, 2010).

12. Donald E. Stokes, *Pasteur's Quadrant: Basic Science and Technological Innovation* (Washington, DC: Brookings Institution Press, 1997).

13. This discussion is partly based on the second section of Paul S. Rosenbloom, "Ubiquity symposium 'What is computation?': Computing and computation," *Ubiquity* (November 2010).

14. Definition of *humanities*. Dictionary.com. *The American Heritage® Dictionary of the English Language*, 4th edition. Houghton Mifflin Company, 2004. Available at http://dictionary.reference.com/browse/humanities (accessed October 08, 2009).

15. Wikipedia entry on *Formal science*. Available at http://en.wikipedia.org/wiki/Formal_science (accessed September 23, 2011).

16. Definition of *mathematics*. Dictionary.com Unabridged. Random House, Inc. Available at http://dictionary.reference.com/browse/mathematics (accessed October 08, 2009).

17. Wikipedia entry on *Analytic philosophy*. Available at http://en.wikipedia.org/wiki/Analytic_philosophy (accessed December 27, 2010).

18. Alex Rosenberg, *Philosophy of Science: A Contemporary Introduction,* 3rd edition (New York, NY: Routledge, 2012).

19. Ibid.

20. Wikipedia entry on *Philosophy*. Available at http://en.wikipedia.org/wiki/Philosophy (accessed September 28, 2011).

21. Elaine Rich and Kevin Knight, *Artificial Intelligence*, 2nd edition (New York, NY: McGraw-Hill, 1991).

22. Feng-Hsiung Hsu, *Behind Deep Blue: Building the Computer that Defeated the World Chess Champion* (Princeton, NJ: Princeton University Press, 2004).

23. Brian Williams pointed out this lack to me, based on ongoing challenges to computing's stature as a scientific domain taking the form of doubts as to whether it has deep questions at its core.

24. John L. Hennessy and David A. Patterson, *Computer Architecture: A Quantitative Approach*, 4th edition, (San Francisco, CA: Morgan Kaufmann, 2007), xv.

25. Richard T. Snodgrass, "Ergalics: A natural science of computation." Available at http://www.cs.arizona.edu/projects/focal/ergalics/files/ergalics.pdf (accessed December 27, 2010).

26. Peter J. Denning, "The great principles of computing," *American Scientist* 98 (Sep-Oct 2010): 369–372.

27. Wikipedia entry on *Formalism (mathematics)*. Available at http://en.wikipedia.org/wiki/Formalism_(mathematics) (accessed October 14, 2009).

28. Ibid.

29. Peter J. Denning, ed., *The Invisible Future: The Seamless Integration of Technology Into Everyday Life* (New York, NY: McGraw-Hill, 2001).

30. This list of surprising results is due to Peter Denning.

31. Time's Best Inventions of 2008: The Best Inventions of the Year. Available at http://www.time.com/time/specials/packages/0,28757,1852747,00.html (accessed November 11, 2009).

32. The Best Inventions of the Year. Available at http://www.time.com/time/specials/2007/0,28757,1677329,00.html (accessed November 11, 2009).

33. The 50 Best Inventions of 2009. Available at http://www.time.com/time/specials/packages/0,28757,1934027,00.html (accessed November 24, 2009).

34. *Time*'s Best Inventions of 2008: The 46th Mersenne Prime. Available at http://www.time.com/time/specials/packages/article/0,28804,1852747_1854195_1854157,00.html (accessed November 11, 2009).

35. The Great Internet Mersenne Prime Search (GIMPS). Available at http://www.mersenne.org/ (accessed November 11, 2009).

36. *Time*'s Best Inventions of 2008: The Orbital Internet. Available at http://www.time.com/time/specials/packages/article/0,28804,1852747_1854195_1854122,00.html (accessed November 11, 2009).

37. The Best Inventions of the Year: Invention of the Year: The iPhone. Available at http://www.time.com/time/specials/2007/article/0,28804,1677329_1678542_1677891,00.html (accessed November 11, 2009).

38. The Best Inventions of the Year: Size Matters. Available at http://www.time.com/time/specials/2007/article/0,28804,1677329_1678130_1678116,00.html (accessed November 11, 2009).

39. The Best Inventions of the Year: Discard the Cord. Available at http://www.time.com/time/specials/2007/article/0,28804,1677329_1678130_1678118,00.html (accessed November 11, 2009).

40. The Best Inventions of the Year: Flexible Fiber. Available at http://www.time.com/time/specials/2007/article/0,28804,1677329_1678130_1678122,00.html (accessed November 11, 2009).

41. The Best Inventions of the Year: The $150 Laptop. Available at http://www.time.com/time/specials/2007/article/0,28804,1677329_1678130_1678125,00.html (accessed November 11, 2009).

42. The Best Inventions of the Year: Reading Glasses. Available at http://www.time
.com/time/specials/2007/article/0,28804,1677329_1678427_1678437,00.html
(accessed January 5, 2011).

43. The Best Inventions of the Year: Water Works. Available at http://www.time
.com/time/specials/2007/article/0,28804,1677329_1678083_1678067,00.html
(accessed November 11, 2009).

44. The Best Inventions of the Year: Bending Reality. Available at http://www.time
.com/time/specials/2007/article/0,28804,1677329_1678130_1678111,00.html
(accessed November 11, 2009).

45. The Best Inventions of the Year: Healing Hand. Available at http://www.time
.com/time/specials/2007/article/0,28804,1677329_1678169_1678150,00.html
(accessed November 11, 2009).

46. The Best Inventions of the Year: An ATM for Books. Available at http://www
.time.com/time/specials/2007/article/0,28804,1677329_1677980_1677970,00.html
(accessed January 5, 2011).

47. J. A. Kahle, M. N. Day, H. P. Hofstee, C. R. Johns, T. R. Maeurer, and D. Shippy.
"Introduction to the Cell multiprocessor," *IBM Journal of Research and Development*
49, no. 4/5 (July 2005): 589–604.

48. *Time's* Best Inventions of 2008: The World's Fastest Computer. Available at
http://www.time.com/time/specials/packages/article/0,28804,1852747_1854195_18
54123,00.html (accessed November 11, 2009).

49. *Time's* Best Inventions of 2008: The Memristor. Available at http://www.time
.com/time/specials/packages/article/0,28804,1852747_1854195_1854131,00.html
(accessed November 11, 2009).

50. *Time's* Best Inventions of 2008: Bionic Contacts. Available at http://www.time
.com/time/specials/packages/article/0,28804,1852747_1854195_1854152,00.html
(accessed November 11, 2009).

51. *Time's* Best Inventions of 2008: A Camera for the Blind. Available at http://www
.time.com/time/specials/packages/article/0,28804,1852747_1854195_1854193,00
.html (accessed November 11, 2009).

52. *Time's* Best Inventions of 2008: The Mobile, Dexterous, Social Robot. Available
at   http://www.time.com/time/specials/packages/article/0,28804,1852747_1854195
_1854135,00.html (accessed November 11, 2009).

53. *Time's* Best Inventions of 2008: The New Mars Rover. Available at http://www
.time.com/time/specials/packages/article/0,28804,1852747_1854195_1854136,00
.html (accessed November 11, 2009).

54. *Time*'s Best Inventions of 2008: Google's Floating Data Center. Available at http://www.time.com/time/specials/packages/article/0,28804,1852747_1854195_18 54190,00.html (accessed November 11, 2009).

55. *Time*'s Best Inventions of 2008: The Everything Game. Available at http://www .time.com/time/specials/packages/article/0,28804,1852747_1854195_1854147,00 .html (accessed November 11, 2009).

56. The 50 Best Inventions of 2009: The Fashion Robot. Available at http://www .time.com/time/specials/packages/article/0,28804,1934027_1934003_1933993,00 .html (accessed November 24, 2009).

57. The 50 Best Inventions of 2009: The Electric Eye. Available at http://www.time .com/time/specials/packages/article/0,28804,1934027_1934003_1933955,00.html (accessed November 24, 2009).

58. The 50 Best Inventions of 2009: Tweeting by Thinking. Available at http://www .time.com/time/specials/packages/article/0,28804,1934027_1934003_1933954,00 .html (accessed November 24, 2009).

59. The 50 Best Inventions of 2009: The Cyborg Beetle. Available at http://www .time.com/time/specials/packages/article/0,28804,1934027_1934003_1933968,00 .html (accessed November 24, 2009).

60. The 50 Best Inventions of 2009: The Eyeborg. Available at http://www.time.com/ time/specials/packages/article/0,28804,1934027_1934003_1933989,00.html (accessed November 24, 2009).

61. The 50 Best Inventions of 2009: The Planetary Skin. Available at http://www .time.com/time/specials/packages/article/0,28804,1934027_1934003_1933962,00 .html (accessed November 24, 2009).

62. The 50 Best Inventions of 2009: Teleportation. Available at http://www.time .com/time/specials/packages/article/0,28804,1934027_1934003_1933950,00.html (accessed November 24, 2009).

Index